According to promise

According to promise

The message of the book of Numbers

Gordon J. Keddie

 EVANGELICAL PRESS

EVANGELICAL PRESS
12 Wooler Street, Darlington, Co. Durham, DL1 1RQ, England

© Evangelical Press 1992
First published 1992

British Library Cataloguing in Publication Data available

ISBN 0 85234 295 0

Unless otherwise indicated, Scripture quotations in this publication are from the Holy Bible, New International Version. Copyright © 1973, 1978, 1984 International Bible Society. Published by Hodder & Stoughton.

Printed and bound in Great Britain at the Bath Press, Avon

To
Deborah Pigott and Ellen McHenry
faithful members of the Tuesday night Bible Study
whose enthusiasm for a study of Numbers
resulted in this exposition

Contents

List of maps and figures

Maps

Figures

Preface

How often do you hear of a preacher giving an exposition of the book of Numbers? Have you ever heard a sermon from this book? Even the name 'Numbers' is enough to set some people to shrugging in incomprehension and wondering if, whatever it talks about, it really is all that relevant to Christians on the threshold of the twenty-first century. Christians agree that all Scripture is equally God-breathed, but in practice often regard some Scriptures as less equal than others. Numbers does not immediately spring to many minds as the book to choose for Bible studies and preaching series. It is nevertheless as much the Word of God as John's Gospel or the Epistle to the Romans! And this certainly ought to be reflected in the reverence and the enthusiasm with which it is handled in the life and ministry of the church.

It is a pity that the book ever came to be called 'Numbers'. This came from the Greek title, *Arithmoi*, which owed its origin to someone some time long ago being impressed by the censuses recorded in its pages. The original Hebrew title is 'In the wilderness' (*b'midbar*), from the fifth word in 1:1. This really expresses something of the essential significance of the book, for it bridges the gap between Egypt and Canaan, when the Old Testament church was in transit between past and present, slavery and freedom, as they passed through the Sinai desert. It is about the church in the wilderness, on a journey from promise to fulfilment. Of course, what was fulfilled for them in the possession of Canaan remained at a deeper level promissary in character, for it looked ahead to its true fulfilment in the advent of Jesus Christ and the coming of the New

Testament era. This is the secret of understanding the Old Testament Scriptures. They are part of God's progressive unfolding of his self-revelation in his only-begotten Son, the Lord Jesus Christ. Rightly understood, Numbers is a milestone to Calvary, a stretch of the road that leads to Christ and ultimately to heaven itself.

The exposition presented in this book began life as a series of sermons in morning worship in Grace Reformed Presbyterian Church, State College, Pennsylvania. The focus upon meaning and application essential for preaching the Word has been preserved in the recasting of that material for publication. Those who are interested in technical and academic questions relative to the text of Numbers are warmly directed to Gordon Wenham's Tyndale commentary, by far the best of recent more academic treatments of Numbers.

The modern church needs the message of Numbers. Like Israel in the wilderness, the church today has compromised the claims of God's Word to a fearful degree and is reaping the inevitable consequences of apostasy. Numbers calls the church to *repentance* for her *sins* against God and man, to *obedience* to the unvarnished *law* of God, and to *trust* in the gracious *promises* of God. Practical discipleship, not lip-service, is the context of the blessing of God. Numbers shows us with uncomfortable clarity why the churches in the pseudo-Christian West are sterile shells of what they might have been, but also holds out, rightly understood, the brilliant prospects of divine blessing for all who will commit their way to the Lord, according to his promises in the gospel of his only begotten Son, the Lord Jesus Christ.

Gordon J. Keddie
State College, PA

Part I

Preparations for the journey

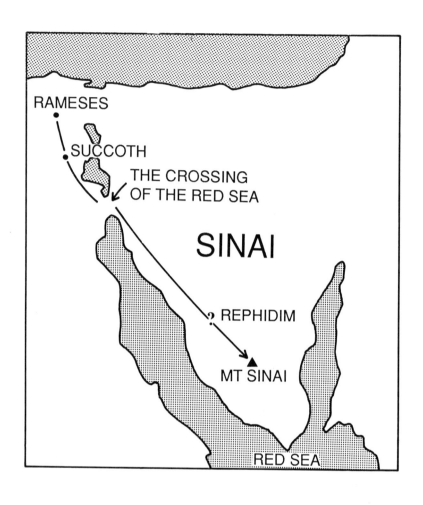

Map 1. — From Egypt to Sinai

1.
Stand up and be counted!

Please read Numbers 1
'So he numbered them in the wilderness of Sinai' (1:19, NASB).

For the first three months after the exodus from Egypt, the Israelites kept on the move through the wilderness. If they entertained the notion that their troubles were over, this was soon dispelled by the onrush of trial and tribulation. They faced 'trial by water' at Mara, 'trial by food' in the wilderness of Sin and 'trial by enemies' at Rephidim. Every time, their trust in the Lord faltered and, every time, the Lord in his grace still provided for them: the springs of Elim and the miracle of the manna gave them food and drink; the water from the rock answered that inner enemy, their querulous unbelief, and the uplifted arms of faithful Moses gave them victory in battle over their external enemy, the Amalekites (Exod. 15:22 - 17:16).

They then camped in the wilderness of Sinai and for most of the year remained in the shadow of Horeb, 'the mountain of God,' as God prepared them for the march to the promised land. Exodus 19-40 records how they were given the Ten Commandments and the laws regulating their society: the regulations for the worship of God and the plans for the building of the house of worship, the tabernacle. We read of how, in spite of all that God had revealed of himself to them and all that he had done for them, they rebelled and turned to the idol-worship of a golden calf. God punished them, but then renewed his covenant with them. They were again given the Ten Commandments on tablets of stone, the laws of the book of

Leviticus were set out for them and they were commanded to build the tabernacle. Thus prepared, they would be ready to renew their journey to Canaan.

The book of Numbers takes up where Exodus leaves off, and tells of the arrangements for the journey, of the journey itself and of the arrival of the people of God at the threshold of the land of promise. The people had to be well organized for their odyssey, and, as a first step, a census was taken of the fighting potential of the nation.

God's people (1:1-16)

The Lord told Moses to count the people, **'by their clans and families, listing every man by name, one by one'** (1:2). But why this laborious process? What was God's interest in having such a census taken?

First of all, God was asserting his *sovereign dominion* over his people. Most modern nations conduct a census about every ten years. What does this signify? Surely it says, at its most basic level, that you who are counted are under the jurisdiction of your national government. Sovereignty is the basis of census-taking and is its primary message for the people so numbered. God said to Israel, 'I am your God and you are my people.' Lordship and ownership belonged to him. He spoke; he commanded; he willed — and they were marshalled according to his decree!

Secondly, God was declaring his *love* for Israel as his particular people. As the Shepherd of Israel, he counts off the sheep (Ps. 80:1). He leads, guides, protects and saves his sheep (Ps. 23). Hence the naming of the heads of the tribes. The Lord knows those who are his (2 Tim. 2:19). It is a picture of the love which moves the Lord to enter, one by one, the names of those who are recorded in the book of life (Phil. 4:3). God's love is personal and particular. He knows his elect with saving love, but he declares to the reprobate lost on the Day of Judgement, 'I never knew you' (Matt. 7:23).

Thirdly, God was reminding them of his *covenant promise*, made so long before, that Israel would be a great nation (Gen. 12:2; 22:17; 32:12). Jacob had taken a family of seventy people into Egypt four centuries earlier and now they were a nation of perhaps 2,000,000![1] God had been faithful and that promised greater things for the future as they looked to the journey to the promised land. The census had a future reference. It organized the people for blessings yet to come! The lesson remains for the church today, for we who were 'not a people' are now, in Jesus Christ, 'the people of God' (1 Peter 2:9-10).

Fighting saints (1:17-46)

The second section records the results of the census. One by one, the fighting strength of each of the twelve tribes is recorded, making a grand total of 603,550. Again, we ask, 'What does this mean?'

Most obviously, it indicates that Israel was going to have to fight for the promised land. The Amorites could not be expected to keel over or run up the white flag. God's covenant promise would involve warfare, with all that implied in terms of blood, toil, tears and sweat. Behind that temporal reality for Israel, however, stands the more profound reality that *God's people*, in Old and New Testaments alike, *are called to a spiritual warfare*, of which the physical wars of Israel were just a shadow and an emblem. The New Testament church, as the 'holy nation' of 1 Peter 2:9, is involved in a mighty contest of arms, even though 'the weapons we fight with are not the weapons of the world' (2 Cor. 10:4). The church's calling is to be a body of believers, going forth in living personal faith in Christ their Saviour, to serve his kingdom in the world. Matthew Henry stresses the necessity of personal commitment: 'The church being militant, those only are [her] true members [who] have enlisted themselves soldiers of Jesus Christ: for our life, our Christian life, is a warfare.'[2] We are to 'put on the ... armour of God' (Eph. 6:13). We are to 'fight the good fight of faith' (1 Tim. 6:12). We are to be fighting saints in God's war! Jesus' kingdom is not *of* this world, but it is certainly *in* it, and Christians are in the thick of the battle!

Secondly, there is a quiet indication in the numbers listed that *God fulfils promises and rewards faithfulness.* The relative strengths of the tribes — and their positions in the camp (Num. 2) — were not mere accidents.

Judah, with 74,600 men, was the largest and most powerful tribe (1:26-27). On his deathbed, Jacob had told Judah, 'Your brothers will praise you,' and

'The sceptre will not depart from Judah,
    nor the ruler's staff from between his feet,
until he comes to whom it belongs
    and the obedience of the nations is his'

(Gen. 49:8,10).

This clearly indicated that Judah would be the foremost of the tribes. And this indeed was the case throughout Israel's history, from the Sinai census to the Davidic monarchy. And it did not stop there. This is a Messianic prophecy. The sceptre ultimately belongs to Christ and the destiny of Judah culminates in the mediatorial kingship of Jesus Christ.[3] 'For it is clear that our Lord descended from Judah' (Heb. 7:14).

Ephraim and Manasseh (1:32-35) were sons of Joseph and together almost as large as Judah. That they were counted equal with their uncles, Reuben and Simeon (Gen. 48:5), marked the fact that their father had been blessed with a double portion — 'Joseph' was two tribes, not just one. Joseph was 'a fruitful vine' (Gen. 49:22), and this is reflected in the census.

These relative numbers are only a little more than hints. They are, nevertheless, encouragements to move us to seek the blessing of God in living faithfulness to his Word. James Philip points out that there is also a warning: 'The tribes that stemmed from men who sinned grievously seldom raised up any great figures, or men of renown.' Caleb and David came from Judah, Gideon and Samuel from Ephraim, Gideon from Manasseh and Paul the apostle from Benjamin. 'No man lives unto himself,' adds Philip. 'We are making our future now, and, it may be, the future of our families also.'[4]

Thirdly, there is, in these numbers, *an implicit promise of supernatural sustaining grace.* The Israelites knew very well that Sinai was no granary, capable of sustaining them through a journey of any length. They did not know, at this point, that it would end up being a forty-year journey. What they did know was that the logistics of even a direct path to Canaan were problematic, to say the least. The grumblings at Marah and Rephidim, and the miraculous provision of the manna and the quail, had already told them that the Lord alone could provide their needs (Exod. 15:22 - 17:7). Therefore, sums up John Calvin, 'The intention of the Spirit is to represent to our eyes the incredible power of God in a conspicuous and signal miracle.'[5] In other words, the passage of Israel from Egypt to Canaan is one stupendous miracle, of which the numbers involved are the clearest testimony. The various schemes adopted by some commentators to explain away the large numbers — '**603,550**' men (1:46) implies about 2,000,000 people — all basically arise, even by their own argumentation, from the assumption that Sinai could never support such a population. This assumption may be correct, but the conclusion that the numbers had to be much smaller is thoroughly rationalistic and misses the whole point, which is that God miraculously sustained Israel through her epic odyssey! Whether Israel was the 2,000,000 implied by the text, or the 100,000 or so suggested by those who try to amend the text, Sinai, even in its ancient, less desertified state, could not have supported them anyway. But God did! God was determined to go with his people and show them a victory over seemingly impossible obstacles and hazards!

Given all God's promises of sustaining grace, why did the Israelites complain so much in the desert? One reason is surely that the desert experience meant that they had to trust God every day. They had no alternative whatsoever, and this rankled. The truth is that none of us wants to have to trust God all day and every day. We want to know there is money in the bank and food in the cupboard. We want a paid-off mortgage and a paid-up pension fund. We like security we can see and touch. We like trusting in our own efforts and in our own things. Take these away and we become scared and embittered. In Sinai, Israelites woke every morning knowing for sure that if they could not trust God, they would go to bed hungry. The manna was indeed as dependable as the Lord who sent it, but every scrap that the Israelites ate reminded them that they had to trust the Lord, wholly, exclusively, for absolutely everything, every single day. That did not sit well with proud hearts and carnal minds.

Devoted ministers (1:47-53)

The tribe of Levi was not numbered with the others, but set apart for the ministry of the '**tabernacle of the Testimony**'. They were to carry it on the line of march. Non-Levites were not to approach it, on pain of death, and the Levites were to camp around it, '**so that wrath will not fall on the Israelite community**'.

Why did God institute this arrangement and attach such draconian penalties to any breach of his regulations? And what does it mean for us today?

Foremost is the reality that *God was in the midst of his people.* The separation of the tabernacle, underscored by the death penalty for transgressing the boundary of separation, told them in unmistakable terms that their God was sovereign, holy and to be worshipped and obeyed in reverence and holy fear, and that he was there with them. God had determined to be visibly present amongst his people in his sanctuary. They had to realize that this privilege had enormous implications for their lives and their conduct. Much was expected from them, because much had been given to them. The same principle lies at the heart of the experience of the New Testament church and believers today. We are called to worship God 'in spirit and in truth' (John 4:24). The very sanctity of the tabernacle, including the severity of the penalty for desecrating it, was in fact a declaration by God of his gracious purpose for his people, his love for them, his desire for their redemption and for their union and communion with him, and his pleasure in them as his believing, worshipping, happy and blessed people. The tabernacle was actually a picture and a symbol of the gospel that would yet be revealed in Jesus Christ — read the Epistle to the Hebrews — and of the consequences of its rejection.

Secondly, this taught Israel that *God had set a spiritual ministry among his people.* The tabernacle was the true heart of Israel's life. The ministry of the priests and Levites was the engine of Israel's national development. God raised up his ministers to guide his people in the godly life. In the New Testament church, the *mediatorial* role of the Levites has been fulfilled in Jesus, our once-for-all great High Priest, and so all believers are priests — Peter calls them 'a royal priesthood' (1 Peter 3:9). We, therefore, have in Christ 'access by faith into this grace in which we now stand' and 'access to the Father by one Spirit' (Rom. 5:2; Eph. 2:18). The *ministerial* function of the Levites, however, lives on in the gifts and offices that the Lord has given to the church for her edification and government (Eph. 4:11-13; Acts 14:23; 1 Tim. 3). Sound ministry, godly pastors, elders and deacons devoted to their calling are vital to the integrity, existence and effective witness of a true gospel church. The Scriptures know nothing of the anti-clerical individualism which has today reduced many pastors to mere 'facilitators', co-ordinating the 'ministries' of everyone else's gifts. The preaching and teaching of God's Word have taken a back seat in favour of concerts, drama, dance, puppets and even magic in what some churches call 'worship'. The Bible is clear that these things have no more place in public worship — whatever their legitimacy in other contexts — than the 'unauthorized fire' which Nadab and Abihu offered to the Lord (Lev. 10:1; Num. 3:4). To be 'in spirit' (i.e. Spirit-led), worship must also be 'in truth' — and vice versa. Blessing flows in the path of faithfulness to God's revealed will.

Finally, *God calls as his ministers a humbled and tested people*. Levi, the father of the tribe, was a bloodthirsty character who, with his brother Simeon, had treacherously slaughtered the Shechemites (Gen. 34). Jacob had declared this to be the reason for the judgement upon Levi, in terms of which he would be a landless tribe, scattered throughout Israel. On the way to Canaan, however, Levi's descendants stood with Moses against the rebellion of the people over the worship of the golden calf (Exod. 32:26). For their faithfulness, the *curse* of landless dispersion was turned into the *blessing* of being set apart as the Lord's ministers, spread throughout the people of the twelve tribes (Exod. 32:29). The ministers of God today share something of this Levitical experience. They are sprinkled across the church. The great themes of their ministry must first humble their own souls before they can proclaim them, in power and demonstration of the Spirit, to their charges. They must be 'instant' in season and out of season. They preach as dying men to dying people, holding out the Word of life in the Saviour who first had to save them from their sins.

Obedient disciples (1:54)

The Lord's people responded in faith. They did everything **'just as the Lord commanded Moses'**. 'To obey is better than sacrifice, and to heed is better than the fat of rams' (1 Sam. 15:22). What makes for a true disciple? Jesus said, 'If you love me, you will obey what I command' (John 14:15). The challenge is plain: from Mount Sinai to the cross, Jesus says, 'Follow me!'

2.
God's order of battle

Please read Numbers 2
'The Israelites are to camp around the Tent of Meeting...' (2:2).

Most of us would like to be better organized than we are. To the degree that our lives, thoughts or habits are disorganized, we find ourselves frustrated and our progress hindered. We know that if we plan nothing, 'nothing' is probably what we will achieve — or maybe something worse!

Israel could not just be a disorganized mob, if they were ever to reach the promised land. A tribal and family structure was already in place, as was an organized judiciary (Exod. 12:41; 18:13-26), but they needed a plan for their march, which would enable them to cope with contingencies as they arose and, not least, keep the people united in both resolve and action to achieve the goals the Lord was setting for them. Order and organization are vital to any army, even the army of the living God. Hence the first phase was to take a census of the fighting men (Num. 1). Every man needed to know how he fitted into the bigger picture. They all needed to know to whom, and for whom, they were responsible. For this reason, phase two details the organization for the journey. As the passage unfolds we are shown not only God's 'order of battle' for Israel, but a picture of the calling and task of God's people in every age, as they go out into the world with the message of his Word. God has called his people to movement (2:1-2), mobilization (2:3-32) and ministry (2:33-34). They are his instrument for the extension for his kingdom upon earth.

Movement (2:1-2)

God organized Israel for movement. His instructions for their
encampment were not the blueprint for a static housing
development, but for a mobile expedition, armed alike for worship
and for war.

Pressing towards a goal

Israel, noted the psalmist, '[found] no way to a city where they could
settle' (Ps. 107:4). They were, in a real sense, passing through. In
consequence, everything in their life reflected this reality. They
were to **'camp'** — and put down no roots until they came to Canaan.
Today, we assume that we should be 'settled' somewhere and live
and work with unvarying stability. Indeed, so powerful is this
conviction in some people that they expect the government to move
jobs to them, rather than that they themselves should move to where
the jobs are. In a more fundamental sense, Christians recognize that
we are passing through: 'For here we do not have an enduring city,
but we are looking for the city that is to come' (Heb. 13:14); we are
'aliens and strangers' (Heb. 11:13; 1 Peter 2:11). As Matthew Henry
put it, we 'are in a movable state' in this world'.[1]

This has profound implications for God's people. It means, first
of all, that *we are going somewhere*. We are not merely 'passing
through', as if our life was no more than an existentialist experience
— all journey and no destination. We are, rather, moving towards
a goal. Israel's immediate goal was the land of promise; ours is that
which Canaan foreshadowed, namely, the kingdom of God.

The journey itself is, however, a part of the destination, even if
the ultimate fulfilment awaits the second coming of Christ. The
church represents the kingdom of heaven amongst humanity. That
kingdom is *now*, in and through Jesus Christ, in transformed lives,
in grace abounding in a fallen world. It is also *future*, in the glory yet
to be revealed, face-to-face with Jesus our Saviour in the fellowship
of the redeemed, where grace abounds and sin is banished — the
eternal glory of heaven. The present witness of the church is to that
salvation which Jesus accomplished in his death on the cross and
which is proclaimed in the gospel to the whole world, and to the
eternal life which is promised to all who believe in him. Believers,
then, are on the move — and they know where they are going.

Secondly, like Israel, we renounce any permanent connection with this world. We are not 'of the world', and 'the things of this world' are not the meaning of our lives. Our eyes are on 'treasure in heaven', for we know how transient and deceptive are the 'treasures on earth' (John 15:19; 18:36; 1 John 2:15; Matt. 6:19-20).

Focused on the Lord

Israel was to camp **'round the Tent of Meeting some distance from it'** (2:2). The distance was probably about one kilometre (see Josh. 3:4). The point is that God was to be the focal point, the very centre and heart of their lives, and his holiness translated into the reverence of keeping the appropriate distance — a constant reminder of their privilege and their need: the privilege of the presence of their Father-God and the need of redemption from sin in all its forms. The meaning, as James Philip so aptly observes, is that 'When God and his Word are in the midst of the church ... it moves forward like a mighty army. Plant the Word of God in the heart of the church's life, and once again it will move forward to some purpose.'[2]

Members of a team

Furthermore, each man was to camp **'under his standard with the banners of his family'** (2:2). They were to relate to one another as tribes and families, each with a distinct role and place in the body. How much strife results from failure to keep to one's own task! The church is called the *body* of Christ in the New Testament, because it is to be a team made up of individuals placed in complementary roles. No one is dispensable and no one is a one-man band. The whole body is 'joined and held together' so that it 'grows and builds itself up in love, as each part does its work' (1 Cor. 12:12-31; Eph. 4:16).

Mobilization (2:3-32)

Having set out the basic idea — an orderly encampment by families around the Tent of Meeting — the Lord then gave specific directions for the position of the tribes (Fig. 1). He assigned each tribe a place

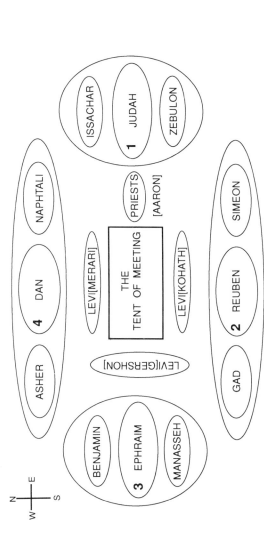

Figure 1. The encampment of Israel

Notes: 1. The order on the march is indicated by the numbers. The Tent of Meeting (carried by Merari/Gershon) marched between the divisions of Judah (1) and Reuben (2), while the Ark was carried (by Kohath) between Reuben (2) and Ephraim (3) (Numbers 10:17-21).
2. Approximately 1 kilometre separated the Tent of Meeting from the secular tribes at all times (Joshua 3:4).

and thereby also fixed their relative responsibilities and the chain of command by which their deployment would be regulated. The tribes were grouped in such a way as to optimize co-operation, while minimizing potential conflicts.

Thus Judah, Issachar and Zebulon, all from sons of Leah, form the vanguard division, signalling the primacy of Judah in spite of his not being Jacob's first-born (2:3-9). Reuben and Simeon were descended from the oldest sons of Leah and might be expected to chafe under the leadership of Judah, and so the Lord with practical wisdom groups them together with the tribe of Gad, who descended from Leah's maid, Zilpah, to form the second division (2:10-16). Rachel's descendants, Ephraim, Manasseh and Benjamin, make up the third division (2:18-24), while the rearguard consisted of Dan, Naphtali and Asher, who descended from Bilhah and Zilpah (2:25-31; Gen. 35:23-26).

Irving Jensen sums up the basic lesson: 'They were taught to keep their places ... and to recognize their dependency on others ... to keep their eyes on the standards ... and to heed the voice of their leaders.'[3] It is a picture of the disciplined order of Christ's church — a temple of living stones, joined together in their Saviour and capstone, Jesus (1 Peter 2:4-8). 'I am with you in spirit,' wrote Paul to the Colossians, 'rejoicing to see your good discipline and the stability of your faith in Christ' (Col. 2:5, NASV). This is what true churches of Jesus Christ are really like.

Ministry (2:33-34)

The Levites were not included in the census of fighting men, as they were to serve the Tent of Meeting. Consequently, they were camped around the tent, within the encircling protection of the twelve tribes.

The separation of the Levites emphasizes *God's special purpose for Israel.* The Levites were to be the mediators between God and his people. The ceremonies and sacrifices they observed all concerned this relationship, and pointed ahead to the final Mediator, who would come in the fulness of time — the Lord Jesus Christ. He is described as Immanuel — God with us — come to save his people from their sins and reconcile them to God. The Levites represent God's presence with his people as a *saving* presence, for the sacrifices spoke of personal redemption through a mediator. The gospel of Christ shines through the ministry of the Levites: salvation was by grace, through faith looking to the substitute sacrifice for sin, which in reality was not the blood of bulls and goats, but the blood of Jesus Christ.

The ministry of the Levites also emphasized *the spiritual core of the mission of Israel.* This mission was not narrowly political. Political freedom, self-determination and democracy were not the point, modern 'liberation theology' to the contrary. They were God's ambassadors. They had the living oracles of God. This meant two things.

First, they had a ministry of *judgement.* The sin of the Amorites was to be repaid. They would feel the cutting edge of God's wrath through the swords of God's people. This is just one vivid picture of a fundamental principle, namely, that 'The saints will judge the world' (1 Cor. 6:2). The real sword of judgement is the Word of God. Unacceptable as this concept is to modern minds, it is the key to understanding life, from the individual and personal to the flow of history and current events. Even when we proclaim Christ, in words or in pattern of life, we judge the world. We assert its lostness and need of a Saviour. We reproach sin with God's standards. To live righteously unavoidably reflects for a watching world the reasons for God's anger with unrighteousness. One fruit of God's blessing is the warning of his curse. And this is why many hate to hear the truth and to see people live it out. They want their sins without the consequences. Nevertheless, the judgements of God are at work in the world, because Christ is 'head over everything for the church' (Eph. 1:22). He is the King of kings and the Lord of lords, who with an unseen hand directs the rise and fall of men and nations. He will not, and cannot, be denied.

Secondly and pre-eminently, this is a ministry of *grace.* God is amongst his people. He speaks his Word. He provides for practical needs and is a strong defence against enemies. He blesses with spiritual blessings. He loves his people with an everlasting love, which will never let them go. And through them, he calls the human race to repentance and faith. Rahab of Jericho understood this message before she ever met one of God's people. She knew that for all God's anger with sinners, he was merciful and willing to save. She trusted the Lord for her salvation. By faith, she received the ministry of grace (Josh. 2:8-13; Heb. 11:31).

The New Testament church is called to be 'to God the aroma of Christ among those who are being saved and those who are perishing'. Paul says that 'To the one we are the smell of death; to the other, the fragrance of life.' 'Who', he asks, 'is equal to such a task?' And the answer? 'In Christ we speak before God with sincerity, like men sent from God... He has made us competent ministers of a new covenant — not of the letter, but of the Spirit; for the letter kills, but the Spirit gives life' (2 Cor. 2:15-17; 3:6).

3.
Saved to serve

Please read Numbers 3 and 4
'They are to be mine. I am the Lord' (3:13).

The most common charge laid against professing Christians today is probably that of hypocrisy. 'You are all hypocrites!' says the world, and they point directly at the sins of erstwhile saints. Here is a man who believes he has 'accepted Jesus' and is 'right with God'. He can talk up a storm — and in all the correct evangelical language — about his new-found 'peace of mind'. But, at the same time he can swear like a trooper and constantly blasphemes the name of our Lord. He is living with a woman to whom he is not married and in many other ways lives a life of manifest ethical, moral and spiritual ruin. This is a real situation. It is not a 'made-for-illustration' story. And, sad to say, it is not as uncommon in today's churches as you might think. The question, of course, must be: 'Why is this so?' How can people think they are followers of Jesus, yet live openly and apparently unashamedly immoral lives, in blatant disregard of the clear teaching of Jesus and the Scriptures?

One obvious place to look for an answer is in the common notion of what it means to come to Christ and to be a Christian. To many people, God, Jesus and faith are more about what we *feel* than about what we *actually do*. The dominant motif has shifted from how we are to please God to what God does to please us! Self-image, self-improvement, self-esteem, self-fulfilment, self-actualization — these are the absorbing concerns of much of the professedly evangelical church today, at least in the Western world. The key word is, of course, 'self'. 'I' want to feel good about myself, and feeling 'saved' goes a long way to fulfilling that desire.

This begs some important questions. Why — and to what end — does God *save* people? What does it mean to be 'right with God', to 'trust in Jesus', to be 'born again' and to be 'saved'? Is it just so we can tell ourselves we are 'forgiven' and feel assured that whatever happens — whatever we do — God will, as some like to say, 'always be there for us'?

At first glance, a passage describing the census of the Levites would not seem to be fertile ground for generating answers to these questions. In fact, it does offer some very relevant and practical teaching. Behind the lists of names and job descriptions, it tells us, in effect, that if we are saved at all, we are saved to serve the Lord.

God's way — authority and discipline (3:1-4, 14-39)

We first have a description of the priestly family. This consisted of Aaron and his sons, Nadab, Abihu, Eleazar and Ithamar, **'the anointed priests, who were ordained to serve as priests'** (3:3). They were the senior division of the tribe of Levi. As the appointed mediators between God and the people, they alone 'had the right to handle the sacrificial blood, to touch the altar and to enter the tent of meeting'.[1] They were the pivotal figures in the lives of the people, for these five men constituted the window on the mind of God for the whole of the covenant nation, and were the chosen channel of the Lord's blessing upon his people. Their responsibility to be exemplary in their public ministry and private conduct cannot be overemphasized. They had been given a truly awesome privilege.

My way (3:4)

'I did it my way,' croons singer Frank Sinatra in a song which sums up the spirit of this age of narcissism and self-fulfilment. Whenever we are told to do something 'this way', it is not long before we consider improving on it. Soon, we may want to do it our own way. This is what happened with the older sons of Aaron. Nadab and Abihu **'made an offering with unauthorized fire before him in the Desert of Sinai'** (Lev. 3:4; 10:1-7). They evidently thought that their way was at least as good as God's way. Perhaps they figured that fire was fire, whatever the source, and couldn't see why God would bother if just this once they didn't use the fire from the altar as he had commanded. God did mind, however, and, no doubt to make the point transparently clear for all time, he visited immediate and decisive punishment upon these miscreant innovators: Nadab and Abihu **'fell dead before the Lord'** for their presumption. This event, later echoed in the death of Uzzah for a similar act of irreverence (2 Sam. 6:6-7), stands as a vivid statement of the regulative principle of Scripture, which says, in a nutshell, that when God has told us something, that is it! There are to be no additions or subtractions, no modifications or corrections, no fudging, no squeezing in of our own 'insights'. The same principle is explicitly applied to the integrity of every word of the book of Revelation — and by implication all of the Word of God — in Revelation 22:18-19: 'If anyone adds anything to them, God will add to him the plagues described in this book. And if anyone takes words away from this book of prophecy, God will take away from him his share in the tree of life and in the holy city, which are described in this book.'

In what happened, we are given a startling picture of the consequences of flouting the Lord's will.

No sin ever escapes God's judgement. Not one. Jesus says that not one 'jot' or 'tittle' — the two smallest marks in Hebrew calligraphy — would pass from God's law until everything was fulfilled, thereby emphasizing God's determination that all his commands should be kept and, if not, would be accounted for before his judgement seat (Matt. 5:18; 2 Cor. 5:10). Jesus also said that 'Every careless word' would require an explanation on the Day of Judgement (Matt. 12:36), and in his depiction of the judgement itself, the specific sins of the unbelieving are cited in detail as the ground of their just consignment to eternal punishment in hell (Matt. 25:41-43).

Those who serve in the church are not exempt from such scrutiny. Judgement must begin at the house of God (1 Peter 4:17). Those who would be teachers will be judged more severely (James 3:1). Jesus makes the vital point when he says, 'Many will say to me on that day...' that they did this, that and the next thing for God, when in fact they never knew him by faith, or did what they did out of anything more than self-serving policy! In consequence, our Lord will say, 'I never knew you. Away from me, you evildoers' (Matt. 7:22).

Sin has a long arm. It reaches far into the future. Nadab and Abihu perished, but so did any posterity they might have hoped for.

In others, who do leave children, sin is passed on to succeeding generations, by habit, example and instruction (Num. 14:18).

There is, nevertheless, nothing invincible about sin and its effects. As long as we do things our way, corruption and condemnation will remain our experience. But there is another way — God's way — and it is a way of redemption, by the grace of God, through faith in the Lord Jesus Christ.

God's way (3:14-39)

The census of the Levites, conspicuously omitted from that of the twelve tribes, highlights their special appointment to spiritual warfare over against the military service of their more numerous brethren. The account not only numbers the Levite males from one month old and up — there were 22,000 (3:39) — but details the assignments of their three main divisions. The Gershonites were responsible for the curtains and covering of the Tent of Meeting and camped on its west side; the Kohathites were in charge of the sacred furniture of the sanctuary and camped on the south side; while the Merarites handled the framework, with its posts, pegs and ropes, and camped on the north side. Moses and Aaron and his sons — the priests — were 'the authoritative teachers of the nation (e.g. Lev. 10:11; Dt. 24:8), the official mediators between God and Israel'.[2] They camped to the east and had exclusive care of the sanctuary, a point underlined by the stipulation that **'Anyone else who approached the sanctuary was to be put to death'** (3:38). Matthew Henry records that it was said that in later years this text was engraved on a golden sword which the Jews hung over the temple door.[3] God is serious about his declared will. We are called to obedience. We have a choice before us all: will it be the way of life or the way of death? (Jer. 21:8).

The very fact that the Lord's instructions are so specific again emphasizes his sovereignty over his people and the privilege that it is to belong to him. God wants us to do things his way, but that way, far from being burdensome, restrictive or tyrannical, is the way of a true and happy liberty! True faith prays,

> 'Teach me, O Lord, the perfect way
>   Of thy precepts divine,
> And to observe it to the end
>   I shall my heart incline.'[4]

God's redeemed — sacrifice and commitment (3:5-13, 40-51)

Why are we supposed to do things God's way, and how are we going to be willing and able to do things his way? If it is a matter of keeping his law perfectly, we know we have already failed! And we are quite aware of the fact that even our best thoughts, words and deeds, fall far short of sinless perfection! The answer therefore is that we need to be *saved*, and since we cannot do it ourselves, it has to come from someone else, and that someone is God. God saves; and when he saves, he gives new life which may be lived for him, his way.

Ownership and salvation (3:5-13)

The Levites were set apart to God for the service and worship of the sanctuary. They were his. They belonged to him. This is elucidated by the symbolic identification of the Levites as the first-born of God's people. God says, **'The Levites are mine, for all the first-born are mine'** (3:12). The concept of the first-born is rooted in the idea of an *unbreakable bond of love*. God owns and sustains them, because he loves them! Furthermore he loves them *before* they love him. The declaration that his first gift of a child to the families of his people belongs to him underscores the covenant bond with his people *as a whole*. If he loves the first-born, that proves how much he loves the parents! So with Israel, the Levites are separated as a living symbol of God's love for all of his people. Sovereign grace and eternal love lie at the heart of the idea of the first-born. Thus Jesus is called the 'first-born among many brothers' — the ultimate first-born, the 'only-begotten' Son (Rom. 8:29; John 3:16) — while the church in heaven is called the 'general assembly and church of the first-born' (Heb. 12:23, AV). The connection is between ownership and salvation — ultimately salvation through the gospel of Jesus Christ, in whom the symbols and shadows of the Old Testament are fulfilled.

Redemption by ransom (3:40-51)

The Levites were not all first-born. They were designated the symbolically first-born of the nation. This was established by the simple procedure of substituting them, one for one, for the first-born males of the twelve tribes. Since the latter had 273 more than the number of the Levites (cf. 3:39,43,46), the Israelites had to pay a ransom of five shekels per person— **'redemption money,'** payable to the priests. The point is that service depended upon salvation. The service of the Levites represented the nature of redemption. The story of the Levites was, if you will, a film with a cast of 22,000, directed by God, to project a message, to everyone who could see it, that redemption is necessary in order for anyone to come to the Lord and to be his disciple. Those set apart for him need to be redeemed by ransom. This was as true in spiritual terms for all of Israel as it was for the Levites. The ransom and substitution of the Levites was an emblem of the need of all for salvation. The actual accomplishment of this salvation is in Jesus Christ, who is the 'ransom for many' (Matt. 20:28). He is the substitute and atonement for his people, of which the Levites were just a foreshadowing. In Christ, the ransom is paid, once for all and in full.

God's team — fellowship and co-operation (4:1-49)

The fourth chapter records a further census of the Levites — this time, that of the able-bodied men between thirty and fifty years of age, who would do the heavy work of the Tent of Meeting. Embedded in this painstakingly repetitive account, we can discern an outline of the principles by which God was to be served. How are we to serve him? Faithfully? Yes! But *together* — not as individualists, but as members of a team, who are workers together with God and with one another in fellowship and co-operation.

Maturity is required for effective service. Levites served from 'thirty to fifty years of age' (4:3,23,30). Both Jesus and John the Baptizer began their public ministries at the age of thirty. There is no fixed rule for the ministry of the New Testament church in this, but it points up a basic principle. An elder is not to be a 'recent convert' and a deacon is to be 'tested' (1 Tim. 3:6,10). The privilege of working for God carries with it a great deal of responsibility and will only be effective when those called to the work know the fruits of the gospel themselves with a degree of understanding and tried and tested experience. The Son of God, who learned obedience in the things that he suffered, did not propel himself into leadership and public ministry until the time was ripe. That timing no doubt included sensitivity to the expectations of his times, one of which was that young lads do not present themselves to the people of God as teachers. It would be no bad thing if those who aspire to minister for the Lord today were to follow his example and get some experience — both of the Christian life or life in the world — before becoming the teachers and pastors of the church. Theological colleges, especially in the United States, have become ministry-mills churning out too many spiritual novices, who go on to church situations with which they cannot cope, and 'burn out' after a few short years. Faithful ministry is a job unlike any other, just because it deals with the deepest things of the human heart. The faithful opening of the Word in preaching and pastoral ministry cannot but expose raw nerves and touch deep feelings. It is arduous work!

Secondly, *there must be a readiness for spiritual warfare.* The Levites were holy soldiers — 'the *militia sacra* of Jehovah'.[5] The Hebrew word for service — as in **'all … who come to serve'** in 4:2 — carries the idea of warfare, of being part of a battle. Serving the Lord is not an easy, painless task. Jesus told us we would have troubles in this world. Paul enjoined Timothy to 'fight the good fight' and to 'endure hardship' with him as 'a good soldier of Christ Jesus' (1 Tim. 1:18; 2 Tim. 2:3).

Thirdly, *the greatest care is to be taken with the things of God.* The Levites' care for the Tent of Meeting and its furnishing is set out in the finest detail. Why? To make absolutely clear that nothing about the Lord is to be treated in a casual or careless manner. Every detail says that the Lord is sovereign and is to be reverenced with holy fear. One detail illustrates this particularly clearly. Wenham points out the predominance of blue and purple — the colour of the heavens and of royalty — in the curtains and coverings of the Tent of Meeting and the sacred articles of the sanctuary (4:6,12).[6] Israel was a theocracy and so is the New Testament church. Christ is King and we are to follow him with careful devotion.

Fourthly, *God's people are to value the gospel ministry as a gift from God.* Moses was to ensure that **'the Kohathite tribal clans are not cut off from the Levites'** (4:17-18). The danger was that they, who were charged with the task of carrying the most sacred objects while on the march and when they were covered up, might overstep the proper bounds and go near them while they were in place in the sanctuary and were uncovered. They were not permitted to **'go in to look at the holy things, even for a moment, or they [would] die'**

(4:20). The priests alone were permitted to see these holy objects. Hence, Aaron and his sons were to take care to ensure these were covered before the Kohathites were assigned their specific tasks in the sanctuary. This is simply to say that the vulnerabilities of God's servants need to be addressed by a caring ministry that seeks the very best of blessings for them.

Fifthly, while the intense rigour seen in 4:17-20 speaks of taking similar care for the Lord's servants today, it also affords *a brilliant contrast with the openness of access which we have to God*, through our mediator, the Lord Jesus Christ. 'Now, through Christ,' writes Matthew Henry, 'the case is altered; we have "seen with our eyes," and our hands "have handled, the word of life" (1 John 1:1), and we are encouraged to "come boldly to the throne of grace."'[7]

Lastly, we have, in the varied tasks of the priests and the three Levitical clans *a picture of teamwork, interdependence and complementarity in the service of the Lord.* It is a picture of the relationship between Christ and his church and between Christians in the church. 'The body is a unit,' says Paul, 'though it is made up of many parts... So it is with Christ' (1 Cor. 12:12). Feet cannot say they do not belong to the body, because they are not hands. Eyes cannot say to hands, 'I don't need you!' In fact, says the apostle, 'Those parts of the body that seem to be weaker are indispensable.'

> Like a mighty army
> Moves the church of God;
> Brothers, we are treading
> Where the saints have trod.
> We are not divided,
> All one body we,
> One in hope, in doctrine,
> One in charity.[8]

4.
Outside the camp

Please read Numbers 5

'Send them outside the camp ... where I dwell among them' (5:3).

Everyone who has camped with the Scouts or Guides will know how much attention is paid to order and cleanliness in the camp. The site for the tents is carefully chosen and neatly arranged — and the latrines are set up down-wind and at a distance. The reasons are the same as those for proper sanitary arrangements in permanent dwellings. Health and well-being are at stake. Disease is as much a threat today as it ever was in the past, and therefore all waste and garbage has to be disposed of as efficiently as possible. We may too easily take for granted the modern facilities we have for these purposes, but we lose sight of the underlying principle at our peril: if we are to live a healthy life, to be 'clean' is in, and dirt must go!

What is true for us was very true for Israel in the Sinai desert. And what is true of the physical necessities of life is also true of the spiritual. Israel was the church of the Old Testament period. She was the people of God, called to be a holy people — in Daniel's words, 'the saints of the Most High' (Dan. 7:18). 'Saint' is a word we immediately associate with excellence of character — a kind of super-goodness, attained by the very few — but in the Bible, the primary emphasis is not on our deeds *per se*, but on our relationship to the Lord. The root of sainthood is separation to God. It is a statement, first, about the condition of belonging to God, and only secondly about what is to flow from that condition, namely, personal godliness and good works. Every believer is a saint, that is, he or she is separated to God. It is because of that fact that the saints strive to live holy lives and grow to spiritual maturity. Israel were God's people, his saints, the people among whom he was present as their Father God. And the implications were tremendous for national and personal life: everything must be clean and dirt must go, for nothing that defiles must enter into the presence of this holy God. This is now expounded in terms of the basic principle that *sin must be put away* (5:1-4) and three pairs of laws, which illustrate and apply the principle. These are the law of restitution (5:5-10), the law of the test for unfaithfulness (5:11-31) and the law of the Nazirite (6:1-27; this will be the subject of our next chapter).

Sin must be put away (5:1-4)

The basic regulation was that those with an **'infectious skin disease or a discharge of any kind,'** or who were **'ceremonially unclean because of a dead body,'** were to be sent outside the camp. This republished in substance the more detailed prescriptions of Leviticus 13-15, which, it should be noted, provided the means by which cleansing and readmittance to the camp could be secured.

Clearly, the quarantine could have usefulness in countering the spread of certain diseases within the crowded confines of the camp. Equally clearly, this does not by itself approach an answer to the question as to why such regulations were laid down. The answer lies in two directions.

The first is that *God was in their midst.* They must put out those so afflicted, **'so that they will not defile their camp, where I dwell among them'** (5:3). God was to be reverenced at all times and nothing that defiled his perfect holiness was to be brought near to him. This is identical to the argument advanced in the New Testament for the necessity of maintaining the purity of the church. The church is the temple of God, indwelt by the Holy Spirit. Therefore, God will destroy those who seek to destroy his temple (1 Cor. 3:16-17). Practical personal godliness is the only acceptable behaviour in the presence of the Lord. 'Lord, who may dwell in your sanctuary?' asks the psalmist, 'Who may live on your holy hill? He whose walk is blameless and who does what is righteous...' (Ps. 15:1-2).

The second reason is to be found in *the ceremonial nature of the defilement.* Why did God single out certain diseases and the handling of dead bodies? After all, were there not sinful minds inside the camp all the time? Why did the unclean thoughts, words and deeds of the Israelites not defile the camp before God? Of course, the Lord knew very well that his people were sinners and that in real terms the sins of the heart were far, far more significant than, for instance preparing a dead body for burial (which was not a sin at all)! But the law focused on ceremonial uncleanness for the reason that these were clear instances of defilement, in that it was self-evident and obvious that disease and death were contradictions of what is good and healthy in normal experience. These *visible* afflictions provided suitable symbols of *invisible* realities relating to the holiness of God and the sinner's condition and need for redemption. The open, observable and highly practical isolation of the ceremonially defiled was a parable for the people of God about the issues of life, which proceed from the hearts of men and women and concern their relationship to the Lord (Prov. 4:23, AV). It taught the Israelites to prepare their hearts before God and recognize the real pollution, of which disease and death were but symptoms and the evil fruit.

As far as the New Testament Christian is concerned, this ceremonial law has passed away, but its lessons remain for ever to guide our attitude to the things of God. We are to be holy as God is holy (1 Peter 1:16). The church as a body is also to be cleansed of scandalous sin through appropriate discipline by the elders (1 Cor. 5:1-5), and the consequences of neglecting discipline and purity are the spread of great evils and the courting of a lost eternity (Heb. 12:15; Ps. 9:17, AV). The Lord is determined to save his people from their sins and sent his only-begotten Son to be the Saviour of all who would believe in him. In the Great Day, when he raises the dead and gathers the living, he will make his people perfect in holiness (Rev. 21:27). In the meantime, sin must be put away (1 Cor. 5:7-8; 2 Cor. 6:14-18).

Sin must be paid for (5:5-10)

The principle that sin must be put away is further elucidated by a pair of regulations teaching that sin must be paid for. This passage repeats the provisions of Leviticus 6:1-7, which has in view certain forms of theft. The two main components are confession and restitution.

Confession (5:6-7)

All sin is against God. Wronging someone else **'in any way'** is to be seen primarily as **'acting unfaithfully against the Lord'** (5:6, NASV). When David committed adultery with Bathsheba and contrived the death of her husband Uriah, he clearly wronged both of them. Nevertheless, he acknowledged his sin as first against God: 'Against you, you only, have I sinned and done what is evil in your sight...' (Ps. 51:4). Why did he do this? Simply because the standard by which sin is defined is God's revealed will. It is sin precisely because it is a 'want of conformity unto, or transgression of the law of God' (*Shorter Catechism,* 14). And it is to the Lord that we will all have to answer for everything we have done in the flesh.

   All sin must therefore be confessed. He **'must confess the sin he has committed'** (5:7). Words are not enough. There must be heart-repentance towards the Lord: 'If we confess our sins, he is faithful and just and will forgive us our sins and purify us from all unrighteousness' (1 John 1:9). Confession, says James Philip, 'is putting things right with God'.[1] It comes before putting things right with the people who have been wronged. The same is true in the case Jesus speaks of in the Sermon on the Mount (Matt. 5:23-24). At first glance, it seems that settling with the people comes before settling with God. Jesus says that if you come to worship God and remember your brother has a grievance against you, you are to 'leave your gift there in front of the altar' and 'first go' and be reconciled to that brother. The order is: reconciliation with people, then worship towards God. Worship is not, however, to be confused with confession of sin. The acknowledgement of sin actually had to precede going to the brother, or the latter would not have happened at all! Leaving the gift at the altar is the proof that the sin was admitted to God, because that is the only basis for going to the brother! Worship is only sincere — and only acceptable to God — when sin has been faced and confessed and is being dealt with. The same is true with the Lord's Supper: 'A man ought to examine himself before he eats of the bread and drinks of the cup' (1 Cor. 11:28).

Restitution (5:7-8)

Restitution is the man-ward side of dealing with wrongs. In Eric Segal's *Love Story*, 'love' meant 'never having to say you're sorry'. This is not only romanticized nonsense; it is the contradiction of the very meaning of love. Real love means always having to say a lot more than 'Sorry!' Real love means acknowledging guilt to God and man, accepting blame, accepting consequences, making amends and seeking forgiveness — and all with a 'broken spirit, a broken and a contrite heart' (Ps. 51:17). Saying sorry is *never* good enough! Without these elements just mentioned, it is tantamount to an evasion of guilt and responsibility and is no more than a sop, a form of words devoid of the essential components that make for genuine reconciliation. The Scriptures always require appropriate restitution for the victims of wrong-doing (5:7-10). This is alone the proof of genuine confession and contrition. We may note the following points (compare Lev. 6:1-7).

1. *Restitution must be in full:* '**He must make full restitution for his wrong**' (5:7). The loss must be made good. The criminal must restore what was taken, or its equivalent. This does not always happen in our judicial system today. 'Going to jail' is often called 'paying the debt to society'. In fact, it is the exact opposite — it is the avoidance of proper, biblical restitution. The mere sequestration of criminals from society is not really justice. It is a palliative for the people on the outside and a vehicle of avoiding responsibility for those on the inside. The principle of restitution is essential to the just resolution of the responsibility of criminals for their victims' losses. Compensation of victims by the guilty is the basic biblical principle.

2. *Restitution must be in full plus* '**one fifth**' (5:7). Such a 20% penalty is punitive, but neither excessive, greedy, nor destructive. Justice must be proportional and keep the emphasis on responsibility for restoration and, ultimately, reconciliation. These 'damages' are, furthermore, transferable to the person's relatives or, if there are none, to the church ('**to the priest**' 5:8). In this way, the righteousness of God is served. James Philip is surely correct, when he says that the Bible's law of restitution is 'considerably in advance of our own'.[2]

Sacrifice (5:8-10)

In reality, it is neither confession and repentance nor restitution and reformation that cancels out sin. This is the significance of the '**ram**

with which atonement is made' (5:8; 'guilt offering,' Lev. 6:6). It is a reminder that, while our obedience is necessary to redress the effects of past wrongs on those we have wronged, it is only substitutionary sacrifice that can atone for our sin and reconcile us to God. In fact, our submission to the Lord in confession and restitution must be seen as flowing from the acceptability of the sacrifice. The sinner, thus received, may then render acceptable obedience, which is the evidence of a saving relationship to the Lord. 'If we say that we have fellowship with him and yet walk in the darkness, we lie and do not practise the truth; but if we walk in the light as he himself is in the light, we have fellowship with one another, and the blood of Jesus his Son cleanses us from all sin' (1 John 1: 6-7, NASB).

Sin must be rooted out (5:11-31)

To the law of restitution is now added the law of the test for unfaithfulness, or the **'law of jealousy'** (5:29-31). This emphasizes that sin problems — real or alleged — must be followed up and resolved, not left to fester out of a squeamish unwillingness to face them.

The case is one of suspected adultery on the part of a wife. Innocence or guilt cannot be determined on the evidence of witnesses, for there are none. This is, of course, the perennial problem in cases of marital infidelity. In its nature, it is private sin, while at the same time a sin which is often 'known' to the betrayed spouse because of the subtle, or not so subtle, changes in his or her relationship with the unfaithful partner. As the relations between husband and wife deteriorate, the marriage becomes clouded with suspicion and resentment and, if one spouse is actually unfaithful, with lies and deceitfulness. The life of the family is impaired and, taking the wider view, the institution of marriage and the very stability of society come under threat. Adultery, it should be noted, carried the death penalty under the law (Lev. 20:10), a clear indicator of God's view of the importance of marital faithfulness.

The question was, how to deal with the case of suspicion of adultery, which, even if unfounded, could be as destructive of relationships as if it had actually occurred. Clearly, an extraordinary method would be required, if this were to be 'nipped in the bud'.

Accordingly, the Lord decreed a procedure by which he would reveal the guilt or innocence of the accused. This rested on the 'basic truth concerning all sin,' namely, that **'God knows and God judges'**.[3] The ordeal to be implemented was, as Wenham points out, 'essentially an elaborate oath'.[4] It consisted of the following main elements:

1. The accused wife was brought to the priest, who presented her **'before the Lord'** (5:15-16).

2. The priest put the woman **'under oath'** as to her innocence, pronouncing the **'curse of the oath'** which would come upon her if she had in fact committed adultery — her abdomen would swell and her thigh waste away (5:17-22).

3. The various components of the ritual associated with the woman's oath of innocence were now enacted. These included making her **'drink the bitter water'** (already prepared from 'holy water' and dust from the tabernacle floor (5:17) and making a **'grain offering'** on the altar (5:23-26).

4. The result would soon follow (5:27-28). The guilty woman would suffer the predicted physical degeneration and **'become accursed among her people,'** while the innocent would be **'cleared of guilt'** and **'be able to have children'**.

The immediate question that arises in modern minds is: 'Is this not a harsh, even "primitive" type of law?' We perhaps learned in schooldays of medieval 'trials by ordeal', in which an alleged witch would be submerged in the village pond: if she drowned, she was innocent and went to heaven (normal people can't survive under water); if she survived, she was guilty and should be burned at the stake as a witch and go to hell (only witches survive under water). Is this not arbitrary and even vicious?

To this it must be replied that the 'ordeal' did not involve doing something in itself life-threatening. The 'bitter water' was in itself harmless. In other words, the so-called 'ordeal' is not at all an ordeal after the torture model of medieval times. The bitter water was not a physical ordeal, but a symbol of the spiritual test — God's test — of the veracity of the oath of innocence. Like every other part of biblical ceremonial law, it was a picture portraying a deeper spiritual reality. The mixture of water from the laver in the court of the Tent of Meeting with dust from the floor of the sanctuary emphasized the holiness of bearing testimony before the presence of God. To ingest these waters and then tell a lie was to invoke the justified anger of

God. And it was direct divine judgement, not the physical result of drinking the water itself, which brought about the curse in the guilty. The same can be said, in different circumstances, of the deaths of Ananias and Sapphira (Acts 5). They proclaimed their beneficence to God, but proved themselves liars by holding back a portion of their declared gift. God therefore made them examples for future generations of the consequences all hypocrites will face sooner or later. Similarly, the abuse of the Lord's Supper in Corinth resulted in sickness and even death in that church. What did this mean? It meant that God is the exposer and judge of liars and hypocrites! Gordon Wenham points out that the ejection of the wicked from the church, as in 1 Corinthians 5:11-13 and Revelation 21:8; 22:15, teaches this truth. 'Numbers 5, Paul and Revelation make the same point: unfaithfulness is incompatible with membership of the people of God.'[5]

Draw the right conclusion: 'Leave your life of sin!'

Is this all wrath and no grace? By no means! The Lord who condemns sin is the same Lord who wants it to be rooted out. That in itself is an overture of grace. The entire sacrificial system of the Old Testament was designed, not to condemn, but to redeem! The God who was ready to expose liars and hypocrites was also full of mercy to the sincerely repentant. The unrepentant 'moral leper' of 1 Corinthians 5:1-5 is excommunicated from the church, while the leper Naaman, 'an outcast and alien from the commonwealth of God,' was 'nevertheless cleansed by the compassion of God'.[6] Jesus passed sentence on the Pharisees, the churchmen of the time, but to a woman taken in adultery, he said, 'Go now and leave your life of sin' (Matt. 23; John 8:11).

5.
Consecration and blessing

Please read Numbers 6
'The Lord bless you and keep you...' (6:24).

The great watchword for God's people in the Old Testament period was the 'Shema' — so called after the first word in the Hebrew, which means the imperative, 'Hear!' — 'Hear, O Israel: the Lord our God, the Lord is One' (Deut. 6:4). The great theme of God's Word is not, as some think, to tell us all about sin, sinners and the wrath of God, but the call to *hear him* and all that that implies — to listen, to come in faith, to follow, to be redeemed, reconciled, united to the Lord, to gain eternal life, to be a child of God. God calls us to live our lives for him, with him and in him. The condemnation of sin and warning of judgement to come are not the Lord's primary interest, but rather the necessary means to his higher goal of saving a people from their sins, that they might love him and glorify his name. Hence the words immediately following the 'Shema': 'Love the Lord your God with all your heart and with all your soul and with all your strength. These commandments that I give you today are to be upon your hearts. Impress them on your children. Talk about them when you sit at home and when you walk along the road, when you lie down and when you get up' (Deut. 6:6-7).

The practical concern, then, is to bring people to be God's people and to live their lives for him — the separated life, one of *consecration*, devotion and practical discipleship. Paul emphasizes this point in 2 Corinthians 6:17, quoting Isaiah 52:11 and 2 Samuel 7:14:

'"Therefore come out from them [the world of unbelievers]
        and be separate,

                                            says the Lord.
    Touch no unclean thing,
        and I will receive you."
    "I will be a Father to you,
        and you will be my sons and daughters."'

Elsewhere he says, 'Since, then, you have been raised with
Christ, set your hearts on things above, where Christ is seated at the
right hand of God. Set your minds on things above, not on earthly
things... When Christ, who is your life, appears, then you also will
appear with him in glory' (Col. 3:1-3). As is clear from these
passages, the theme of *the blessing of God* in our lives is inextricably
bound up with that of separation to be the Lord's people. 'Blessings
crown the head of the righteous' (Prov. 10:6) is writ large across the
Lord's relationship to his believing people.

These twin themes — consecration and blessing — meet in the
conjunction of the law of the Nazirite (6:1-21) and the priestly
benediction (6:22-26). They are two sides of one coin in the
experience of the child of God. No consecration — no blessing! No
blessing — no consecration! In the heart of the Christian, however,
they chase each other in the ascending heavenward spiral of the
Spirit-filled life.

Consecration — the law of the Nazirite (6:1-21)

The Nazirite law stands in sharp contrast to the previous chapter's
concern with the judicial exclusion of uncleanness from the people
of God. The Nazirites were people who devoted themselves to the
Lord in a special way and became examples to the people in general
of the meaning of discipleship. The present section tells us who they
were and what they did.

Who were the Nazirites? (6:1-2)

They were ordinary Old Testament believers — whether men or
women — who of their own volition, took **'a special vow'** to
dedicate themselves to the Lord. This was *entirely voluntary* and

was *for a specified period of time*, at the discretion of the individual. It was for purposes of personal godliness.

The Hebrew word, *nazir*, means 'separate'. It therefore had to involve practices that made the separation obvious to the community. Consequently, God gave precise regulations to make this separation clear and, in so doing, to prevent the excesses of super-piety which might well be adopted if it were left to people to decide on their own what they ought to do. It was a carefully limited regimen of spiritual exercises, designed by God to promote genuine piety, while avoiding spiritual pride. Its very simplicity stands in contrast to the elaborate ritualism of the Pharisees of Jesus' day, which, of course, was devotion gone to seed — external observance prostituted to the service of spiritual pride! Naziritism was popular for centuries among the Jews, down to the New Testament period. The most famous Nazirites were Samson and Samuel, both of whom were lifelong Nazirites, by divine appointment and dedication. Paul may have taken a Nazirite vow (Acts 18:18) and is known to have paid the expenses of the purification rites of four Nazirite men (Acts 21:23-36).

What Nazirites were not to do (6:3-12)

The most visible points of separation from everyday behaviour are those things we do *not* do, but which everyone else takes for granted. The Nazirites were required by the Lord to separate *from* normal practice at just three points.

The first of these was separation from *everything that came from the grapevine*, whether alcoholic wine, grape juice, grapes or even raisins (6:3-4). We are not told why, but it seems probable that the fruit of the grape was chosen because of its association with sensuality and excess, perhaps especially when abused in its fermented form. The other major fruits of the east, olives and figs, are just not in the same league as vehicles of worldly pleasure, however useful or nutritious they might be. Total abstinence from grapes, from skin and seeds to fermented wines, therefore provided a suitable, highly visible symbol of holiness over against the worldly pleasure represented by the grapevine.

The second marker of the vow was to be separation from *cutting the hair* (6:5). Hair was to be allowed to grow long and, as the most obvious of all Nazirite practices, was probably chosen for that very reason — as a symbol of visible separation from society in general, where the grooming of the hair was, and remains, expressive of a desire to project oneself in the most favourable and impressive manner. *Not* to cut the hair symbolized effectively the denial of self and concentration upon the Lord signified in the Nazirite vow.

The final point of separation was from *contact with a dead body and attendance at funerals* (6:6-12). Proximity to a dead body was always ceremonially unclean for God's people, so the Nazirite vow represents a heightened awareness of that point, which was symbolic of the fact that God is the Lord of *life*.

What Nazirites were to do

On the positive side, they were called to general personal godliness (6:2,5,6,7,8,14,17,21). They were given to the worship of God and the study of his Word. They were actively involved in community life — see, for example the public ministries of Samson and Samuel. Nazirites were not generally hermits, even if they did live distinctly separated lives. It was not a monastic order in any sense.

After the period of the vow expired, Nazirites *returned to normal life* (6:13-21). Offerings were to be brought to the priest and presented to the Lord. These offerings were costly — a Nazirite had to sacrifice three lambs, whereas anyone else could substitute doves (Lev. 5:7). From start to finish, the Nazirite was denying himself as he reverenced the Lord. The uncut hair was to be shaved off and burned with the fellowship offering. They could then drink wine, eat grapes, cut their hair and go near dead bodies.

What does this mean for Christians today?

Aside from Paul's apparent, but oblique, involvement in Nazirite vows, the nearest we come in the New Testament to a self-denying periodic vow would seem to be in the apostle's position that marital relations should only be discontinued 'by mutual consent and for a time' for the purpose of prayer (1 Cor. 7:5). Vows just do not figure very largely in New Testament piety. This is wholly consonant with the transition from the old covenant, for New Testament devotion is never mere ritual, shadow, or type, but is an open-faced, absolute standard of discipleship, set by Jesus himself, in example and precept. Even in the Old Testament, vows were entirely individual and voluntary and the great concern was not to promote such observances, but to make sure that they were not entered into lightly and that, once made, they were kept (Prov. 20:25; Eccles. 5:4-6). We have nothing of this in the New Testament, and cannot agree with G. J. Wenham when he suggests that there may be a place for such vows today as a means of 'pointing to the total dedication to God's service that is the goal of all Christian disciples'.[1] Jesus himself did no such thing. He simply lived out the perfect example of a godly life and called us to follow him.

Still less is there any warrant for the church requiring vows on matters not explicitly required by God's Word. An example of this would be requiring a vow of total abstinence from fermented wine as a condition of membership or office in the church.[2] The Bible says a great deal about alcohol abuse, and enjoins sobriety in the use of *all* God's gifts, but it nowhere requires a pledge of total abstinence. We may be ready, with Paul, to abstain from meat (offered to idols) — or fermented beverages — while the world lasts, for the sake of a brother with a tender conscience about such things (1 Cor. 8:13), but that remains a matter for informed, sanctified, *individual* consciences. This was the case for the Nazirites with respect to wine, and it remains so for us. Those who would impose a new asceticism on the church should note that the Nazirites, once released from their vow, returned to the enjoyment of haircuts, grapes, raisins … and fermented wine.

The Nazirite vow was a vivid symbolic picture of consecration to the Lord. Even after the institution has passed away, what stands is the basic claim to serve the Lord with heart, mind and strength. We are told in Scripture: 'Present your bodies a living and holy sacrifice, acceptable to God, which is your spiritual service of worship. And do not be conformed to this world, but be transformed by the renewing of your mind, that you may prove what the will of God is, that which is good and acceptable and perfect' (Rom. 12:1-2, NASB). This is the focus and message of the Nazirite vow.

But what does this mean in practice? What is consecration? It is, on the one hand, separation *from* the 'desire of the flesh' and 'the deeds of the flesh' (Gal. 5:16-21, NASB). On the other hand, it means separation *to* the 'fruit of the Spirit' (Gal. 5:16-21). Gifts and energies are dedicated to the Lord. This may mean choosing a path of specific self-denial, for the sake of Christ. I am not suggesting taking vows as did the Nazirites. God's Word does not require that.

But I think, for example, of Paul's commitment to his ministry (see Phil. 4:12; 1 Cor. 4:12-13; 7:31).

The implication is that Christians will live very differently from the world. The difference will be visible, like a city set on a hill (Matt. 5:14). Christians will be seen to live for Jesus Christ. The Nazirites symbolized, in a heightened way, the separation of believers to their Lord as a kingdom of priests and a holy nation (1 Peter 2:9). And, in this respect, they anticipated the Lord Jesus Christ, the gospel of his saving grace and the church which is the body of Christ.

The blessing — the Aaronic benediction (6:22-27)

It is no accident that this blessing is recorded in the Word next to the Nazirite law. Holiness and blessing are inseparable. Indeed the blessing of God precedes our desire to do his will, undergirds our present obedience and rewards and reinforces us for future discipleship.

The giver of the blessing (6:22-23)

The blessing was to be pronounced by the priests in the name of the Lord and indicated, then as now, the gracious intention of the Lord towards his people. The modern pastoral benediction is its direct descendant and, indeed, the Aaronic original is widely used today in the church. It may be that when Jesus, in his last act before his ascension, blessed his disciples with uplifted hands, it was in the utterance of these words (Luke 24:50-51). The apostolic benediction, which is explicitly trinitarian in form, may well be echoing the structure of the Aaronic blessing, in which 'the Lord' is mentioned three times (2 Cor. 13:14; cf. 6:24-26).

The content of the blessing (6:24-26)

The blessing is a poem with three lines consisting respectively of three, five and seven Hebrew words.[3] Wenham points out that if the three occurrences of 'Lord' are subtracted, there are twelve words left, 'no doubt symbolizing the twelve tribes of Israel'.[4]

Each of the three blessings follows the same pattern, and falls into three divisions, consisting of the Lord's name between two verbs, the second of which reinforces the first, as follows (in the order of the Hebrew text):

Bless you ... the *Lord* and ... *keep* you (6:24);
Shine on you ... the *Lord* his face and to you ... *be gracious* (6:25);
Turn ... the *Lord* his face to you and ... *give you peace* (6:26).

The force of each blessing is plain. In the first, the declared blessing of God issues in his keeping us under his protection and care. In the second, the shining of his face indicates a benevolent intent and results in our experiencing his grace and favour in many ways. Finally, the turning, or lifting up, of his face towards us means that he is attentive to our needs and meets them with his peace. He cares for us, he surrounds us with his favour and he brings forth peace in our hearts. This is the unconditional promise of his free grace! The threefold nature of the blessing speaks of fulness and points, say Keil and Delitzsch, to 'the threefold way in which it is communicated to us through the Father, Son, and Spirit'.[5] Echoing this sentiment, Wenham beautifully observes that 'In Jesus the full meaning of peace is revealed: he gave peace, made peace and is our peace (Jn. 14:27; Eph. 2:14f.).'[6]

The confirmation of the blessing (6:27)

'So they will put my name on the Israelites, and I will bless them.' The Lord places his name on us: the name that will live for ever; the name that is above every other name; the name that saves (Ps. 72:17; Phil. 2:9; Ps. 54:1). How then shall we wear his name upon our daily lives? We have turned full circle: from consecration to blessing, to consecration again, we are called to walk with our Lord, in dependence upon his grace.

6.
Gifts for God's altar

Please read Numbers 7
'These were the offerings for the dedication of the altar' (7:88).

The common saying, 'Why don't you put your money where your mouth is?' encapsulates a vital truth. And it is this: what people do with their material wealth says something about their commitments. It is always easier to spend money on things in which you are interested, than on things to which you are indifferent. We enjoy giving gifts to those we love, but are less enthusiastic when it comes to others.

The same is basically the case when it comes to the things of God and his church. Jesus said that 'Where your treasure is, there your heart will be also' (Matt. 6:21). What he meant was that when you love the Lord, your heart is bound to him and he is your real treasure; money, material things, hedonistic pleasures are no longer your gods. And because of this, your material wealth, such as it may be, becomes part of your service of the Lord. You 'give to the Lord's work as He [has] prosper [ed] you'.[1] Tithing, then, is no legalistic burden, but a joyous grace-driven privilege, born of the happy conviction that the Lord has saved you by the giving of himself as the only sacrifice for sin, thereby enabling you to present your body as a living sacrifice, 'holy and pleasing to God' (Rom. 12:1).

In our passage, we are shown something of this great principle in the lives of God's people. The setting is the establishment of the tabernacle (7:1; Exod. 40). This means, of course, that Numbers 7-9 record events that took place before the census of Numbers 1-4 —

in fact, a full month before. Why is this so obviously, and deliberately, out of chronological order? The answer is principally to be found in the nature of the first gifts that the leaders of the Israelite tribes brought to Moses. They were for the transportation of the tabernacle during the wilderness journey. It was therefore more appropriate to tell of these gifts in connection with the preparations for the journey than in the middle of the description of the structure of the tabernacle (Exod. 40) or embedded, perhaps incongruously, in a book devoted to details of the nature and task of the priesthood (the book of Leviticus).[2] So, as we consider the way the Lord prepared his people for their pilgrimage to Canaan, we have a picture of God's people bringing gifts to the Lord, which were not only relevant to their imminent journey of faith, but which also afford some timeless practical insights into the way in which the Lord's people today should bring their gifts for God's altar.

The roots of giving to the Lord (7:1-9)

Why do people give to a particular cause? The well-known American syndicated columnist, Cal Thomas, often speaks for Crisis Pregnancy Centres (CPC). These are Christian pro-life organizations which, throughout the United States, offer free pregnancy tests, counsel and pre- and post-natal support to mostly unwed mothers-to-be, to the end that the babies will be saved from being put to death in the womb by abortion. Having spoken of the issue of abortion and given testimony to his own Christian convictions, Thomas calls his audience to ask themselves how much saving a baby's life is worth, and so to give support to their local CPC, whether of time or money or clothes and toys. Now why do hundreds of thousands of American Christians respond positively to such a call? Because they are persuaded that the cause is truly worth supporting. It is a good cause. For Christians, it is good because it serves the purposes of God.

This leads us to the roots of all Christian giving, whether of time, effort, money or material. It arises from basic convictions about the value, importance and worthiness of the project or cause. We can see this in the gifts which the Israelites brought to Moses. Three essential elements stand out: worship, willingness and evident need.

Worship to the Lord (7:1-2)

Worship is essentially a recognition of worth. The Lord is 'worthy to be praised' — that is, to receive the worship of the men and women he has created. Jesus, 'the Lamb, who was slain,' is 'worthy' to receive 'power and wealth and wisdom and strength and honour and glory and praise' (Rev. 5:12). So it is no accident that the leaders' presentation of gifts arises from the actual completion of Israel's house of worship and the inaugural descent of the glory-cloud upon that tabernacle (cf. Exod. 40:34-35). With Moses' consecration of the tabernacle, we are brought to the very centre of Israel's worship — and, indeed, her national life as the Lord's people. Here God manifested his glory, visibly but in a way that transcends description. Here was the arena in which atonement was offered for the sins of the people. Here was the mercy seat, from which was dispensed the redeeming grace of God. Here was the focus of the worship of Israel.

Everything begins here, with God and with the adoration of his holy name. The gifts arose from worship and not in a dry and formal sense, like so much ritualized tribute designed to placate some dimly understood and darkly threatening deity. God's people worship their Father-God with the personal attachment of hearts transformed by his free grace. Their gifts are the response of those who know forgiveness and who feel his everlasting love. And this is true of the giving of Christians today, who experience these truths with the vastly greater clarity which comes from New Testament faith in Jesus Christ, as they give of themselves and their resources to the service of his cause and kingdom.

Willingness to serve (7:3)

It is important to notice that the **'gifts'** of the tribal leaders were voluntary, free-will offerings. These were distinct from the tithes, which were required by the Lord as matters of right and law (Gen. 14:17-21; 28:20-22; Lev. 27:30-33; Num. 18:20-24). These leaders gave willingly and out of a desire to serve the Lord. This highlights an important point: namely, that giving to the Lord's work, in the Old Testament no less than in the New, was to be motivated by love and spontaneous generosity of spirit. The Lord has always loved cheerful givers (2 Cor. 9:7). The grace of gospel giving was always implicit in the tithes of the patriarchs. In the New Testament, giving is constrained by the love of Christ and the dictates of a free and sanctified conscience. It is joyful (2 Cor. 9:7); systematic and proportional (1 Cor. 16:2); substantial (Acts 2:45); voluntary (Acts 5:3-4); and is related to the twin aims of supporting the ministry of the gospel (1 Cor. 9:13-14) and the ministry of mercy to those in need (Gal. 2:10; 2 Cor. 8:13-15; 1 John 3:17). This flows from the very nature of Christian stewardship as a trust from God in which Christians devote themselves with whole-hearted willingness to the work of the kingdom of Jesus Christ in the hearts and lives of men and women.[3]

Responding to a need (7:3-9)

The Israelite leaders saw a need. The Tent of Meeting would need to be transported. Its aggregated components constituted a tremendous burden, which would have to be carried on human shoulders. The silver sockets, which held the framework in place, alone weighed 100 talents — something over four tons! The sheer logistics argued the necessity of wheeled transport, at least for the bulky elements. So they presented **'six covered carts and twelve oxen'** (7:3).

Firstly, they presented their gifts **'before the tabernacle'**. That is to say, they offered them for the Lord's acceptance, or refusal. They recognized that God had as yet made no disposition on this question, so they came with a readiness to bow to whatever might be his will in the matter. They wanted to please God, rather than themselves.

Secondly, the Lord told Moses to **'accept these from them, that they may be used in the work at the Tent of Meeting,'** and ordered their distribution to the Levites as their work required (7:4). God has given us the framework of our lives and discipleship in the commands and principles of his Word. Within that context, he calls us to think and act with spiritual discernment and informed intelligence on the wider range of matters in which he has left it to us to apply these principles. This is what the leaders did in giving their gifts, and it is what Moses did in apportioning the carts. Two-thirds of the carts — four — went to the Merarites, who were responsible for the frames, posts, crossbars, pegs and ropes — the heavy stuff (4:31-32). The other two carts went to the Gershonites, who handled the lighter load, the curtains and coverings (4:25-26). The Kohathites received nothing, for they were to carry the 'most holy things' — the ark of the Testimony, the gold lampstand and the other furniture of the sanctuary (4:4-15), and to do so **'on their shoulders'** (7:9). This 'hands-on' responsibility emphasized, in the simplest way, the focused reverence with which the Lord himself is always to be regarded. These 'most holy things' represented God's provision for the redemption of his people, and the devoted care to be lavished upon them indicates something of the response of our heart to the mercies of God in Jesus Christ. We are to come to him, to embrace him in faith, to trust him for salvation and to receive eternal life.

There are a couple of sidelights on human experience worth noting here. One is that God's church is always 'on the move' and therefore always has new needs, which call for prompt, discerning and generous responses. New spheres of ministry require new facilities. Think how audio equipment has helped ministry to those whose hearing is impaired or to shut-ins. In a multitude of ways, our gifts can spread God's Word. The other is the more general reality that we must be prepared for changes. We too easily long for a settled, unmoving *status quo*. 'No sooner is the tabernacle set up,' notes Matthew Henry, 'than this provision is made for the removal of it... Even when we are but settled in the world, and think we are beginning to take root, we must be preparing for changes and removes, especially for the great change.'[4]

The response of the Lord to such giving (7:10-89)

This long section seems forbidding at first glance — a sterile litany of gifts to the tabernacle. It is, however, one of the simplest passages in the Bible. One list of gifts is repeated twelve times, one for each tribe, followed by the record of their sum total, together with the beginning of the Lord's response.

God received the gifts (7:10-11)

When the time arrived for the formal dedication of the altar, the Lord told the Israelite leaders, through Moses, to bring their gifts for the tabernacle itself. These gifts were apparently as spontaneous as the earlier gift of carts and oxen, and were also warmly accepted by the Lord for use in the service of his sanctuary. They were to be brought, one tribal gift per day, for a period of twelve days.

God does not always receive the gifts people give him. Only those gifts given in faith are acceptable to God. Without faith it is impossible to please God and anything that is not motivated by faith is simply sin (Heb. 11:6; Rom. 14:23). From Cain and Abel to Mary of Bethany and Ananias and Sapphira, and on to the separation of the 'sheep and the goats' on the Day of Judgement, the Lord applies this principle with perfect fairness (Gen. 4:3-5; Matt. 26:6-13; Acts 5:1-10; Matt. 25:31-36). This is why Jesus said that we had better be reconciled to our brother, before we bring our offerings to God (Matt. 5:23-24). God does not like us 'just the way we are'.[5] To be acceptable to God means first becoming right with him.

God recognized the givers (7:12-88)

Why one per day? Why not all together? The only answer must be that God meant it to be absolutely clear that he recognized every tribe particularly. They all belonged to the Lord and were accepted by him. One tribe could not say of another that they were less a part of the proceedings, less a part of God's people. God does not love 'humanity' in the abstract: he loves particular human beings, who make up his people. The very repetitiveness of the account demonstrates vividly the particularity of his grace towards those he has purposed to redeem. This is in the nature of a personal encouragement to devoted discipleship. When I am assured that God loves me, personally, I have a powerful motive to love him back with my whole heart. This experiential reality is marvellously evident in the psalms, which track the ups and downs of life and always find the answer in communion with the Lord.

The gifts themselves were very suitable as emblems of a deeper spiritual commitment. They were costly and practical. They revolved around the idea of sacrifice, and the necessity of coming to the Lord seeking his forgiveness and his blessing. They are connected with three specific sacrificial offerings.

1. The **'grain offering'** consisted of fine flour mixed with oil and incense (7:13-14). A handful was burned on the altar, while the rest belonged to the priests for food (Lev. 2). In this first observance in the tabernacle, the flour and oil were presented in two silver

vessels — a plate (1.4kg) and a bowl (0.8kg) — and the incense in a gold spoon (120g). The precise meaning of the offering is not clear, but it may be assumed to be concerned with reaffirmation of dedication to God. Since it followed the burnt offering, it can be seen as the response of gratitude to God for the forgiveness represented by that sacrifice.[6]

2. The **'burnt offering'** was to be a young bull, a ram and a year-old male lamb (7:15). This was for the acknowledgement of sin and the making of atonement to seek the mercy of God (Lev. 1). The New Testament presents the Lord Jesus Christ as the once-for-all burnt offering — the Lamb of God who takes away the sin of the world (John 1:29; Heb. 7:27; 1 Peter 1:18-19).[7]

3. The **'sin offering'** was a male goat (7:16). This was for specific transgressions of God's law (see Lev. 4-5; 12:6; 14:19; 15:15) and for dedications, as in the present case, or a person's release from a Nazirite vow (Num. 6:14). The sprinkling of the blood cleanses from sin. Again, Jesus Christ is the one to whom this points (Heb. 9:22; 1 John 1:7; Rev. 7:14).[8]

4. The **'fellowship offering'** comprised two oxen, five rams, five male goats and five year-old male lambs (7:17). These were sacrificed, blood sprinkled on the sides of the altar, certain parts burnt, certain parts given to the priests and the rest consumed by the worshipper and his family (Lev. 3). The focus appears to have been upon peace with God and the enjoyment of his presence among his people.[9]

Together, these represent the covenant relationship which God established between himself and Israel. They were his people and he was their God. In Jesus Christ, this is a fulfilled reality for Christians today (1 Peter 2:9-10).

God revealed himself in grace (7:89)

The seal of God's approval was to speak to Moses from the 'mercy seat' (NIV **'atonement cover'**) on the ark of the Testimony. The words, **'And he spoke with him,'** indicate the continuing experience of Moses. He heard the voice of God with his own ears. God was really present with his people! 'The tabernacle was no empty shrine,' says Gordon Wenham, 'but the palace of the living God.'[10]

This speaks of *the necessity of atoning sacrifice for human sin.*

Neither the blood of the animals themselves nor the proper form of the ceremonies of the tabernacle constituted the actual atonement. It was rather that which they symbolized: the blood of the promised Messiah, Isaiah's 'suffering Servant', who alone was 'good enough, to pay the price of sin' (C. F. Alexander).

It also speaks of *the sufficiency of Jesus Christ* as that atonement. He is the meaning of the Old Testament sacrifices. He is the only Redeemer of men and women. 'Why is the Son of God called "Jesus" meaning "Saviour"?' asks the *Heidelberg Catechism*, (Q.29). 'Because,' comes the answer, 'he saves us from our sins. Salvation cannot be found in anyone else; it is futile to look for salvation elsewhere' (Matt. 1:21; Heb. 7:25; Isa. 43:11; John 15:5; Acts 4:12; 1 Tim. 2:5).[11]

Finally, it speaks of *the power of the Word of God* to bring lost people to saving faith. Jesus says that people will hear the voice of the Son of God and those who hear will live (John 5:25). His sheep, he says, hear his voice and follow him (John 10:3-5, 14-16, 27). God speaks — then at the mercy seat, and now in Jesus who is both sacrifice and mercy seat to save his people from their sins! The gifts at the dedication of the tabernacle lead us to Christ! They are not a plug for funds, but a plea for faith! The Word has come amongst us and to those who receive him, who believe in his name, he gives the right to become children of God (John 1:12).

7.
Living lamps

Please read Numbers 8:1 - 9:14
'Every first-born male in Israel, whether man or animal, is mine'
(8:17).

Worthwhile projects are never accomplished by ill-considered decisions and lackadaisical actions. They all need a plan, some careful preparation and then perseverance in pursuance of the plan. Such was certainly the case for Israel if her expedition to Canaan was to succeed, or even get under way. Nevertheless, like everything in life — contrary to the wisdom of the world — this was more a spiritual and theological problem than one of logistics or weaponry. They were already organized as a 'nation in arms' (Num. 2-3). What they now needed was the right condition of heart and soul for their great venture. This was more than a matter of mere morale; it meant being right with the Lord, being committed to his will as the believing recipients of his redemptive grace.

Central to this was the dedication of the Tent of Meeting and those who served it, the Levites. The Levites were the 'living lamps' of God.[1] They embodied both the consecration of Israel to be God's people and the determination of God to be their God. The establishment of their service at the heart of Israel's life was essential to the march on Canaan, because, in the last analysis, this was integral to God's plan of redemption, but also because, experientially, the Lord's people needed to know the power of God in their lives and in their counsels. It is this essentially spiritual preparation which is the subject of Numbers 8:1 - 9:14.

The light of the Menorah (8:1-4)

If much of the Book of Numbers seems distant and exotic to modern readers, the inclusion of a section on the lampstand, or *Menorah*, seems decidedly odd. What connection does this have with the dedication of the tabernacle and the Levites? It is, on the face of it, merely a description of the object and its general function.

Nothing in Scripture, however, is merely incidental and an examination of the nature of the Menorah soon suggests some answers. It stood in the Holy Place of the Tabernacle (Fig. 2).

The *Menorah* was a seven-branched flowering tree made of gold (Exod. 25:31-40; Num. 8:4), with a lamp on each branch, fed by oil and 'kept burning continually' (Lev. 24:2-4). This stood on the south side of the Holy Place and was the only light, as there were no windows. Aaron was to set up the seven lamps, so as to **'light the area in front of the lampstand'** (8:1).

The lamp is a picture teaching that *God is the source of light*. The lamp is 'an emblem of spiritual light',[2] while the seven branches symbolize 'the Lord's church, fed by the oil of the Spirit'.[3] Together, the light and the fire on the altar of incense represent the 'life-giving presence and blessing of God' with his people.[4]

The light shone forwards upon the Table of the Showbread. Upon this table were laid twelve loaves of bread, one for each tribe. This was the 'Bread of the Presence', which signified that God was the sustainer of his people's lives, the giver of the 'bread of life' (Ps. 36:8; Luke 22:30; John 6:32-35). The light shines on the bread. In other words, God is *our* light. We experience that light as a lamp to our feet and a light for our path (Ps. 119:105). He keeps our lamp burning and turns our darknesses into light (Ps. 18:28). The Bible is to us as a 'lamp shining in a dark place' (2 Peter 1:19). The Lord makes his face to shine upon us (Num. 6:25). Jesus is 'the light of the world' and, because of this, believers in turn become 'the light of the world' as they witness for Christ (John 8:12; Matt. 5:14).

The first step from Sinai towards the promised land was, then, the acceptance of God's light — his revealed will — as the plan to guide them through their journey. The message is timeless. Those who would come to God must believe that he is and that he is the rewarder of those who diligently seek him (Heb. 11:6).

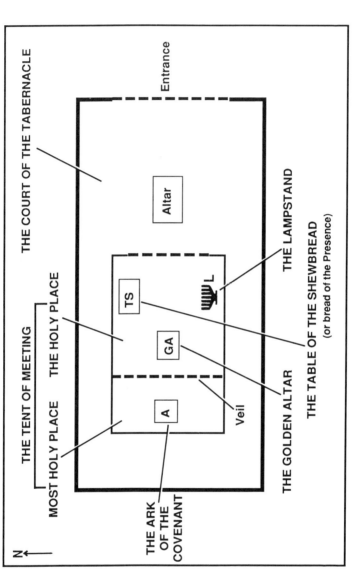

Figure 2. The tabernacle

The cleansing of the Levites (8:5-14)

The next step was to make the Levites **'ceremonially clean'** (8:5). The assumption is, of course, that actual purification could not be achieved by means of a mere ritual. Why, then, have ceremonies at all?

The key point to be grasped is that the entire ceremonial system, with its laws, tabernacle and the sacrifices, was a series of pictures, the components of which were symbols pointing to the Lord, his people and the relationship between the two. Just as a parable can be called 'an earthly story with a heavenly meaning', so the ceremonial laws of the Old Testament are visual aids to invisible truths.

They were, however, far more than mere symbols, for they were to involve the spiritual exercises they often portrayed. Thus, while a sin offering was made and the blood of the animal was sprinkled on the altar, the worshipper was from the heart to look to the Lord as the Redeemer — as opposed to trusting in the death of the animal. Godly Hebrews understood the spirituality of these external actions, just as modern Christians, for example, realize that the blessing of participation in the Lord's Supper relates to faith in the heart, and is not some automatic consequence of hearing the words of institution and ingesting the bread and wine.

Ultimately the ceremonial law pointed to Jesus Christ and was bound to become obsolete in the aftermath of his fulfilment of its meaning and promise. The ceremonial cleansing of the Levites, therefore, must be seen as a picture of the salvation which God brought to his people through the blood of the real sacrificial Lamb, slain before the foundation of the world.

The immediate purpose of the ceremonial cleansing was to set apart the Levites for the service of the sanctuary. The ceremony enshrined the necessity of 'clean hands and a pure heart' for anyone who would 'stand in his holy place' (Ps. 24:4), and so emphasized the holiness of the living God, who cannot look upon sin. Those who worship him, said Jesus to the woman at the well, must worship him 'in spirit and in truth' (John 4:24).

Cleansing from defilement (8:5-7)

The Levites were first subjected to a threefold regimen of personal cleansing. They were sprinkled with water, shaved off all body hair and washed their clothes. This imagery underlies such New Testament expressions as 'the washing of rebirth' or regeneration and 'hearts sprinkled to cleanse us from an evil conscience' (Titus 3:5; Heb. 10:22) and is symbolic of the spiritual cleansing of the renewed heart of the believer from the corruption and defilement of sin.

Redemption from condemnation (8:8-13)

The second series of ceremonies focused on the curse or penalty of sin. This was in two linked phases.

The people were to **'lay their hands'** on the Levites and the latter were to be presented as **'a wave offering from the Israelites'** (8:8-11). In other words, the Levites were offered to God as a sacrifice for the nation. They were, firstly, living substitutes for the first-born of the twelve tribes of Israel, secondly, representatives of the dedication of the whole nation to God and, thirdly, the symbolic sacrifice for the sins of the people (cf. Rom. 12:1-2).

The Levites, in turn, were to lay their hands on the two young bulls presented for the sin offering and the burnt offering (8:12-13). These animals were then sacrificed for the sins of the Levites — and, by association through the earlier laying on of hands, those of Israel as a whole. This is the second link in a chain of symbolic identification, connecting the people, the Levites, the sacrifices for sin and redemption. With the subsequent celebration of the Passover, this last focus centres on the sacrificial lamb, which foreshadows Jesus Christ, the once-for-all Passover Lamb (9:1-14; 1 Cor. 5:7; Rev. 13:8).

'The Levites will be mine' (8:14)

In this way, the Levites were set **'apart'** and declared by the Lord to be his (8:14). The ceremonial defined the actual. They were his already. But everyone needed to know that people had to be cleansed from sin by a substitutionary atonement, for without the shedding of blood, there is no remission of sins (Heb. 9:22).

The commitment of the Levites (8:15-26)

Many a venture is launched in a fanfare of enthusiasm, only to founder on the shoals of flagging interest and grudging performance. Assessing the cost of commitment is too easily put off until later and by that time the unanticipated burdens become reasons for reneging on earlier pledges. Israel had already been through three such episodes — at Marah and at Rephidim and in the incident of the golden calf (Exod. 15:22-27; 17:1-7; 32:1-33:6) — and it was therefore essential to lay out plainly what they had to do to be in the path of God's blessing.

First, there must be *undivided loyalty* (8:15-19). After the preparation, came the work — to which they were to give themselves wholly. The rationale that they were representative of the first-born redeemed from Egypt is given here to underscore the point. 'From everyone who has been given much, much will be demanded; and from the one who has been entrusted with much, much more will be asked' (Luke 12:48). The devotion of the Levites was to be seen as a great **'gift'** to the Lord's people, which was accordingly to be prized and nurtured, **'so that no plague will strike the Israelites when they go near the sanctuary'** (8:19). The parallel with the sickness and death that attended the abuse of the Lord's Supper in Corinth is inescapable. The ordinances of God are to be observed with reverence and holy fear. The ministry of the gospel is a precious privilege to be respected and encouraged by the Lord's people. God gave the gift of ministry to the church for the blessing of the whole body (Eph. 4:11-16). When churches lose, or abuse, the ministry God has given to them, the results cannot but be catastrophic, for the simple reason that it is the rejection of the Lord himself!

Secondly, there had to be *unswerving obedience* (8:20-22). Moses and Aaron **'did ... just as the Lord commanded Moses'**. The Levites **'purified themselves'** and Aaron presented them as a **'wave offering'** and **'made atonement'** for them before the Lord. God spoke, and they acted, willingly and gladly. And so must we, for, as Jesus says, 'If you love me, you will obey what I command' (John 14:15).

Godly obedience is far more than merely 'doing what you are told'. You know how it often is. Mum asks Johnny to tidy his room, or help set the table, and is greeted with a 'Why?' Too often the answer comes, 'Because I tell you!' Or even just, 'Because...' Or, worse, a threat, 'Get cracking, or I'll tan your hide!' The Lord commands obedience for good reasons; which are stated clearly in his Word, the Bible. He also commands obedience as a conscious response of love on our part. This is the only true obedience in any case. Loveless obedience is only a policy, adopted because it serves our self-interest. It cannot be true obedience, because it is not obedience from the heart. It is a simulation, rather than the real obedience of a holy love for God, his kingdom and his righteousness.

This is the significance of the connection of obedience and atonement in the dedication of the Levites. God saves by providing atonement for sin. The fruit is that those who are saved love him and give their lives to him willingly and joyfully. 'We love,' says John, 'because he first loved us' (1 John 4:19). The result is the fruit of the Spirit's work, 'love, joy, peace, patience, kindness, goodness, faithfulness, gentleness and self-control'. And the reason? 'Those who belong to Christ Jesus have crucified the sinful nature [flesh, AV] with its passions and desires. Since we live by the Spirit, let us keep in step with the Spirit' (Gal. 5:22-25).

Finally, they were to give of their *best* (8:23-26). Theirs was to be prime-time service. The **'regular service'** of Levites was between the ages of twenty-five and fifty. Thereafter they would 'retire' and assume lighter duties, assisting the younger men. Early years would be taken up with preparation of one sort or another. The point is that the prime of life must be given to the Lord's work. The establishment of a definite term of service also ensured a regular succession, as each age group moved into the responsibilities appropriate to their age.

It ought therefore to be unthinkable for anyone to entertain the notion of the modern church-member who, when challenged about her non-attendance at church, gave the reason that she was too tired because of her work, but promised to come back after she retired in a few years! Discipleship is *now*, not when you have some time left over, later on.

We are also given a caution against another scourge of the modern church — people who never hand on responsibilities to others, because they refuse to see their own growing incapacities, or else have come to see themselves as indispensable. The 'mandatory retirement' of the Levites is not a rule for pastors, elders, Sunday School teachers etc., in the New Testament church, but it is a principle which ought to be corrective of certain abuses as they arise. Churches which have no room for the active involvement of men and women in the prime of life, because certain people are determined to go on doing what they have been doing for fifty or sixty years (forgetting that someone older had then stepped aside to let them take up the work when they were still young), are churches which become self-fulfilling prophecies—namely, churches of old people. Young, active Levites knew exactly when they had to take over full responsibility for their service to God. Young Christians need a similar incentive, and churches that refuse to mobilize them for service, until, at the age of sixty, they step into the shoes of retiring octogenarians, are virtually telling them that they are just not needed in the prime of their lives, except to fill pews on Sunday and raise the church's budget! God wants our energies, when we still have some to put forth!

The celebration of the Passover (9:1-14)

The first Passover had been celebrated in Egypt on the fourteenth day of the first month, and this was to be a 'lasting ordinance' for Israel, to be celebrated even after they had come to the land of promise (Exodus 12:25).[5] The tabernacle was completed by the first day of the first month in the second year since the Exodus, so it was exactly the moment for the Lord to fix clearly in the minds and calendar of the Israelites what he wanted done with the Passover in future. This was a 'lasting ordinance' to be observed annually on the fourteenth of every first month (9:1-5).

A problem arose, however, over some men who could not participate on account of ceremonial uncleanness through contact with a dead person (9:6-14; Lev. 7:20). What were they to do? The Lord's answer through Moses was to permit them a delay of one month, with the proviso that any who used this as an excuse to miss the regular Passover, when they were really able to be present, were to be **'cut off'** from the people. Unworthy participation by reason of ceremonial uncleanness, and non-participation without a good reason, both incurred the displeasure of God. To be 'cut off' was to suffer sudden judgement at God's hand, even death. There is a parallel penalty in the New Testament, in the case of the Corinthians' abuse of the Lord's Supper (1 Cor. 11:27-30).

What did this Passover observance mean to the Israelites? Certainly, the Exodus, of which the Passover was the centre-piece, was a mighty complex of miraculous deliverances for God's people.

The first Passover marked the redemption of Israel's first-born. The first-born, so redeemed, in turn symbolized the redemption of the nation as a whole and were a sign of all Israel's belonging to the Lord. To observe it thereafter was to celebrate the mighty acts of God in his love for his people. It was a celebration of salvation, personal and corporate. God loved his people. He kept his covenant with Abraham, Isaac and Jacob. He provided the way of escape and set them on the road to the fulfilment of promises given long before. The annual Passover looked back to deliverance from Egypt and forward to the promises of God's covenant.

At the heart of the Passover was the accomplishment of redemption through the blood of the sacrificial lamb. The lamb substituted for the people, atoned for their sin and washed it away. This was, of course, a symbol of the real sacrifice of the final Lamb, who was yet to come and take away the sin of the world (John 1:29). Christ is the true Passover Lamb — and the fulfilment of Israel's Passovers (1 Cor. 5:7). It is the blood of Jesus Christ that *alone* achieved what the lambs of the Israelites only represented — namely, cleansing from all sin (1 John 1:7).

The necessary consequence of this truth is the requirement of joyful obedience to the Lord's will. Paul expresses the logic of the Passover when he says, 'For Christ, our Passover lamb, has been sacrificed. Therefore let us keep the Festival, not with the old yeast, the yeast of malice and wickedness, but with bread without yeast, the bread of sincerity and truth' (1 Cor. 5:7-8). When Jesus identified himself as 'the bread of life', he said, 'I tell you the truth, unless you can eat the flesh of the Son of Man and drink his blood, you have no life in you' (John 6:35,53). All this highly figurative language is rooted in the imagery of the Passover and is talking about its salvation, living faith and practical obedience.

The consecration of the Levites and the celebration of the Passover called the people to be living lamps, shining for the Lord through the luminescence of holy lives. Fulfilled in the promised Messiah, the one true and final Lamb, slain from the foundation of the world (Rev. 13:8), that light shines in succeeding generations of Christians:

> The Lord's my light and saving strength;
>   Who shall make me dismayed?
> My life's strength is the Lord; of whom
>   Then shall I be afraid?

One thing I of the Lord desired
 And will seek to obtain:
That all days of my life I may
 Within God's house remain:

That I the beauty of the Lord
 Behold may and admire,
And that I in his holy place
 May rev'rently enquire.[6]

8.
Guided by God

Please read Numbers 9:15 - 10:10
'They obeyed the Lord's order...' (9:23).

The eighteenth-century Welsh preacher, William Williams, began his most famous hymn with the words:

> Guide me, O thou great Jehovah
> Pilgrim through this barren land.
> I am weak but thou art mighty
> Hold me with thy mighty hand
> Bread of heaven, feed me till I want no more.[1]

His inspiration for these marvellous lines was, of course, the wilderness wanderings of Israel some thirty-five centuries ago and the way this touched the real experience of Christians in every generation. Williams knew that he was a pilgrim and that Christians are passing through a spiritually barren land, a world blasted by evils, great and small.

The leading motif is not, however, the barrenness of the land, but rather our need for the presence and guidance of our Lord, and his assurance of provision for our very real needs. The Bible teaches us to have certain expectations of our God. One of these is that he will show us where we are to go with our lives, how we are to walk, what our goals and aspirations ought to be. He has promised to 'guide [us] always', with the assurance that 'If the Lord delights in [our] way, he makes [our] steps firm' (Isa. 58:11; Ps. 37:23).

In spite of their complaining, the Israelites had seen plenty of evidence that this was true, that God was as good as his word. They had camped for nearly a year at the foot of Mount Sinai. God had revealed his law — the Ten Commandments, the plans for the Tent of Meeting and the sacrifices and the book of Leviticus. The Tent of Meeting had been dedicated. The people had been organized for the march. Now, on the eve of departure, the Lord made provision for their guidance: first, through the cloud they were given a clear vision of the way they were to go (9:15-23) and second, through the silver trumpets they were given a clear call to what they were to do (10:1-10).

A clear vision — the cloud above the tabernacle (9:15-23)

God first manifested his presence with Israel in the cloud and fiery pillar, which went ahead of the people out of Egypt at the Exodus (Exod. 13:21-22; also 14:14-20; 24:15-18; 33:9-10; 40:34-38). Night and day, he led them to Sinai and showed to them the truth, later expressed by the psalmist, that 'He who watches over Israel will neither slumber nor sleep' (Ps. 121:4).

This now changed in certain important respects. From the day that the tabernacle was dedicated, **'The cloud covered it, and at night it looked like fire'** (9:15-16). Whenever the cloud lifted, they were to move. When it settled, they were to camp. These movements also determined how long they were to camp — whether **'two days or a month or a year'** (9:17,22). It appears that specific instructions, perhaps as to direction, were given **'through Moses'** (9:23). It is easy to see what this all meant for Israel, but what, if anything, does it mean for us today? I would suggest three main points: God reveals himself to us, God is present with us and God promises his blessings to us.

God reveals himself to us

The cloud was visible proof to Israel that God was revealing himself to them. The revelation in words that God gave through Moses, whether of the Ten Commandments and the Law, or the more everyday communications of his will, were proof positive that God was opening a view of himself to his people. God did not hide anything from them that they needed to know about him. He was not like the inscrutable gods of the heathen, who had to be placated with endless prayers and sacrifices out of a vague hope that such devotion might 'work'. Pagans today, as then, live fear-filled lives, never knowing what judgements may lurk around the corner from unknown, impersonal and terrifying deities. Israel knew exactly where they stood with the living God, because he had explicitly, repeatedly and clearly revealed his will for their lives. One powerful example of this, in very short compass, is found in Exodus 34:5-7, on the occasion of the Ten Commandments being issued for the second time. It is an evocation of the very character of God and of his programme for the human race. Notwithstanding the insistence upon just judgement, it is primarily and essentially redemptive: 'Then the Lord came down in the cloud and stood there with him and proclaimed his name, the Lord. And he passed in front of Moses, proclaiming, "The Lord, the Lord, the compassionate and gracious God, slow to anger, abounding in love and faithfulness, maintaining love to thousands, and forgiving wickedness, rebellion and sin. Yet he does not leave the guilty unpunished; he punishes the children and their children for the sin of the fathers to the third and fourth generation."'

God still reveals himself today. He does so in his creation, including our own very being as people made in his image (Ps. 19:1-6). This is quite sufficient to leave us without an excuse for rejecting our Maker, but only reveals God's wrath against our rebelliousness and provides no way of salvation (Rom. 1:18-20). The Lord has also revealed himself in his Word and with that the message of salvation (Ps. 19:7-14). Jesus is the living Word, of whom the written Word speaks (John 1:1,14). Jesus is the revelation of the Father's glory and the express image of his person (1 Cor. 11:7; Heb. 1:3). His claims are explicit and exclusive: 'I am the way and the truth and the life. No one comes to the Father except through me ... Anyone who has seen me has seen the Father' (John 14:6,9). And we know this from the Scriptures, which are the power of God unto salvation for all who believe. The cloud and fiery pillar are no more, but the Word of God endures for ever.

God is present with his people

The cloud was visible over the tabernacle, twenty-four hours a day. As such, it proclaimed to Israel that the Lord was with them, that he would protect them and that he would lead them. This is just as true for the New Testament church. The Lord *is with us*, 'to the very end of the age' (Matt. 28:20). He has promised never to leave us or forsake us (Heb. 13:5). He is able to *keep us* when we face troubles, because he has 'overcome the world' (John 16:33). True Christians will 'never perish', because 'No one can snatch them out of [his] hand' (John 10:28-29). And he has promised to *guide us*, for the children of God are led by the Spirit of God into the sure understanding of the Word of God (Rom. 8:14; John 14:26).

God assures his people of his particular love and blessing

The movements of the cloud determined the movements of Israel. When God waited, they waited. When he moved, they moved. And in every turn of events, the hand of the Lord was upon them in his particular love for his people.

This was true in their *waiting*, when the cloud descended. Waiting is always a challenge to patience. Like the dancing swarms of mayflies — those aptly named 'Ephemeroptera' which live as adults only to breed and never even to feed — restless and frustrated men and women will flit from one thing to another, always seeking an elusive satisfaction. In contrast, the Lord gives peace and a spirit of contentment to those who simply trust in him. In the midst of a hard and bruising life as a missionary, the apostle Paul could testify, 'I have learned the secret of being content in any and every situation' (Phil. 4:12). How did this happen? It happened because he knew 'the God of peace' and was persuaded by his experience of God's dealings with him that he could 'do everything' through the Lord who gave him strength (Phil. 4:9,13). If this is true of you, then you will be enabled to wait with patience for God's timing in your life. 'There is no time lost when we are waiting God's time.'[2]

The same is true of our *going on* with the Lord. In the doing of his will, the tokens of his particular care for us become clear to discerning hearts. It was not given to the disciples on the road to Emmaus to recognize their companion at the time, but after the risen Jesus did reveal himself, the penny dropped: 'Were not our hearts burning within us while he talked with us on the road and opened the Scriptures to us?' (Luke 24:32). Think too of Paul's assurance that the Lord was with him, even when he was facing terrible troubles: 'dying, and yet we live on ... sorrowful, yet always rejoicing ... having nothing, and yet possessing everything' (2 Cor. 6:3-10).

The 'secret' is, of course, *communion* with the Lord. Asaph describes the believer's guidance system in a sentence: 'You guide

me with your counsel, and aferwards you will take me into glory.'
He explains further:

> 'Whom have I in heaven but you?
>   And earth has nothing I desire besides you.
> My flesh and my heart may fail,
>   but God is the strength of my heart
>   and my portion for ever'
>
> (Ps. 73:24-25).

Other psalmists, the sons of Korah, let us look through heaven's window: 'For this God is our God for ever and ever; he will be our guide even to the end' (Ps. 48:14). Genuine communion with the Lord — believing prayer and meditation on his Word — is a means of grace to our souls (Ps. 104:34).[3] A most touching instance of how spiritual communion gives rise to fresh and indescribable experiences of assurance of God's goodness to us is that of the aged Simeon, a godly man who had been assured by the Holy Spirit that he would see the promised Messiah before he died. Jesus was eight days old when his parents brought him to the temple for circumcision, the sign of the covenant. Simeon took the baby Jesus in his arms and, discerning instantly who he was, uttered the most glorious epitaph anyone ever declaimed over his own life:

> 'Sovereign Lord, as you have promised,
>   you now dismiss your servant in peace.
> For my eyes have seen your salvation,
>   which you have prepared in the sight of all people,
> a light for revelation to the Gentiles
>   and for glory to your people Israel'
>
> (Luke 2:29-32).

The cross was still three decades in the future, but godly Simeon knew the promises of God's Word and believed in Christ as the only Saviour! Like Abraham, he believed 'the gospel in advance' — not quite so far in advance, to be sure, but still entirely in anticipation, by faith, of events he would not see in his lifetime (Gal. 3:8).

The meaning of God's guidance in the cloud above the tabernacle is, in the end, to be found in Jesus the promised Messiah. He delivers his people by the sacrifice of himself in their place and he walks with them and talks with them along the pathways of life.

Again this is the testimony of William Williams:

> Open now the crystal fountain,
> Whence the healing stream doth flow;
> Let the fire and cloudy pillar
> Lead me all my journey through:
> Strong deliverer
> Be thou still my strength and shield.

A clear call — the silver trumpets (10:1-10)

In addition to the visible movement of the cloud, the Lord ordered that **'two trumpets of hammered silver'** be made **'for calling the community together and for having the camps set out'** (10:1-2). These were to be made and blown by the priests — that is, Aaron and his sons — and they were to be blown according to a simple code.

1. Twice (10:3) — for the calling of the people to a general assembly around the Tent of Meeting.
2. Once (10:4) — for a conference of the leaders of the people.
3. With a different, louder sound (10:5-7) — each **'blast'** would signal the successive divisions to move off in order.
4. In Canaan (10:8-9) — an alarm for battle and a call for the Lord's help.
5. In Canaan at **'your times of rejoicing'** (10:10) — as a memorial before the Lord, calling upon him to accept the sacrifices for sin and for blessing.

What is striking in the provision of the trumpets is the emphasis here on the element of human responsibility. Whereas the cloud was the visible manifestation of God and of his sovereign will, the blowing of the silver trumpets was something the servants of God did. Both were a response to God's guidance and, in the wilderness at any rate, concerned the alternate encampment and movement of Israel. The use of the trumpets, however, necessitated faithful mediation by the priests, between the will of God as revealed to them and the conveying of that will to the people.

The primary message of the trumpets, then, is not God's guidance as such, but the faithfulness of responsible human leadership, under God. If the cloud moved, everybody saw it and knew God's will. If the priests did not blow the trumpet, nobody knew what God had revealed. You will notice also that the sacrificial and ceremonial aspects of the priestly task are not in view here. The trumpets point to the pastoral aspects of their ministry. They were to be blown as an aid to the practical mobilization of the people of God, in other words, their use was analogous to the pastoral role of the ministers of the gospel in the New Testament church. God gave the church, among others, 'pastors and teachers,' in order to build up the people of God, so that they would come to 'unity in the faith ... and become mature, attaining to the whole measure of the fulness of Christ' (Eph. 4:11-13).

Indeed, the message reaches beyond the ordained officers of the church, to the priesthood of all believers. Anything any Christian may say comes under the exhortation to give a very clear note to the trumpet, which is your personal witness for your Saviour. Paul says, in criticism of charismatic excesses: 'If the trumpet does not sound a clear call, who will get ready for battle? So it is with you. Unless you speak intelligible words with your tongue, how will anyone know what you are saying?' (1 Cor. 14:8).

The promise of the silver trumpets is timeless, even if the instruments themselves are long gone, with all the other symbolic accoutrements of the old covenant. The Lord has promised to lead us. He issues the call for us to follow him. Yet we — his ministers and his people — are charged with the fullest responsibility to provide the wind to sound the clarion call of the gospel to worship, adore and serve him. The proclamation of the Word of God is, pre-eminently, that call. It must be clear, or preachers and people alike will perish under its deceiving and deadly notes. When it is clear, the Lord's people respond with an exalted sense of God's love for them and they march onward, rejoicing to do the Lord's will, confident of fulfilling his purpose and assured in their heart of hearts that he will bring them home to glory!

> When I tread the verge of Jordan,
> Bid my anxious fears subside!
> Death of death; and hell's destruction,
> Land me safe on Canaan's side!
> Songs of praises
> I will ever sing to thee.
>
> (W. Williams, 1717-1791).

Part II

From Sinai to Kadesh

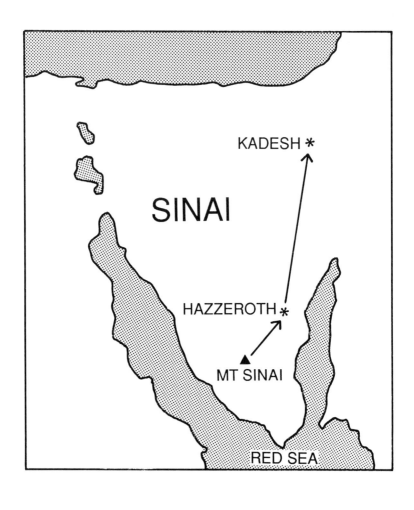

Map 2. — From Sinai to Kadesh

9.
Promise and compromise

Please read Numbers 10:11 - 12:16
'Now the people complained about their hardships...' (11:1).

Sometimes when things go wrong at work, you hear someone say,
'I've come up against a few hurdles lately.' Life can be like a hurdles
race. You start out of the blocks with a bang and head for the finish,
but instead of sailing over the hurdles, you start clipping them or
knocking them down altogether, and you may even get completely
out of your proper stride, and come crashing down on the track. You
may get up, to be sure, but it hasn't been a good run for you.

Israel had many hurdles to negotiate in the journey from Egypt
to Sinai and from Sinai to the promised land. Like many an athlete,
she had a good coach (the Lord speaking through Moses) and plenty
of motivation to run her race with patience with her eyes fixed on the
goal (the presence and the promises of God). In spite of these
advantages, she had something of a habit of faltering. Several times
the journey had ground to a halt in griping and complaining (Exod.
15:24; 16:3; 17:3; 32:1). Each time, the Lord dealt mercifully but
firmly with this recalcitrance and they returned to the straight and
narrow.

After three months, they arrived at Mount Sinai. There they
camped for some eleven months, during which time they received
from the Lord the Ten Commandments and the law as a whole
(Leviticus). They constructed the Tent of Meeting and its sacred
furniture according to God's special instructions. The priests and
Levites were consecrated, the Passover was observed, the census

was taken, the tribes organized for the journey to Canaan and final orders given about guidance on the line of march (the cloud and the silver trumpets).

The day duly arrived for them to strike camp and set out for Canaan. Our passage covers the beginning of that journey. It was to have taken just eleven days to walk from Sinai to Canaan (Deut. 1:2), but in the end it took over thirty-eight years! Succeeding chapters tell us why this happened, but even in the record of what began as a good start, we can see the rise of the problems which were to result in all but two[1] of the generation that came out of Egypt living and dying in nomadic peregrinations through the wastes of Sinai.

The promise — a good start (10:11-36)

Beginning a new venture is always exciting. The passage conveys a vivid sense of that fresh enthusiasm, and does so in three stages: first, by describing something of the panoply of Israel's power as the nation moved off at God's command (10:11-28); second, in Moses' invitation to the non-Hebrew Hobab to come to Canaan with them (10:29-32); and finally in the picture of a people led by their God towards their unfolding destiny (10:33-36).

'They set out ... at the Lord's command through Moses' (10:11-28)

The account of the order of the column parallels the layout of the camp described earlier (10:13-28; 2:1-31). Here was the Old Testament church, 'terrible as an army with banners' stepping forth in the will of the Lord (S. of S. 6:4; Ps. 60:4). We know that a generation later, the Canaanites trembled at Israel's approach (Josh. 2:9-11) and it certainly seems reasonable to believe that even at this early stage, reports of the advance of Israel had already reached their ears and given them some cause for concern.

The principle that shines through is, of course, that of obedience to **'the Lord's command'** (10:13). When the cloud rose in the sky, they marched! They did not have an itinerary which assured them of all the places they would visit, where they would stop, what battles they might have to fight, and so on. In this respect, we are no different from them. None of us knows what a day may bring forth, however careful our plans and preparation. Our diaries may be full of obligations and intentions, but our frequent experience is not far removed from what the Americans call 'Murphy's law' — 'Anything that can go wrong, will!' Christians are not, however, left there, at the mercy of chance. *We* don't know, but we believe that *the Lord* knows the end from the beginning (Isa. 46:10). Comments Matthew Henry, with that wonderful pithiness of English Puritan piety: 'Those that have given themselves up to the direction of God's Word and Spirit steer a steady course, even when they seem to be bewildered. While they are sure they cannot lose their God and guide, they need not fear losing their way.'[2]

'Come with us and we will treat you well' (10:29-32)

Exemplifying a marvellous confidence in the Lord, Moses invited his brother-in-law, Hobab,[3] to pitch in his lot with Israel. Moses' argument was straightforward: on the one hand, he would share in the blessing the Lord would bring to Israel (10:29); and on the other hand, he would be a blessing to Israel, because he knew the country like the back of his hand and could advise on good camp-sites and, in general, **'be [their] eyes'** (10:31). This latter inducement should not be seen as a contradiction of God's leadership through the movement of the cloud but rather as a supplement which offered detailed help in arranging certain practicalities while in camp.

Hobab was not a Hebrew, but a son of Jethro, the priest of Midian. It would appear that this family were believers in Moses' God (Exod. 18) and, although nothing is said of Hobab's response, the evidence is that he accepted the invitation, for his descendants, the Kenites, were later to be found in Canaan, associated with the Israelites (Judg. 1:16; 4:11). This is a lovely intimation of the later universality of the call of the gospel to all nations. Moses did not see the blessing of God as something denied to non-Hebrews on narrowly racial grounds. He did not imagine that Hobab's gain would diminish Israel's share of God's grace. 'We shall never have less of the treasures of the covenant,' writes Matthew Henry, 'for others coming in to share with us.'[4] Yet, practically speaking, many Christians seem to act as if they believed the contrary. We have heard folk say that it would ruin the fellowship and the atmosphere if too many people came into a particular church. In other words, the blessing can't expand to take in more; it can actually be expected to contract! The sad reality is that this sin blights churches and reduces

them to special-interest clubs for groups of people who feel com-
fortable with their narrow circle, but uncomfortable with others for
whom Christ died.

Moses' overture to Hobab stands, comments James Philip, as 'a
useful and important illustration, in Christian terms, of the invitation
to pilgrimage'. Indeed, 'Where men know Him and are persuaded
of the good He has promised in the gospel, they will be so gripped
and mastered by it that their lips will be touched with holy fire. Thus
they will speak persuasively to others concerning Christ, and, like
Moses, refuse to take no for an answer.'[5]

'The ark of the covenant ... went before them' (10:33-36)

Much fruitless debate has centred on the position of the ark. Did it
precede the whole column, as seems to be the case in 10:33, or was
it with the Kohathites in their assigned position between the second
and third corps (those of Reuben and Ephraim) as in 10:21? These
allegedly contradictory accounts have even been used as evidence
for source-critical views that different authors penned them ('P' for
v.21 and 'J' or 'E' for v.33). The argument is utterly contrived. The
ark definitely preceded the entire nation at the crossing of the
Jordan, but was between a vanguard and a rearguard at the fall of
Jericho (Josh. 3:3; 6:8-9). Other permutations were apparently
permissible on special occasions. Is it so improbable that on this
inaugural stage of the journey to Canaan, the ark was advanced to
the front, while the bulk of the Kohathites bore their burdens in the
appointed place? In any event, the meaning of the passage is clear
and there are three main points to grasp.

1. *Trust the Lord to guide you every day (10:33-34).* God was
with Israel, through thick and through thin, every day of their
wilderness wanderings. He was faithful and trustworthy. They
could be confident in him and the cloud hovering over them was a
visible token of God's covenant love and a challenge for them to
look to him alone for guidance and for success.

2. *Begin each day with prayer for his blessing (10:35).* As the
ark set out each day, Moses called upon the Lord to prepare the way
before them by scattering his enemies and theirs. David later uses
Moses' words as the opening verse of Psalm 68, a song of the church
militant, beside which 'Onward Christian soldiers' seems pallid and
somewhat trite:

'As smoke is blown away by the wind,
   may you blow them away,
as wax melts before the fire,
   may the wicked perish before God...
When you went out before your people, O God,
   when you marched through the wasteland,
the earth shook,
   the heavens poured down rain,
before God, the One of Sinai,
   before God, the God of Israel'

(Ps. 68:2,7-8).

The forces of evil are at work in the world and are the enemies of God's people. Our struggle is not against 'flesh and blood', but against 'spiritual forces of evil' (Eph. 6:11-12). Jesus tells us to 'watch and pray' just because the threat is real (Matt. 24:42; 26:41).

3. *Close each day with prayer for his presence (10:36).* When the ark rested, Moses prayed, **'Return, O Lord, to the countless thousands of Israel.'** It is a prayer for the nearness of God. It says, in the words of Henry Lyte:

Abide with me: fast falls the eventide;
The darkness deepens; Lord, with me abide.
When other helpers fail, and comforts flee,
Help of the helpless, O abide with me.

And having prayed, the psalmist could say, 'I will lie down and sleep in peace, for you alone, O Lord, make me dwell in safety' (Ps. 4:8).

Israel made a good start. The first hurdle had been negotiated and they were on their way. They ought to have continued as they began. They had every reason to expect great things from God and every motive to attempt great things for him.[6] But, as we shall see, their progress was soon to be compromised by a spirit of discontent and rebellion against the Lord.

Compromise — the spirit of discontent (11:1 - 12:16)

'A murmuring spirit,' said Jeremiah Burroughs, 'is the evil of the evil and the misery of the misery.'[7] What the great English Puritan meant was that, however grievous the affliction which has come upon us might be, a 'murmuring heart within ... is more grievous'. Why more grievous? Because it denies the attitude of faith, trust, gratitude and dependence upon the Lord which ought to characterize the Christian. It therefore brings to any problem, real or imagined, a disposition to be frustrated, angry, bitter, fault-finding and recriminating, with the inevitable result that far from being resolved, the difficulty becomes further fuel for the fires of discontent in that person's innermost being. It is the antithesis of the peace that God gives to his people, the denial of the grace-filled lordship of Christ over all of our life and withdrawal from the healing power of gospel grace.

Three instances of complaint arose in that first week out of Sinai. Two involved large numbers of people, while the third was between Moses and his siblings, Aaron and Miriam. All involve challenges to Moses' leadership and each one vividly illustrates the spirit of discontent, which, then as now, casts its long dark shadows across the human experience.

'This is just too much!' (11:1-3)

The people **'complained[8] about their hardships in the hearing of the Lord'** (11:1). No specific reasons are given, but it must be concluded from the record of God's response that this was a profound and significant repudiation of his will for Israel. It was no trivial whining. Of course there were deficiencies and hardships in that wilderness. Three days' march in such an inhospitable clime would test anyone's mettle, especially after more than a year of camping out. But that isn't the whole story. Matthew Henry, with characteristic pithiness, puts it all in perspective: 'When we consider how their camp was guided, guarded, graced, what good victuals they had and good company, and what care was taken of them in their marches that their feet should not swell nor their clothes wear (Deut. 8:4), we may ask, "What more could there be done for a people to make them easy?"'[9] The fact is that many of them harboured reservations deep in their hearts about the whole project. They failed — or rather *refused*, for there was no lack of information and evidence on the subject — to grasp with submission and discernment what the Lord was doing in his plan and providence.

For this reason, God's **'anger was aroused'** and he sent fire which **'consumed some of the outskirts of the camp'**. The place was called **'Taberah'**[10] from the Hebrew *ba' ar*, 'to burn' (11:2-3). R. K. Harrison notes that the 'source of the fire is not stated other than that it proceeded from the Lord rather than from an extraneous natural occurrence, and as such it was reminiscent of the situation that involved Nadab and Abihu (Lev. 10:2).'[11] It was, in other words, a warning, a vivid picture of his righteous anger. It as good as says to us, 'When we complain without cause, it is just with God to give us cause to complain.'[12]Israel had *everything* to be thankful for and their complaining was sin, the evil that turned their real difficulties from occasions of victory into blueprints for defeat.

'Things were better before!' (11:4-35)

The second complaint arose from **'the rabble'** — the 'other people,' not ethnic Israelites, who left Egypt with Israel — who **'began to crave other food'** (11:4-9; cf. Exod. 12:38). Manna was boring — but, oh, for the good old days in Egypt, where the eating was so rich and varied! R. K. Harrison gets to the heart of the matter: 'The "complaining motif" of Exodus and Numbers constitutes a serious spiritual offence, because it describes open rebellion against God and not simply a monotonous diet.'[13] Old miseries are so easily reborn as rosy memories, when deeper discontent needs to be justified.

This, in turn, elicited from Moses the kind of complaint with which anyone who has exercised responsibility — whether at work, at home or in the church — will be sympathetic (11:10-15). Leadership is a heavy load, even when the led are eagerly supportive. When they mump and moan, the pressure can be crushing. Moses was ever faithful, but felt the need of relief, even the relief of death. The 'followers' of this world, who are so ready to criticize their leaders, rarely see how childish and ill-informed they really are. Still less do they see why leaders so often become weary of leading them. Moses felt keenly the thanklessness of his ministry to these people, for whom he had expended himself unceasingly and unselfishly. The Lord understood even more clearly what Moses was feeling. He too was troubled, but not with the careworn frailty of his servant Moses. He was **'exceedingly angry'** with the perfect anger of offended holiness.

First of all, the Lord *answered the prayers* of the two parties (11:16-23). Before dealing with the rebellious people, however, God responded to Moses' plea.

The Lord told Moses to set aside **'seventy of Israel's elders'** to help him **'carry the burden of the people'** (11:16-17). These may have been the same seventy who were with Moses on Mount Sinai (Exod. 24:9-11). They were to be specially endowed with the Spirit of God to equip them for their task. The Lord answered Moses' prayer with the promise of a gifted and sympathetic leadership team. To this present day, the leadership of the Lord's people is to be corporate, by elders appointed by God from among the people and endowed with the gifts of the Holy Spirit.

Turning to the people, the Lord promised that they would indeed eat meat, but made it clear that this would not be the great blessing they might imagine it to be (11:18-23). In fact, the 'blessing' — the answer to their prayers — would turn out to be a curse! They would eat meat for **'a whole month — until it comes out of your nostrils and you loathe it'**. The Lord not only answers the faithful prayers of believers; he also answers the unbelieving prayers of the faithless. The ultimate expression of this is the eternal condemnation of those who die in their sins having rejected the gospel message of salvation in Jesus Christ. As they pass into a lost eternity, for ever to be separated from the Lord, they receive the answer to their deepest prayer, which was that God keep out of their lives and leave them, as the saying goes, to 'do their own thing'. They did not want the grace of Christ, the love of the Father, or the fellowship of the Holy Spirit, and in hell that wish is granted with endless finality. Hell, said J. C. Ryle, 'is truth known too late'.[14] God is not mocked.

Secondly, the Lord *fulfilled his promises* (11:21-35). He always does, sooner or later. Even Moses, who had seen the mighty and miraculous deeds of God, found it hard to imagine how God could feed Israel on meat for a month (11:21-23). This is only to be expected, for it is impossible for God's promises not to test our faith to the utmost. Here, there was no hiatus between word and action — God's answers were immediate and unmistakably decisive. The seventy elders received the Spirit (*ruah*), while a wind (also *ruah*) brought the meat, in the form of vast numbers of quail (*Coturnix coturnix*). The double use of the Hebrew *ruah* (Spirit/wind) is echoed by the double-sided action of the Lord in blessing Moses and judging the people.

On the other hand, the public inauguration of the elders, sealed by a once-for-all prophetic utterance, demonstrated God's approval of Moses. The circumstance that two of the elders, Eldad and Medad, received the Spirit in the camp, rather than at the Tent of Meeting, reinforced this point before the people at large (11:24-30).

On the other hand, the judgement of those who complained extended beyond the diet of quails to a **'severe plague'**, surely an indication that the chorus of rebellion had continued without abatement. **'Therefore the place was named Kibroth Hattaavah** [literally, 'graves of craving'], **because there they buried the people who had craved other food'** (11:31-35).

So much for 'the good old days'! 'Why did we ever leave Egypt?' they had wailed (11:20). Testing times always provide the temptation to indulge vain regrets. Not only is this worthless, because we cannot turn back the clock anyway, but it, in effect, dethrones God as the Sovereign Ruler of our lives. Since, as the Scripture says, 'everything' works together for the good of those who love the Lord — even the bad things — the only proper response to past events is to press on with thankfulness towards the promise of God that good things lie ahead. When past events have been wonderful providences of God's goodness towards us — as they were with Israel — it is sheer unbelief to reinterpret them as if they were great evils. This is to deny God altogether and operate as if he did not exist, as if his promises were a lie and as if the facts of our experience meant exactly the opposite of what they actually signified! God called Israel back to reality — the reality of his grace towards them. He still calls us today to press on, with unreserved trust in him and spiritual contentment in all his dealings with us, towards the goal of our heaven-ward calling in Christ Jesus.

'Our gifts aren't being recognized!' (12:1-16)

The third episode of complaint comes from Moses' own relatives — his sister Miriam and his brother Aaron. It unfolds in five phases.

1. First, **'Miriam and Aaron began to talk against Moses because of his Cushite wife'** (12:1). The fact that Miriam is mentioned first, and that the complaint is about a sister-in-law, suggests that she was the instigator. This also would explain why Miriam was later struck with 'leprosy'.

Cush is often identified with Ethiopia, but has also been linked with Midian (Hab. 3:7), so it is quite likely, if not certain, that this 'Cushite' is Zipporah.[15] In any event, the complaint latches on to an ethnic difference and in belittling Moses' wife's origins displaces the supposed odium onto Moses himself. It is, of course, a cheap and and nasty pretext. It was no better than a rabbit punch. And if it hadn't been this, it would have been something else. People often hide their real complaints behind 'cheap shots' and trivialities, just because even they have a niggling sense of shame about exposing what is really on their minds. The real cause of the disaffection of Miriam and Aaron went far deeper than Zipporah's non-Hebrew parentage. In the language of modern psychology, this was 'sibling rivalry'. They were jealous of Moses. They resented his paramount position. They were put out about being 'second fiddle' to their little brother! Had God spoken **'only'** through Moses? Had he not also spoken through them? The answers to these questions were, of course, 'No', and 'Yes', respectively: Aaron was Moses' mouthpiece and Miriam was a prophetess. But these facts were never in dispute. The problem lay in what the facts were being made to say. It did not follow that, because God spoke through others than Moses, they should be equal in authority over God's people. So the real complaint was that God had made Moses the leader — and that too was a fact of which they were all aware, even if it was never mentioned. This was the heart of the matter and its significance was not lost on the Lord. He heard not only what they said: he read what was in their hearts.

2. Moses seems to have remained silent (12:3). The NIV puts the verse in parenthesis, in mute acceptance of the view that Moses did not write it himself, but that, like the account of his death in Deuteronomy 34, it was inserted by a later editor. It would certainly be rare for a humble man to write about himself in this way, but if anyone could do so with candid humility it would be Moses. He was **'a very humble man'** and the evidence is that, as on other occasions when faced with opposition, he quietly cast himself upon the Lord. Sometimes we must simply leave our defence in the hand of the Lord. The Lord's people are to be 'the humble of the land', in imitation of their Saviour who was 'gentle and humble in heart' (Zeph. 2:3; Matt. 11:29). 'Blessed are the meek, for they will inherit the earth' (Matt. 5:5).

3. The Lord duly vindicated Moses (12:4-8). He set forth the logic of the position. Aaron and Miriam were prophets. He revealed

himself to prophets in visions and dreams. But to Moses, he spoke **'face to face, clearly and not in riddles. He sees the form of the Lord'.** Therefore, **'Why were [Aaron and Miriam] not afraid to speak against [his] servant Moses?'** How, indeed, could anyone who really believed that God is who he is imagine they could malign his faithful servants with impunity? Human rebellion is preposterous in its irrationality. But that is the nature of sin. Sin, in the act, overwhelms the logic of sober truth.

4. The Lord chastised Miriam: **'The anger of the Lord burned against them, and he left them ... there stood Miriam — leprous, as snow'** (12:9-10). Whatever the disease — it was not leprosy as we know it (Hansen's Disease), but some other ailment(s) of the skin — its import was to render Miriam instantly and visibly ceremonially unclean and so to necessitate her banishment from the camp (Lev. 14:1-9).

5. The Lord showed mercy to Miriam (12:11-16). Aaron appealed to Moses, in an evidently repentant tone, and Moses interceded with the Lord for her healing. The Lord's reply is instructive: if in a family argument, her father had spit in her face, she would have been regarded as unclean (Lev. 15:8). The present case was far more serious, therefore she would be confined outside the camp for seven days, after which time she would be healed and could be restored. The whole nation was witness to this rebuke of Miriam, for they could only move on after her restoration to the camp.

The message of all of these complaints — the 'people' and their alleged hardships (11:1), the 'rabble' and their desire for meat (11:4), and Miriam and Aaron over Moses' leadership (12:1) — is, as James Philip aptly comments, 'not that they were finally lost, but that they were disqualified in the purposes of God — a grim and solemn reality. This murmuring, complaining, critical spirit ... got into them, and did something to them, rendering them progressively incapable of rising to their divine calling until, at a moment of crisis, they crashed.'[16] The seeds of compromise soon flourish as the weeds of failure.

The promise of God, nevertheless, remains the principal theme. Conviction of sin calls for repentance and new obedience. 'If we confess our sins, [God] is faithful and just, and will forgive us our sins and purify us from all unrighteousness' (1 John 1:9).

Part III

Kadesh — the four-decade delay

10.
So near and yet so far

Please read Numbers 13 and 14
'Wouldn't it be better for us to go back to Egypt?' (14:3).

We are conscious, are we not, of how often we get 'so near to and yet so far from' completing a project or achieving some personal goal? Sometimes these experiences have been public events. One thinks of the great English runner, Jim Peters, who led the Commonwealth Games marathon into the stadium at Vancouver in 1954, only to be overcome by exhaustion before he could cross the finishing line. A myriad of times, in events mundane and epoch-making, men and women have faltered and fallen back — so near and yet so far from their goal.

Perhaps, though, it is surprising, even shocking, to find this kind of tragedy in the lives of God's people, ancient and modern. God leads his people, is Lord over all things for them, has bound them to himself in his everlasting covenant promises and is their loving heavenly Father-God. Yet he does not lead them to success and glory irrespective of what *they* do, or of the choices *they* make, or the responsibility — or lack of it — that *they* exercise! Israel had the presence of God and many precious promises, but they failed again and again to believe God and do his will. Hundreds of thousands of Israelites, one by one and as a people, failed to lay hold on God's blessing and blighted their lives for the rest of their days. Why? Because they chose their own way at vital moments of decision and set in motion consequences which were as predictable as they were disastrous. None of those crossroads of faith versus unbelief was more significant in their lives than their decision at Kadesh Barnea on the borders of the promised land. We see how defeatism (13:1-33) and discontent (14:1-4) led to God's disposition (14:5-45). We must also see that there is an alternative, that failure is not inevitable, and that in the Lord we will be 'more than conquerors'.

Defeatism — the report of the spies (13:1-33)

Israel stood on the threshold of Canaan at a place called Kadesh Barnea (Deut. 1:19-20). R. K. Harrison notes that the site generally agreed to be Kadesh — the oasis of Ain el-Qudeirat — was first identified by the researches of Leonard Woolley and T. E. Lawrence ('Lawrence of Arabia').[1] It was prudent to spy it out and formulate invasion plans. Twelve spies, one from each tribe, were appointed to reconnoitre the land and given detailed instructions as to the information to be gathered (13:1-20). Mention is made of Moses' renaming **'Hoshea** ['Salvation'] **son of Nun'** as **'Joshua** [*Jehoshua* = 'the Lord saves']' (13:16). 'Jesus' is the Greek equivalent of the Hebrew Joshua.

The reconnaisance took forty days and covered the whole country from the **'Desert of Zin'** in the south to **'Rehob, towards Lebo Hamath'** in the far north — the extent of modern Israel (13:21-25). Mention is made of the descendants of Anak, noted for their great size (Deut. 9:2). These were to figure significantly in Israel's later loss of resolve, but, later still, were driven from Hebron by Caleb and killed by the forces of Judah (Josh. 15:14; Judg. 1:10) Grapes and other fruits were brought from Eshcol, an indication that the expedition was in September-October, at the time of the vintage.[2]

Upon their return, the spies reported their findings to Moses and Aaron and the whole community (13:26-33). The essential points are as follows:

1. They first *reported the facts*, accurately enough, but with a negative cast sufficient to agitate the people (13:26-29; cf. v.30). Yes, the land was fruitful, but the people were powerful and the cities fortified. To cap it all, they had even seen the giants of the land, the descendants of Anak!

2. Caleb, of Judah, countered this with *a confident call to arms* and a reminder of their mission from the Lord: **'We should go up**

and take possession of the land, for we can certainly do it' (13:30). The fact that Caleb had to 'silence the people' indicates how rattled they were by the potential obstacles as reported by the spies. This is a word for Christians everywhere, for we are too easily awed by the apparent power of wickedness and forget that the church is called to spiritual conquest through the spread of the gospel and the conversion of lost people. Some Christians seem to regard the present age with a siege mentality and view the Second Coming as little better than a 'Dunkirk' evacuation of what is left of the Lord's armies. It is certainly true that the struggle with evil will rage back and forth across history until the Day of the Lord. Along the way, the church will have her defeats as well as her victories. The fundamental attitude, nevertheless, must be one of holy optimism looking to the promises of God. He has not left us to 'hold the fort', but to take the battle to the enemy, in the spirit imbued with the conviction that even the gates of hell cannot prevail against the church (Matt. 16:18).

3. The majority of the spies — all except Caleb and Joshua — then *openly opposed going forward* (13:31-33). Their defeatist attitude is aptly summed up in their own self-evaluation: **'We seemed like grasshoppers in our own eyes.'** We cannot but contrast the attitude of David the shepherd, when he faced Goliath armed with only a sling and a few stones. He was certainly 'a grasshopper' in the eyes of the gigantic Philistine. In his own, however, he was the instrument of God: 'I come against you in the name of the Lord Almighty ... whom you have defied' (1 Sam. 17:45). The point is that the ten spies made themselves grasshoppers, through their own unbelief in the Lord. The fact that they could apparently confess this without shame tells us what unbelieving fear can do to human self-respect.

But look at the Israelites' actual situation. They had 600,000 men capable of bearing arms. Not a drop of blood had been spilled so far. God had protected them and provided for them throughout the year-and-a-half odyssey from Egypt to Kadesh. God had promised victory. It was right to fight, because it was God's declared will for them. Even so, in their minds they were already defeated: they were too weak, the Canaanites too strong, and God — well, they made no mention of him. It was as if he were less than a grasshopper — as if he did not exist at all!

This is the true nature of unbelief. God is out of the picture. For all practical purposes, he is dead. He can do nothing for us. Our fears are justified; more, they are 'being practical'! Real faith sees things differently. Caleb knew they would win, because he took God at his word! In the New Testament, Paul encourages Timothy: 'For God did not give us a spirit of timidity, but a spirit of power, of love and of self-discipline' (2 Tim. 1:7). Does the Kadesh syndrome ring any bells in your personal experience? God is able: he has better things for us than craven fear and paralytic doubt. Trust him. Israel did not. Don't make the same mistake! In Christ, you will be more than a conqueror, for he has overcome the world!

Discontent — the people rebel (14:1-4)

It always takes a little time for a loss of nerve to crystallize into a plan of inaction. If the Israelites took their faithless hysteria to bed that night, they certainly were not able to 'sleep on it'. **'That night'** they could not rest. Fear coursed through their minds with ferocious intensity, as they set their faces towards the denial of their calling as the people of God. This unfolded in three phases.

First of all, the people *wallowed in self-pity*. They **'raised their voices and wept aloud'** (14:1). 'Like foolish children, they fall a-crying yet know not what they cry for,' writes Matthew Henry. 'But those that cried when nothing hurt them deserved to have something to cry for... Unbelief, or distrust of God, is sin that is its own punishment.'[3]

Secondly, they *grumbled against their leaders* (14:2). This is rather reminiscent of the way in which modern public-opinion polls swing back and forth, not out of any discernible application of principle, but apparently on the basis of little more than perceived self-interest and irrational forebodings of future woes. Like a cinema crowd startled by a cry of 'Fire!', **'all the Israelites'** stampeded for an exit. The measure of just how irrational their terror was is seen in their pathetic moanings: **'If only we had died in Egypt! Or in this desert!'** It is useless to ask why death in Egypt or the desert is preferable to death in Canaan. There is no reasoning with people when they are in the grip of an overwhelming fear of the future. The opposite of, 'Be still, and know that I am God' (Ps. 46:10) is,

'But the wicked are like the tossing sea,
    which cannot rest,
    whose waves cast up mire and mud.
"There is no peace," says my God, "for the wicked"'
                                                (Isa. 57:20-21).

Finally, when they did collect some thoughts, they *decided to return to Egypt* (14:3-4). This was the construction of a rationale for the essentially irrational. All unbelief comes down to this: a wicked and foolish decision is laundered by a show of rightness and wisdom. Notice how this pretence of doing the right thing is put together.

1. *Doubt is cast as to the Lord's will.* **'Why is the Lord bringing us to this land only to let us fall by the sword?'** (14:3). This is unbelief masked behind the hint of a suggestion that maybe — just maybe — 'the Lord' really meant to do no such thing. 'Maybe Moses misinterpreted God's will. Yes! That's it! We need to consider other viewpoints. Does God want us to die here? How could that be?' And so, with pseudo-theological sleight of hand, the real will and promise of God is utterly rejected and replaced by a lie dressed up as new light!

2. *A high-minded reason is advanced.* **'Our wives and children will be taken as plunder'** (14:3). This was not the last time men hid their real motives for their decisions behind the supposed good of their families. 'We're doing it for the children', is a great excuse for doing what *you* want to do!

3. *It was resolved that they return to Egypt.* **'Wouldn't it be better...? We should choose a leader and go back...'** (14:3,4). People who decide to sin generally want to retain a good reputation. This is especially true of backsliding believers. They want others to think well of them, and they want to feel good about themselves. They even want God to approve of what they are doing. So they rationalize and engage in a revision of their own personal history. They redefine the past to justify the present, so that their apostasy comes up smelling like a rose. So the Israelites persuaded themselves that it was good to ditch Moses and go back to Egyptian bondage! 'Madness!', you might say — but it is the 'madness' of every lost sinner that ever lived.

Is there an answer to this? Matthew Henry points to it clearly in a passage that is unforgettably illuminating. We must learn, he says, 'the folly of discontent and impatience under the crosses of our outward condition. We are uneasy at that which is, complain of our place and lot, and we would shift; but is there any place or condition in this world that has not something in it to make us uneasy if we are disposed to be so? The way to our better condition is to get our spirits into a better frame; and instead of asking: "Were it not better to go to Egypt?" ask, "Were it not better to be content, and make the best of that which is?"[4] The grass is not greener on the other side of the hill and, as Israel would discover yet again, God's grace is not greater on the other side of his will.

Disposition — appeal and judgement (14:5-45)

Human sin, like the blood of righteous Abel, cries out to God from the ground (Gen. 4:10). It is a tribute to his longsuffering mercy that we are not consumed (Lam. 3:22). The Israelites had, once again, challenged the Lord to do something about them. They would not have seen it in these terms, but the essence of the matter was whether or not God could be denied by his erstwhile people and, consequently, whether or not God would have a people at all on the earth. The whole church was in revolt, worshipping her own will instead of her God. Would the rebels succeed? What would God do? The narrative unfolds in terms of three cycles of appeal and disposition: an appeal to the people to reconsider, their response and the Lord's initial disposition (14:5-10); an appeal to the Lord to have mercy and his revised disposition (14:11-38); an appeal to the battlefield and the Lord's final disposition (14:39-45).

First appeal: to the people (14:5-10)

Moses and Aaron did not say a word. They cast themselves on the ground in submission to the mercy of God, but also, Wenham thinks, 'expressing their awe at the sacrilegious blasphemy of the people' (14:5).[5] There are times when silence is a witness and a testimony, and our defence is left entirely in the hands of the Lord. Let the world and the masses think of us as they wish, it will be more than enough to be enabled to say with David,

'Vindicate me, O Lord,
    for I have led a blameless life;

I have trusted in the Lord
    without wavering'

                                        (Ps. 26:1),

or with Moses himself on another occasion,

'May the favour of the Lord our God rest upon us;
    establish the work of our hands for us —
    yes, establish the work of our hands'

                                        (Ps. 90:17).

Joshua and Caleb, the two faithful spies, rose to Moses' defence and reiterated the point made earlier (by Caleb), that they could indeed take the land, provided the Lord was pleased with them. They appealed for an end to the rebellion and to fear of the Canaanites, for, they said, **'Their protection is gone, but the Lord is with us'** (14:9). They correctly discerned that God is the Lord of history and nations rise and fall according to his will. This did not sit well with the majority. Faithful facts do not mix with fantastic fears. Only the intervention of God saved the two men from death by stoning (14:10). The appeal to the people's consciences had failed.

First disposition by the Lord: total destruction (14:10-12)

God was justly angered by their ingratitude and told Moses that he would **'destroy them'**, and make, from Moses' family, a new nation **'greater and stronger than they'**.

Second appeal: to the Lord (14:13-19)

Moses immediately responded by interceding on behalf of his erring flock, exemplifying his compassion for people in trouble as well as his lack of interest in any aggrandizement for himself or his family (cf. 12:3).

Moses advanced a threefold argument for God to be merciful to Israel. Firstly, he argued from *the glory of God* (14:13-16). The total destruction of the people would be perceived by the nations as meaning that **'The Lord was not able to bring these people into the land he promised them on oath; so he slaughtered them in the desert.'** How would God's glory be served if he appeared incapable of keeping his own promises? Secondly, paraphrasing

Exodus 34:6-8, he appealed to *the love of God* (14:17-19). Finally, he reminded the Lord of *his own past actions* — how he had **'pardoned them from the time they left Egypt'**. Why, then, could he not once more bring them back to faithfulness?

Second disposition by the Lord (14:20-38)

The Lord returned a five-part answer, which 'sings both of mercy and judgement' (Ps. 101:1).[6]

> 1. He *pardoned* the nation as a whole of the sentence of death (14:20).
> 2. He *punished* them, however, by depriving them of their inheritance in the land (14:21-23).
> 3. He *promised* faithful Joshua and Caleb that they would enjoy their inheritance in the land (14:24).
> 4. He *proscribed* the whole community, by sending them back to the wilderness (for thirty-eight more years), to ensure the fulfilment of his judgement upon them; and he fully explained his reasons for doing so (14:25-36).
> 5. He *purged,* through plague, the ten spies, whose 'majority report' had precipitated the apostasy of Israel (14:37-38).

The Lord's explanation of his judgements is very revealing, not only of his offended righteousness, but of the nature of sin. He says, **'I will do to you the very things I heard you say: In this desert your bodies will fall... Not one of you will enter the land...'** (14:28-29). God took their words seriously, even if they really had not. They wanted to die in the desert — they would! They didn't want to go into Canaan — their wish would be granted! God is not mocked. He gives the lost the lostness which they prefer to his offered salvation. Those who, to the end, declare they do not want Jesus will get their wish — in hell! Those who choose to reject the Lord of life are making their covenant with death.

The Lord also says that the children they said **'would be taken as plunder,'** would be taken in **'to enjoy the land** [they had] **rejected'** (14:31). The Lord was determined that the next generation would not be deprived of their birthright because of their parents. Their parents' sins would descend upon the children to the extent that they would have to suffer as **'shepherds'** in the desert **'for forty years'**. These would be, for them, years that the locusts would eat (Joel 2:25) — 'a discipline,' remarks James Philip, 'which they must endure ... for the apostasy and faithlessness of their fathers'.[7]

Third appeal: to the battlefield (14:39-41)

When Moses conveyed God's decision to the people, they **'mourned bitterly'** (14:39). They felt sorry. But did they *repent* and commit themselves to *doing God's will*? Not for a moment! They were still just sorry for themselves. And it was what Scripture calls 'worldly sorrow' — the kind of unhappiness that 'brings death' (2 Cor. 7:10). Like Esau, they 'could bring about no change of mind' in themselves, even though they 'sought the blessing with tears' (Heb. 12:17). Their false repentance was worse than their real sin! They felt bad about being judged, but deep down they still refused to accept the true nature of their sin.

Why can we say this so definitely? For the simple reason that they now attempted to reverse God's will just as much as they had before! They decided to attempt the conquest of Canaan, after God had made it plain that all the fighting men (except Joshua and Caleb) were never to enter the land! True repentance means, among other things, accepting God's will with a chastened and humbled spirit. It is not enough to 'acknowledge you are a sinner' (**'We have sinned,'** 14:40), and then go on to decide how you want to serve God! Repentance means accepting God's interpretation of your actions and attitudes. The Lord is certainly not fooled by our mere words, even if we manage to fool ourselves!

Third disposition: defeat (14:41-45)

Moses duly told them that they were bound to be defeated, since they were not only going against the Amalekites and Canaanites, but against the Lord's will. Defeat followed in the battle at Hormah (lit., 'destruction') and confirmed the truth of Moses' warnings. It was **'presumption'** and they paid the price!

'Warnings for us...' (1 Cor. 10:11)

The great lesson is made plain for us by the New Testament. 'Now,' says Paul, 'these things occurred as examples to keep us from setting our hearts on evil things as they did' (1 Cor. 10:6). What did they do? Paul says they were idolaters (v. 7; Exod. 32:6), immoral (v.8; Num. 25:1-9), they tested the Lord (v.9; Num. 21:6), and grumbled at the Lord (v. 10; Num. 14:2). Learn from all this, says the apostle, and serve your Lord with gladness. He suggests that there are three lessons to be received for our blessing.

A truth for your theology

The Old Testament is full of examples, good and bad, of what it means to be a child of God. Paul is saying, 'Take seriously the message of all of God's Word, for there is, rightly understood, a continuity of teaching throughout the whole unfolding revelation of God in the Scriptures. And the heart of it all is, in fact, Jesus Christ. The Israelites 'drank from the spiritual rock that accompanied them, and that rock was Christ' (1 Cor. 10:4). We are, in turn, pointed to Jesus that we may follow him as his disciples.

A caution for your conscience

The errors of God's people, so honestly reported in the Scriptures, are warnings to us to conform to Jesus Christ with all our heart and mind and strength. 'So, if you think you are standing firm, be careful that you don't fall' (1 Cor. 10:12). Subjective feelings that you are right are not the same as the God-given grace of assurance. The Spirit leads into *all truth* (John 16:13), and truth is what God has said in his Word. Receive with meekness the ingrafted Word, which is able to save your soul (James 1:21).

A stimulus for your soul

It might seem that there is nothing but discouragement in all this talk of examples and warnings. No, says Paul, there is abundant grace for fainting saints. 'No temptation has seized you except what is common to man. And God is faithful; he will not let you be tempted beyond what you can bear. But when you are tempted, he will also provide a way out so that you can stand up under it' (1 Cor. 10:13). God is faithful! Therefore, we can and will live for him, in his strength and by his grace.

11.
Reminders of God's goodness

Please read Numbers 15
'Then you will remember ... and will be consecrated to your God' (15:40).

After the dramatic account of the failure of Israel at Kadesh and her subsequent defeat by the Amalekites and Canaanites at Hormah, a chapter on laws concerning offerings and tassels looks oddly out of place. Stuck in the middle of a continuous narrative, it makes us wonder what was Moses' purpose in including them at this point. There are commentators who see no connection and basically shrug their shoulders.[1]

There is, however, no reason for not taking the sequence of the text at face value and, assuming the order to be not only deliberate as to placement, but accurate as to chronology, to look for the connections with the Kadesh disaster and the subsequent wilderness wanderings. Can we discern something of the logic of God's dealings with Israel in the giving of these seemingly out-of-place regulations? I believe we can and that these are in the nature of reminders, all of which were designed to point the Israelites to various aspects of God's dealings with them and their calling to be his people. The Old Testament is helpfully understood as an illustrated guide to God's will — a picture-book into which his spiritual children can look and from which they can learn. If we view it as a series of pictures, we shall see, not vague and exotic rites and customs, but reminders of basic truths — of God's promises (15:1-16), his provision (15:17-21), salvation (15:22-29), holiness (15:30-

36) and will (15:37-41) — and we shall find them of ever-fresh application to ourselves.

Reminders of his promises (15:1-16)

In spite of his recent judgements, God made it clear that *he had not gone back on his promises* to Israel. They would certainly, one day, **'enter the land'** that God was giving them **'as a home'** (15:2). This is God's definitive answer to any questions which the failure at Kadesh might raise in the minds of the people. If God's purposes are not thwarted by the 'gates of hell', still less are his promises going to be made null and void by the weaknesses of his own people. This is not only a statement about God's gracious, longsuffering attitude. It is a reflection of his eternal decree to save people from their sins throughout the future generations of human history. A generation might die in the desert, but the seed of Abraham would still be raised up — a nation more numerous than the sand on the seashore. God is faithful, even when we are not.

Furthermore, in detailing the various burnt offerings and grain offerings, the Lord again showed Israel that *through atonement and repentance, they might know a happy communion with the Lord.* The import of the sacrificial **'aroma pleasing to God'** is the enjoyment of reconciliation to God and the concomitant reception of his blessings, spiritual and temporal (15:3). The promises of God are to be experienced in holy living. You will notice that the specified sacrifices — which parallel and augment the regulations as stated in Leviticus 1:3-17 and 3:1-17[2] — all involved produce which presupposed settlement and prosperity in the land of promise, a clear indication of what was certain to come in the future (15:4-12). They had every encouragement, in spite of the débâcle of Kadesh and Hormah, to begin again to live in faithfulness to the Lord — to live, as it were, out of the future, in anticipation of the promise of God. And even if they had been disqualified from their inheritance in Canaan, their children would enter the land and offer these sacrifices. There were glories to come for God's people.

Last, but not least, there is even *a slight foretaste of the gospel,* in that there were **'the same rules'** for the Hebrews and the aliens living among them (15:13-16). In terms of faith, they share a redeemed relationship to God and this was to be reflected in a genuine fellowship before the Lord. 'Communion in religion is a great engagement to mutual affection, and should slay all enmities,' observes Matthew Henry.[3] The practical application reaches to the Christian community today: our homes, our fellowships and our churches may and must be opened to new people, but it is the Word of God that is held out and is the standard upon which we conduct ourselves. The 'alien' may come in, but the 'world' must be kept out. **'You and the alien shall be the same before the Lord,'** means that while the alien is to be embraced within the bosom of the church, the church is to do so on the one and only basis of the worship and service of God, according to his will. Incorporation, not accommodation, is the goal. The church extends by conversions to Christ and the engrafting of new people into his body.

Reminders of his daily provision (15:17-21)

The Lord also called for a portion of **'the food of the land'** to be presented — through a priest[4] — an an offering in recognition that he provided their daily bread.

Acknowledging the gift (15:17-19)

This **'cake from the first of your ground meal'** is given in token of the recognition that the whole fruit of the harvest is the gift of God. Contrast this with the increasingly neo-pagan language used in the West today, attributing good harvests to 'Mother Nature' and 'lucky' weather patterns! Thanksgiving Day in the United States traditionally commemorates God's preservation of the Pilgrims through their first winter in the New World. Secularism, aided and abetted by the poultry and greeting card interests, is progressively turning it into 'Turkey Day'. People are thus encouraged to focus on the gift and forget the Giver. The first-fruit offerings of Israel unmistakably exalt God as the provider of our daily bread.

Priority praise (15:20)

The grain offering was to be given **'from the threshing-floor'**(15:20). In other words, it is appropriate to acknowledge the Lord's goodness promptly and gladly. Our giving to the Lord's work ought to be the first thing we do with our energies and our incomes. Attendance at worship and time for corporate prayer and fellowship are priorities for those who love the Lord. They do not play second fiddle to football and television. Tithe cheques should be made out before spending money on other things, and every week (1 Cor. 16:2; 2 Cor. 9:7).[5] Our practical commitments are very telling. They reveal where the Lord stands in our priorities. Are you a 'first-fruit' disciple or an 'afterthought' giver? Is Jesus your Lord, or only your fire-insurance policy? Remember this: if he is your Lord at all, he must be Lord of your all!

Daily dependence (15:21)

Another implication of the grain offering is that God's people are to *depend on the Lord* every day, for even the most basic things in life. The Lord's Prayer expressed this in saying, 'Give us today our daily bread' (Matt. 6:11). Prayer before meals, prayer in family worship and the daily private prayer of the secret place all encapsulate the meaning of the Mosaic grain offerings. We thank the Lord for his faithful provision and we anticipate with joy his future blessings.

Bountiful blessing (15:21)

The offerings were to be given **'throughout [Israel's] generations'**. They would experience God's blessing precisely as they lived by faith (Ezek. 44:30). 'Test me in this,' God said, in reference to faithful tithing, 'and see if I will not throw open the floodgates of heaven and pour out so much blessing that you will not have room enough for it.' The blessings specified were very practical indeed: crop pests and plant disease would be prevented and, on account of the resulting prosperity, they would be known among the nations as possessing God's special favour (Malachi 3:10-12). Note that this is not the promise of 'a rose garden' — an easy, pampered, pain-free life. It is the promise of *fruitful labour*, provided that labour is done 'with all your heart, as working for the Lord, not for men' (Col. 3:23; 1 Cor. 10:31).

Reminders of his salvation (15:22-29)

The Bible does not tell us so much about sin in order to make us feel bad about ourselves or merely to let us know why we are lost and condemned. The law of God is, says Paul, a 'schoolmaster' to lead us to Christ (Gal. 3:24, AV). Just as our teachers are not paid to convince us of our ignorance, but to fill us with knowledge, so every sin recorded in Scripture is a pointer to right living. Of course, Scripture makes it clear that we cannot do good works on our own. We need a Saviour to take away our sins and give us a new heart, so that we may believe in him and live for him. The gospel bridges the gap between our need and new life. Even in Sinai, this connection is made. God speaks to Moses about *unintentional sin* and connects it with the provision of *atoning sacrifice*, to the end that the transgressor may receive forgiveness and the whole community enjoy the Lord's blessing.

Unintentional sin (15:22-23)

It was easy to fall into sins of ignorance, when regulations such as those governing the above-mentioned burnt and grain offerings were so complicated and so numerous. It has been just as possible in every age, and with the whole range of God's revealed will, to sin unintentionally. People, in fact, cannot avoid such sin, simply because they cannot know even God's revealed will perfectly comprehensively. Hence Jesus could say from the cross, 'Father, forgive them, for they do not know what they are doing' (Luke 23:34). Paul could say of himself, 'I was shown mercy because I acted in ignorance and unbelief' (1 Tim. 1:13). This is not to say that Jesus' murderers and the unconverted Paul were *innocent*, but that they were *ignorant* of the true extent of their guilt, and that ignorance, as a sub-division of spiritual blindness and deadness, is the target of God's purpose to save people from their sins. 'Ignorance of the law does not constitute an excuse for violating it,' as Roland Harrison rightly observes, but it does engender compassion in the heart of the living God.

Atonement is necessary (15:24-27)

Even for unintentional sins, atonement was to be made according to the prescribed form (cf. Lev. 4:1 - 5:13). 'Sins committed ignorantly need to have atonement made for them; for, though ignorance will in a degree excuse, it will not justify those that might have known their Lord's will and did it not.'[6] This also involved the whole community — a point that emphasizes the separation of God's people as a body.

Pardon is provided (15:28-29)

The way of forgiveness is stated plainly: **'When atonement has been made for him, he will be forgiven,'** and, as before, it is equally applicable to the Israelite and the alien. We have another gentle breeze of the gospel grace that would be revealed in fulness to all nations in the New Testament, in Jesus Christ, 'the great sacrifice ... offered up ... once for all upon the cross'.[7]

Reminders of his holiness (15:30-36)

The other obvious case is that of intentional sin — in particular, that category of aggravated or presumptuous sin denominated in the literal reading of the text, 'sins with a high hand'. The picture is of a fist lifted up against heaven. It is openly, knowingly, deliberately and defiantly committing sin and, in the process, virtually challenging God to do something about it — the 'boastful tongue' which says, 'We will triumph with our tongues; we own our lips — who is our master?' (Ps. 12:3-4). Two components of this sin are noted: such a transgressor **'blasphemes the Lord'** (15:30) and, secondly, has **'despised the Lord's word and broken his commands'** (15:31). That is to say, he regards God as unworthy of being obeyed, unreasonable in his commands and incapable of enforcing them anyway. God is held in contempt and decisively rejected. For such sin, no atonement was prescribed: **'That person must surely be cut off; his guilt remains on him'** (15:31). To be 'cut off' means to be removed from the covenant community by execution (Lev. 24:11-16).[8]

An example of this was then given — that of *a sabbath-breaker* who was put to death by stoning (15:32-36). The sabbath was instituted at creation (Gen. 2:2-3), hallowed by God's own example (Gen. 2:2), made explicit in the fourth commandment of the Decalogue and the Mosaic law (Exod. 20:8-11; 31:14-15; 35:1-3) and its relevance and the way it was to be applied affirmed by Jesus (Mark 2:27-28; Matt. 12:3-12; Heb. 4:9).[9] The Mosaic penalty for breaking the Fourth Commandment was death. 'Reverence for the Sabbath,' comments James Philip, 'symbolized reverence for God

Himself, and violation of its sanctity was therefore ... an insult to His majesty. It is in this regard that we can best understand the widespread contemporary neglect and desecration of the Lord's Day. It symbolizes our generation's neglect and contempt of the things of God. It is man's refusal of God.'[10]

The fact that the specifically Mosaic ceremonial regulations governing the sabbath no longer apply in no way lessens the force of the moral law as a principle applicable today. The notion that the Fourth Commandment is abolished while the other nine are still in force has become quite widely entertained, but is entirely indefensible. Not unrelated is a modern myth that God is less concerned about lawlessness in general, and sabbath-breaking in particular, under the New Testament. After all, it might be argued, when compared with the Old, the New Testament offers no explicit warrant for the Mosaic death penalty to continue to this day. This is to misunderstand the character of God and the nature of his dealings with us under the gospel. 'True it is,' says Charles Simeon, 'that under the Gospel we have a sacrifice for presumptuous sins as well as others: but if the Gospel be the object of our contemptuous disregard, we cannot possibly be saved, but must perish under a most accumulated condemnation.' Simeon goes on to explain why 'Contempt for the Gospel is in itself more heinous than a contempt of the Law.'[11] The law, compared with the gospel, consisted in 'weak and beggarly elements' (Gal. 4:9, AV). The gospel fully reveals the wisdom of God, the work of Christ and the influences of the Holy Spirit. So the writer to the Hebrews can say, 'Anyone who rejected the law of Moses died without mercy on the testimony of two or three witnesses. How much more severely do you think a man deserves to be punished who has trampled the Son of God underfoot, who has treated as an unholy thing the blood of the covenant that sanctified him and who has insulted the Spirit of grace?' The writer reinforces his point from the Old Testament — citing Deuteronomy 32:35-36 and Psalm 135:14 — and ends with the epitaph for all antinomianism and unbelief: 'It is a dreadful thing to fall into the hands of the living God' (Heb. 10:28-31; cf. 6:1-6). God is holy and he will not be mocked.

Reminders of his will for our lives (15:37-41)

In a world of God-given details, the fringe tassels of the Israelites' garments were arguably the least obtrusive, yet ever-present, reminders of the Lord's will. Tassels were required on the four corners of their outer garments — the same hem of Jesus' garment which figured in the healing of a sick woman (Deut. 22:12; Matt. 9:20). A **'blue cord'** was to be included in each of the tassels, so that they would look at them and **'remember all the commands of the Lord ... and not prostitute [themselves] by going after the lusts of [their] own hearts and eyes ... and ... be consecrated to [their] God'**. Blue was the colour of lordship — hence the blue covers for the sacred furniture of the tabernacle (4:6-7, 11-12). The blue thread was perhaps the simplest form of 'royal warrant'[12] ever issued by any king — it said, in effect, that the bearer was 'By appointment to the living God, child of his heavenly Father.'

There is no encouragement in the New Testament for the continuation of this kind of practice — or, indeed, of any distinctive form of dress. There is no such thing as a Christian 'uniform', notwithstanding the written and unwritten rules of many denominations and groups. Jesus wore the tassels (Matt. 9:20; 14:36), but condemned the way in which some had enlarged their tassels and made them badges of their orthodoxy and piety (Matt. 23:5). The passing of such regulations places the focus for discipleship upon living faith and attention to the Word of God and undercuts any tendency to invest more importance in the things themselves than in the spiritual realities to which they pointed. Under the guise of 'aids to devotion', crosses, pictures, statues, so-called relics, 'holy places' and all sorts of religious trinketry have become objects of veneration. 'St Christopher,' who never even existed, protects cars and 'St Joseph', buried in the front garden, will help sell your house! This is superstition, not biblical faith. The very notion that things or rituals convey some automatic grace in themselves (*ex opere operato*) is no better than heathen magic and was as foreign to the Old Testament ceremonies and regulations as it is to the New Testament gospel. What we need is God's law written *on our hearts* and that is precisely the nature of new covenant faith in Jesus Christ (Jer. 31:33; Heb. 8:10). The Bible is itself God's book of 'reminders to stimulate [us] to wholesome thinking' (2 Peter 3:1) and to 'clothe [our] selves with the Lord Jesus Christ' (Rom 13:14) and to be 'steadfast, unmovable, always abounding in the work of the Lord'. We will then discover that our 'labour in the Lord is not in vain' (1 Cor. 15:58, AV).

12.
Showdown in the desert

Please read Numbers 16:1-40
'Woe to them! ... they have been destroyed in Korah's rebellion'
(Jude 11).

On 17 January 1991, war broke out between a coalition of almost thirty countries, led by the United States and including the United Kingdom, and the Middle East country of Iraq, which on 2 August 1990 had conquered her tiny neighbour, Kuwait. This first ever 'television war' made riveting viewing, especially in the opening days of hostilities. The American CBS network aptly headlined its coverage, *Showdown in the Gulf*, and that is what it was — a showdown, and a highly lethal one at that, between an immovable object and an irresistible force. The Allied ground offensive went in on 24 February and in exactly 100 hours an Iraqi army of over half a million men was decisively demolished. The 'irresistible force' had moved the 'immovable object'!

These events illustrate a most profound reality in human life — namely, that God often brings us to our own personal showdowns. For a while he lets us go our own way. Indeed, at such times, we seemed so immovable in our sins and he seemed very resistible. Subsequent experience taught us otherwise. However long he waited, the day of reckoning arrived! This is, of course, exactly what happened with Israel in the desert — and not just once, but many times. God led them out of Egypt. He did them a great deal of good. Yet they repeatedly got themselves into serious trouble. Even then, the Lord tracked their ups and downs to confront, to chastise and to correct them. Korah's rebellion was one of their most decisive moments.

Rebellion (16:1-3)

The rebels were led by a 'gang of four' consisting of a Levite named **'Korah'**, and three Reubenite accomplices, the two brothers **'Dathan'** and **'Abiram'**, together with a fellow named **'On'**, of whom we hear no more. The 'foot-soldiers' of the rebellion were **'250 Israelite men, well-known community leaders'**. Like most revolutions, this was a movement of the educated upper classes (16:1-2).

Their complaint, as one might expect from disaffected people in secondary leadership, concerned alleged high-handedness on the part of their superiors. They made three basic points: they alleged that Moses and Aaron had infringed the rules, they protested their own high-mindedness in bringing their objections and they ended with an accusation of unworthy motives on the part of the leaders (16:3).

First, *the alleged infringement of the rules.* They told Moses and Aaron, **'You have gone too far!'** In other words, they had exceeded their authority. The unspoken implication was that they were guilty of presumptuous sin against God. What made them think that they knew the Lord's will better than Moses and Aaron, they did not say. They certainly did not see that they were actually guilty of the very thing they charged against their leaders (cf. 16:7). We are most blind to our own sins and most prone unjustly to attribute them to others.

Second, *their own supposed high-mindedness:* **'The whole community is holy.'** False accusers never fail to attempt to launder their own bad attitudes. They never have an ulterior motive, far less a bad one! They act for the good of all. The whole congregation of Israel is as good as Moses. Indeed, they might have said, 'We are as good as you ... so why should you rule us, preach to us, and so on and so forth? We are all fine people, and we four feel a moral obligation to set things straight.' The truth is, however, elsewhere, for 'A malicious man disguises himself with his lips, but in his heart he harbours deceit' (Prov. 26:24). 'Not a word from their mouth can be trusted' (Ps. 5:9). 'The poison of vipers is on their lips' (Ps. 140:3).

Finally, we have *the imputation of unworthy motives*. They charged God's servants with a self-aggrandizing spirit: **'Why do you set yourselves above the Lord's assembly?'** The truth was that Moses and Aaron had taken none of their honours to themselves, but had been clearly called by God (Heb. 5:4). It was their critics who had unworthy motives, for it later became apparent that Korah wanted to be a priest and that the others resented Moses' and Aaron's authority (16:10,13).

If we are not spiritually content — that is, in our hearts — then discontented frustration will always fill the gap between our actual situation and our view of where we think we should be. Paul learned to be content 'whatever the circumstances', because he discerned the hand of God in these circumstances and did not believe that the discouragements especially were the result of others overruling God's providence to his detriment (Phil. 4:11). You will have noticed that those in the grip of a spirit of discontent always blame others, or even God, for their being held back from realizing their imagined potential. It is always somebody else's fault! The truth is, however, that where the grace of spiritual contentment is found in the human heart, humility is also found — humility which praises God for the privileges he has given others but denied to me, and rejoices in the blessings he has given me, in spite of my being undeserving of the very least of his benefits! Complaining is simply sin, because it accuses God of unjustly depriving me of something I might otherwise have had. Korah and his companions never explicitly charged God with error, but that was nevertheless the actual meaning of their rebellion against God's servants. This was not lost on the Lord. He was not fooled by their pious words. And, as we shall see, he did not allow their presumption to go unchecked. The Lord is not deceived by the unbelieving church leaders and contentious, self-righteous church members of our day. The reckoning comes sooner or later — it always comes.

Response (16:4-17)

Before that reckoning came, however, it fell to Moses and Aaron to respond to the crisis. This falls into two parts. Moses first deals with Korah and his Levite supporters, who had come to him as a group, and then with Dathan and Abiram, who remained at a distance in their tents.

Korah and the Levites (16:4-11)

Moses did three basic things, and they constitute a model for all crisis management.

First, *he cast himself completely upon the Lord and his mercy* (16:4). He was utterly submissive in his heart to the Lord. He first recognized that this problem was beyond his control. He refused to dissolve into abject terror and so go on to compromise with the rebels. He simply acknowledged his utter helplessness. The meaning for every Christian is that when trouble strikes, the first action of our minds must be to trust the Lord to keep us, whatever happens. We do not need to understand what is happening, still less what will happen. We only need to be still and know that God is our loving heavenly Father.

Secondly, *he referred the case to the Lord* (16:5-7). Since the Lord was alone the Guide and Sovereign of Israel, he declared that the matter would be decided by him at the tabernacle the next day, at which time Korah and his followers should appear with their **'censers and ... put fire and incense in them before the Lord'** (16:7). Too often, we rise up to defend our personal integrity and explain our past actions. Moses never refers to himself. He keeps the focus where it belongs — with God. For New Testament Christians, this means going to the Word of God and, instead of being concerned to defend ourselves, leaving the Lord to vindicate himself, and us, through his truth. Even to 'give the reason for the hope that you have' is not strictly speaking *self*-defence, but rather proclamation of the truth as it is *in Christ* (1 Peter 3:15; Rom. 9:1). Confronted by the claims of the spiritualists, Isaiah emphatically exhorted God's people to go 'to the law and to the testimony! If they do not speak according to this word, they have no light ... ' (Isa. 8:20; see also 2 Tim. 3:15).

Lastly, *he challenged them directly in terms of the meaning and implications of their rebellion* (16:8-11). With respect to *God's people*, they had broken fellowship (16:8). Moses reminds them of who they are: **'Hear now, you sons of Levi'** (16:7, NASB). Moses himself was a son of Levi. In fact, Korah was his cousin! But, more than that, they were in a spiritual relationship, bound by God's covenant. The Levites were to be God's sons in a particular and special way. They were to serve him at the tabernacle. In other words, their calling and fellowship were established by the Lord for his glory and their happiness. But they had broken this bond.

With respect to *their own spiritual life*, they were gripped by the spirit of discontent (16:9-10). Moses reminded them of their great privileges and gifts as Levites: **'Isn't it enough for you...?'** Had God been stingy in his blessings? No, he had not! But for selfish ambition, God's gifts are never enough. Moses hit the nail on the head: **'Now you are trying to get the priesthood too.'** Discontent is the cancer of the soul and it inevitably develops into a consuming desire for greater recognition, increased influence, more prestige and a coveting of other people's gifts and positions. How different is the counsel of God's Word! 'Should you then seek great things for yourself?' the Lord asked Baruch, 'Seek them not' (Jer. 45:5). 'Not many of you should presume to be teachers, my brothers,' says James (3:1). God distributes gifts among his people in order that they may complement one another, as members of one body, and honour one another in their service to the Lord, however humble it may seem to be (Rom. 12:4-8; 1 Cor. 12).

With respect to *the Lord*, they had rejected him and his will (16:11). They complained against Aaron, but that was not the whole story. **'Who is Aaron that you should grumble against him?'** asked Moses. Aaron was only the agent and instrument of God's will. He certainly was not perfect. But that is beside the point, which was that the appointment of imperfect Aaron as priest was the perfect will of the Lord! The real problem, exposed here by Moses, was that Korah's attack on Aaron was a cover for an attack on God! Korah was using Aaron as his 'stalking horse', just as hunters long ago would stalk their quarry, preceded by specially trained horses whose size and smell would shield the hunters from being detected. The real target was God himself. His will obstructed Korah's ambition.

I dare say Korah and friends would have hotly denied all of these assertions. Such is the nature of spiritual blindness — and a fearful thing it is, for it means that people can convince themselves that they are right with God when in fact they are in danger of a lost eternity under his righteous judgement. To those who have an ear to hear, this sombre passage calls for reflection, repentance, reformation and reconciliation to the Lord. Moses' challenge, when taken in reverse, calls for a 180° turn-around on each point.

There must be a *turning to the Lord* in gospel repentance and faith, 'seek[ing] his face always' (Ps. 105:4; 17:15; 69:17). Flowing from that must come the *cultivation of spiritual contentment*. The

Lord told the church at Ephesus to return to her lost 'first love' (i.e., the things of God) and 'do the things [they] did at first' (Rev. 2:4-5). Exercise the gifts that God has given! Run with patience the race set before you. Learn contentment in whatever circumstances the Lord has placed you! (Phil. 4:11-12). And finally, there must be a *commitment to true fellowship*. This means being 'living stones' that work at being built up into a 'holy temple' in the Lord, by loving God's people out of love for the Lord himself (1 Peter 2:4-10).

Dathan, Abiram and the Reubenites (16:12-15)

The Reubenite faction had remained in the background, although they had clearly made their disenchantment known to Moses through Korah. Letting others do your dirty work does not mean, however, that you will escape facing the consequences directly. Moses duly summoned Dathan and Abiram. But they refused to appear and excused themselves by heaping outrageous accusations upon him. Leaving Egypt was a mistake — it was a land flowing with milk and honey. Indeed, far from bringing them to any inheritance, it seemed that Moses wanted them to die in the desert. And maybe he would, if he could, even **'gouge out the eyes'** of Korah's people! In other words, Moses was a demagogue, who only cared for his own power and glory and didn't give twopence for the people! (16:12-14).

This breathtaking piece of false accusation finally stung Moses into righteous anger and a declaration of his innocence (16:15). Significantly, Moses only defended himself *after* he had first put the whole problem in the Lord's hands. It is never improper to defend oneself, but our first consideration is always the honour and glory of God and the progress of his cause and kingdom. This is why Jesus chose to remain silent before his accusers, whereas Paul appealed to Caesar. In neither instance was mere self-vindication the primary goal. Silence took Jesus quickly to the cross and secured redemption for all his people in every age. Claiming his rights as a Roman citizen took Paul to Rome and brought the gospel message to the heart of the Roman empire. In both cases, the plan of redemption was pushed forward.

Final instructions (16:16-17)

It only remained to remind the rebels that they should appear the next day **'before the Lord'**, each man with his censer, ready to put the matter to the test. We cannot but be reminded here of the fact that 'We must all appear before the judgement seat of Christ, that each one may receive what is due to him for the things done while in the body, whether good or bad' (2 Cor. 5:10). How unutterably solemn that so many are ready to face the living God in the apparently sure conviction that they will be vindicated, even when, by all biblical standards, they are in open rebellion against God! Many, says Jesus, will protest their achievements for the Lord when they give an account of their lives to him, but in the most devastating surprise of their lives, they will hear him say, 'I never knew you. Away from me, you evildoers!' (Matt. 7:23). Still, they rush on towards their fall! The warning remains as urgent today: 'It is appointed unto men once to die, but after this the judgement' (Heb. 9:27, AV). The reckoning will come for everyone. It is no secret and it is very near. And implicit in the fact is a vital question: 'Where will you spend eternity?' 'Whoever believes in [Christ] is not condemned, but whoever does not believe stands condemned already because he has not believed in the name of God's one and only Son' (John 3:18).

Reckoning (16:18-40)

The following day, Korah and his followers appeared before the Tent of Meeting, blindly confident in the justice of their case and apparently expecting that the Lord would bring down Moses (16:18). So will the unconverted protest their innocence to the foot of God's throne, if not indeed to the very lip of hell!

Showdown (16:19-35)

It would appear that others, besides Korah's group, had come to the Tent of Meeting, no doubt out of curiosity but perhaps also with a readiness to see Moses get his come-uppance. There is no record of any expression of support for Moses and Aaron. The Lord manifested himself decisively and passed sentence on the rebellion, ordering Moses and Aaron to separate themselves from the assembly **'so that I can put an end to them at once'** (16:20-21). Since this involved the bystanders as well as rebels, Moses was moved to appeal for God to be merciful and not 'sweep away the righteous with the wicked' (Gen. 18:23; Num. 16:22). In answer, the

Lord gave the assembly opportunity to remove themselves from the vicinity of the rebels, which they did, leaving the conspirators and their families to face the justice of God (16:23-27).

The judgement would be plain to all. If they died natural deaths, then they would indeed know for sure that the Lord had not sent Moses. On the other hand, if the ground opened up and swallowed them, then they would know that **'these men have treated the Lord with contempt'** (16:28-30).

The punishment fitted the crime in each case. Dathan and Abiram had unjustly complained that Moses intended to kill them in the desert. For their unbelief, the desert opened up and swallowed them. Korah and his 250 aspired to the Aaronic priesthood and were consumed in their presumption by the fire of God (16:31-35; Lev. 10:1-2; Jude 11). Sin, like Moloch, consumes her children. Specific sins have specific consequences. Spiritual death begets eternal death. It is important that modern readers of God's ancient judgements draw the proper conclusions from these distant and dramatic events. The fact that God does not directly reveal and immediately execute his judgements in the same way today, but rather merges them into the regular flow of history (i.e., providence), tends to lull people into imagining that he punishes no one and even leads some to conclude that he is not there and that the old stories of the Bible are just that — old stories of no more than legendary significance (2 Peter 3:3-5). The reality is otherwise. His judgements are manifested in the earth (Rev. 15:4). If they are less dramatically obvious than the more sensational episodes recorded in Scripture, it remains true that 'the Lord knows how ... to hold the unrighteous for the day of judgement, while continuing their punishment' (2 Peter 2:9) and that a day is coming when God will judge the world with righteousness by his appointed King, the Lord Jesus Christ (Acts 17:31). The lost still descend into a pit every bit as real as the fissure which swallowed the 'gang of four' (Ps. 9:15; 55:15). 'It is a dreadful thing to fall into the hands of the living God' (Heb. 10:31).

Sign (16:36-40)

As a perpetual sign attesting the divine appointment of the priesthood exclusively to the descendants of Aaron, the bronze censers of the Korahite rebels were fashioned into an overlay for the altar of burnt offering. Since this altar already had such a cover, this addition only served all the more pointedly as a reminder that the Lord is determined to do his will and not be thwarted by apostates and rebels.

The continuing message of this incident is one of warning that we might flee the wrath to come. This does not sit well with people, even many professing Christians, who find the notion of a God who judges with perfect righteousness unsettling and even offensive. We live in an age when, in the dreamy theory of shallow minds, '"Love" means never having to say you're sorry.' The most popular religious proposition in the world is that God will never judge people who try to be good. It does not seem to register with people who believe this that no one finds it even rational, far less emotionally feasible, to operate that way towards those who wrong *them*! The world is full of people who feel completely justified in responding vigorously against the slightest offenses others offer them, while blithely assuming that God will be falling over himself to forgive their sins — and all this in spite of the clear and unmistakable teaching of the Word of God. 'Could we but hear the cry of those who are in hell,' wrote Charles Simeon, 'we should no longer sit supine and confident. O let us realize this thought before it is too late, and "flee in earnest from the wrath to come!"'[1]

13.
In wrath, remember mercy...

Please read Numbers 16:41 - 17:13
'In the midst of the years make it known, in wrath remember mercy' (Hab. 3:2, NASB).

Surely there is nothing more obvious in the world than the reality that the result of human wickedness is always misery and often death. At every level of human society — whether international, national, community or family — the effects of the kinds of behaviour which the Bible defines as 'sin' are relentlessly painful. Where do the strife and sadness originate? They all come from 'desires that battle within' people: 'You want something but don't get it' (James 4:1; Rom. 6:23). This is the most fundamental key to understanding the wretchedness of so much human experience in the world. People want but don't get, and so they take what they want, by hook or by crook! All our great social evils are reducible to this fact. Millions of children are executed *in utero*, because people want freedom from the responsibility of child-rearing and/or the consequences of sexual sin. AIDS, divorce, drugs, war, theft, oppression, racial prejudice, violence and so on, are all consequences of the 'I want...' syndrome. God's way is, by all standards of rationality, the practical answer to these scourges. But sin is not rational. It is slavery to 'I want...!' And it is boldly blind to the inevitable results.

Look at Israel after the rebellion of Korah. They had seen what God had done to the rebels. God's perfect justice had been demonstrated. The rebels did not have a leg to stand on — quite literally, for the ground opened and they were gone! Yet, the very next day, the people as a whole rebelled against the Lord, apparently oblivious either to their error or their danger (16:41). They had learned nothing from the Korah incident! Well might we ask, 'Is there any hope for humanity?' The answer is that if you expect rational argument and the facts to change people, you can forget it. Sinners will sin on and just try to dodge the bullets! There is, however, a real hope and it is from the hand of the Lord. Our passage shows how, even in his just wrath, the Lord remembers mercy and provides a way — the only way — of salvation.

Sacrifice — Aaron stands between the living and the dead (16:41-50)

As we have already observed, new and more widespread grumbling against Moses and Aaron arose the day after Korah's rebellion was crushed (16:41). In a number of ways, this was even worse than Korah's rebellion.

For one thing, these people had seen 'the gang of four' punished and the true nature of their complaining exposed as an unbelieving rejection of the Lord's will. Evidently, they did not connect their own complaining with Korah's rejection of Moses' leadership. Nevertheless, they were actually doing the same thing, with the essential difference being that they did it in the face of the Lord's plain demonstration of the nature and consequences of such an act!

They were also aware of the sign God had given of his seal on the Aaronic priesthood — the bronze overlay for the altar made from the censers of Korah's dissident Levites (16:38-40). Yet they still murmured against their God-given leadership.

More than even this, they contradicted God's verdict and declared the guilty to be innocent and the innocent to be guilty! They accused Moses and Aaron of killing **'the Lord's people'** (16:41). Thus they 'canonized the rebels'[1] and execrated the Lord's faithful servants. Such is the madness of all unbelief in the living God.

The wrath of God against sin (16:42-45)

God's response was to appear in his glory-cloud over the Tent of Meeting and to pass the sentence of death upon the mob. **'Get away**

from this assembly,' the Lord said to Moses and Aaron, **'so that I can put an end to them at once'** (16:44). God is saying, 'Why should those live another day who hate to be reformed, and whose rebellions are their daily practices? Let just vengeance take place and do its work, and the trouble with them will soon be over…'[2] In this way, the Lord defines the essential seriousness of sin.

Aaron stood between the living and the dead (16:45-50)

Moses and Aaron fell on their faces — as before, in submission to the Lord's will, but also as a plea for mercy (cf. 16:4). Moses then told Aaron to take his censer, with incense, and fire from the altar, and **'Hurry to the assembly to make atonement for them,'** because the plague — the instrument of God's wrath — had already started to take a toll (16:46). Aaron then **'ran into the midst of the assembly … offered the incense and made atonement… He stood between the living and the dead, and the plague stopped,'** although, by that time, some **'14,700 people'** had died (16:47-49).

This dramatic event offers several pictures of vital spiritual truths.

First is a picture of *compassion for the lost*. Moses and Aaron interceded for the people, on the sole basis of their terrible danger and need. They could have said, as we often do, if the truth were known, of those whom we see reaping the well-deserved evil fruit of their own actions, 'They've got it coming to them! They should have known this would happen! We told them so!' Intercession, in its very nature, takes its eyes off the judicial aspect of the problem and focuses exclusively on the redemptive need of one who is otherwise lost. It is love that seeks mercy for those who deserve only to be condemned.

Second is a picture of *the grace of God*. Even as God judged the people with perfect justice, he did so in such a way as to demonstrate the sovereignty of his grace in salvation and his love of showing mercy. Aaron, who had been the focus of Korah's rebellion, proved to Israel that the priesthood was the mediator of God's grace to people who will not and cannot save themselves. Had God not delighted in mercy, there would have been no priesthood and no sacrifices. The conjunction of plague and priest, of mercy in the context of justice, said to lost people that God had provided a way of salvation by grace — a way of salvation to be received, on their part, through faith (see 21:8-9).

Third is a picture of *ministerial self-denial.* Aaron unhesitatingly ran into a hostile, and now plague-stricken, crowd. 'Were there more tender compassion amongst us,' writes Charles Simeon, 'more ardent love, more self-denying zeal, more active exertion to "pluck our people as brands out of the fire," and more willing to perish in the attempt, we might not stop the mouths of gainsayers, it is true; but "we should save many souls alive," and have them to be "our joy and crown of rejoicing" to all eternity.'[3] Therefore, says the same writer, 'I call you..., every one of you, to forget yourselves, as it were, and your own personal concerns, and to be swallowed up with love and pity for your perishing fellow-creatures.'[4]

Fourth is a picture of *Jesus Christ atoning for sin.* There was no animal sacrifice here. Aaron was, in effect, the sacrifice. He was the advocate with God. He stood between the living and the dead, mediating between God and sinners. To understand this, we must 'look through the shadow to the substance'.[5] The substance is Jesus Christ (1 John 2:1-2). Aaron's actions point ahead to the one and only real Saviour, who died, rose again, makes intercession and saves to the uttermost all who come to God through him. Jesus stands between the living and the dead — the acceptable and sufficient sacrifice for sin (Rom. 8:34; Heb. 7:25).

Sign: Aaron's blossoming staff (17:1-13)

Mercy is God's 'darling attribute'.[6] He accordingly gave Israel a sign, which would seal for ever his appointed priesthood, head off any future rebellion against Aaron and his descendants and so encourage them to faithfulness towards their God **'so that they [would] not die'** (17:10). The sign God chose to give was the miraculous blossoming of Aaron's staff.[7]

The test (17:1-9)

The Lord directed that **'twelve staffs ... one from the leader of each of their ancestral tribes,'** be placed **'in the Tent of Meeting in front of the Testimony,'** that is, before the Ark of the Covenant.[8] The name of each tribe would be inscribed on its own staff, with **'Aaron's name'** on **'the staff of Levi'.** God promised that the staff of his chosen priest would **'sprout'** and he would thereby **'rid [him]self of this constant grumbling ... by the Israelites'** (17:1-7).

The next day, Moses went into the Tent of the Testimony and discovered that **'Aaron's staff, which represented the house of Levi, had not only sprouted but had budded, blossomed and produced almonds'** (17:8). This was made known to the people when the staffs were taken out and returned to the tribal leaders. Two significant declarations immediately followed: one from the Lord interpreting the meaning of the sign, and the other from the Israelites, expressing their fear that they would all die should they come too near to the tabernacle.

The message (17:10-11)

God commanded Moses to place Aaron's staff **'in front of the Testimony, to be kept as a sign to the rebellious'**. It was later kept *in* the ark, presumably until the time of the Babylonian exile in 586 B.C. when the ark was destroyed (Heb. 9:4). But of what was Aaron's staff a sign?

First, it testified to *God's sovereignty*. It was placed before **'the Testimony'** or Ark of the Covenant, which was itself the evidence of God's will for his people and of the holiness of his ordinances. The specific focus, already emphasized in the symbolism of the bronze covering fashioned from the censers of Korah's men (16:36-40), was the divine appointment of the priesthood in the family of Aaron. The general message, however, was that God's revealed will must stand. The staff symbolized authority: Aaron's authority as priest and the ultimate authority from which it was derived, that of God himself. In New Testament terms, this is fully revealed in Jesus Christ, to whom, in virtue of his death and resurrection, 'all authority in heaven and on earth' has been given. This, in turn, issues in Christ's commission to the church to make disciples of all the nations (Matt. 28:18-20). The church preaches the gospel, administers the sacraments and exercises pastoral care and discipline on, and with, the authority of her Lord (see Matt. 18:15-20). She proclaims God's will as revealed in Scripture alone and calls everyone everywhere to repentance towards God and faith in the Lord Jesus Christ.

Second, Aaron's staff speaks of *God's covenant mercy*. It was **'kept'** in the ark as a constant witness to the Lord's determination to save his people from their sins — **'so that they will not die,'** even if they had been rebels before!

Closely related to this, in the third place, is *God's promise to maintain an ordained ministry* among his people. Neither the Aaronic priesthood nor the New Testament ministry exist merely because of some sociological necessity or organizational convenience. God has covenanted to provide his church throughout history with a ministry called, gifted and ordained according to his will. He has promised to 'give pastors after [his] own heart' who are to 'feed the flock of God' (Jer. 3:15, AV; Acts 20:28; 1 Cor. 4:1; Eph. 4:11-12). And he has promised to protect them and bless them (Ps. 105:15).

Fourth, the staff reminded the people of *God's unchangeable justice*. It was **'a token against the rebels'**. God keeps mercy for thousands, but will not clear the guilty (Exod. 34:7). It calls for the confession that the Lord is always 'proved right when you speak, and justified when you judge' (Ps. 51:4).

Fifth, we have an intimation of *God's purpose to send his Son*. There is a breeze of gospel grace here. Christ is a shoot out of the stem of Jesse, the Branch that will bear fruit and 'build the temple of the Lord' (Isa. 11:1; Zech. 6:12). He is a root out of dry ground (Isa. 53:1-2). The gospel is 'the rod' of his strength, which comes out of Zion (Ps. 110:2, AV). Christ is, of course, the 'great High Priest,' whom Aaron only prefigured (see Heb. 4-10).[9]

Finally, there is a promise of *God's future blessing of his people*. The miraculous blossoming and fruiting of an otherwise dead staff was 'a figure of things to come,' speaking of all that God would do for his people.[10] They were to cease their **'grumbling against [God]'**. The sign spoke of sanctification — of dead sinners bearing live fruit, of former rebels loving God and keeping his commandments with joy in their hearts.

The response (17:12-13)

The Israelites were powerfully struck with the fear of death. **'Are we all going to die?'** they asked. This has sometimes been interpreted as indicating a resigned, despairing attitude towards God's judgement in the matter — the sort of outlook that says, 'All right, we get the message, but don't expect us to like it!' A better and certainly more charitable interpretation is that they were so profoundly humbled under a sense of their sin, and therefore of their danger of suffering God's just condemnation, that they could only give expression to the thought that if God took notice of our sins, no one could very well expect to stand (Ps. 130:3). Their approach to Moses implies a desire that he intercede for them, that God would be merciful and save them.

When we consider that God's stated purpose for causing Aaron's staff to blossom was to silence Israel's grumbling, precisely so that they would not die, it seems clear enough that that aim was immediately fulfilled in the Israelite response. The positive challenge for all of us is surely one that leads us to the very heart of the gospel of Jesus Christ. Believe and be saved! Hear, and your soul will live! 'If we reject Christ,' says Charles Simeon, 'we have nothing to hope for; if we cleave unto him, we have nothing to fear.'[11] Yet the fear of God is the beginning of wisdom and the very law of God which is precisely what gives us reason to fear him is also the schoolmaster to lead us to Christ (Gal. 3:24, AV). So does Aaron's blossoming staff call us to trust in the Lord with all our heart, soul and might.

14.
A gift of grace

Please read Numbers 18
'I am giving you the service of the priesthood as a gift' (18:7).

The charge has often been levelled against the Old Testament that it dwells rather heavily on wrath, judgement and death, and pays relatively little attention to God's love, redemption and life. In the popular mind, the Old Testament portrays God as a vengeful deity, as opposed to one who is full of grace.

To anyone who has actually read the Old Testament with intellectual honesty and grasped the scope and balance of its teaching, the exact opposite seems clearly to be the case. God is good: the giver of life, who pours his blessings upon mankind. And what response does he get, but rebellion, unbelief, rejection and every kind of evil imaginable? Yet, with a longsuffering none of us would accord those who treat us half as badly, God keeps back his anger and continues to spare his people, calling again and again for repentance and reformation. The point is illustrated so vividly from Israel's wilderness experience. Twice, they provoked God so badly that he might, with perfect justice, have removed them all from the face of the earth (16:21, 45). Nevertheless, the Lord heaped grace upon grace on them, all wholly underserved. He not only spared Israel from the judgements they certainly had coming to them, but even led them to new and larger blessings than they had known in the past! God demonstrated himself to be the God of free and sovereign grace to people who, by their own choice, were well on their way to destruction!

Notwithstanding the fact that the Lord had twice spared them through the intercession of Moses and Aaron and had given a sign of future blessing in the blossoming of Aaron's rod, the people were quite understandably terrified at the awesome judgements of God (7:12-13). This is so true to life. Calamities make more powerful impressions than pleasures. So even when Israel had been spared, they remained shattered, weak, confused and fearful — just like any child in the aftermath of severe chastisement by a parent. This was the problem that now needed to be dealt with, if they were to be a whole and healthy people for God. They needed to know and experience with deep power that God loved them and cared about them. In modern parlance, they needed 'affirmation' that God was their Father-God and they were his children.

To achieve this, and to reinforce the place of the priesthood in the light of Korah's rebellion, the Lord gives an account of the ministry he has given to the church — the priests and Levites — and presents it as a wonderful gift of grace to his people. He affirms his gracious fatherhood towards his people and points to the promise of future blessings.

The tasks of the ministry — gifts of God (18:1-7)

Why was the ministry of the priests and Levites to be regarded as a great gift to God's people? The answer is that it represented mediation between God and otherwise lost people. It provided access to God and to all that this meant for their redemption and reconciliation to God. This distinctly mediatorial core of the Old Testament priesthood was later to be fulfilled in the person and work of our 'great High Priest', Jesus Christ (Heb. 4:14; 9:28). He is the *only* Mediator between God and man (1 Tim. 2:5). As a result, the New Testament ministry has shed the mediatorial character of the Old Testament ministry, but retains, in more highly developed form, its teaching and pastoral functions. The ordained ministers of the Christian gospel are not 'priests' in the Aaronic sense of mediators, but the mantle of the general ministerial role of the Aaronic priesthood among the people has descended to them. We may therefore discern legitimate applications of principle from the Aaronic priesthood to the Christian ministry, always taking into account that which has definitely passed away on account of the gospel of Christ. We should also remember that New Testament

Christians have boldness of access to God and share in the priesthood of all believers (1 Peter 2:9). With this in mind, we may note five characteristics of duties of the priests and Levites which stand as timeless evidences that the ministry God has given his church is an unequalled blessing to both the church and the world.

An accountable ministry (18:1)

The priests (**'You, your sons'**) and Levites (**'and your father's family'**) were responsible for **'offences against the sanctuary'** and the priests alone were responsible for **'offences against the priesthood'**. The former offences related to any 'approach to the tabernacle by unauthorized individuals,' while the latter put the priests 'under obligation to abide strictly by the ceremonial regulations or else suffer the fate of Nadab and Abihu'.[1]

The central and abiding principle is that of accountability to the Lord for the faithful exercise of their ministry. 'Obey your leaders and submit to their authority. They keep watch over you as men who must give an account' (Heb. 13:17). They are to be workmen 'who [do] not need to be ashamed and who correctly [handle] the word of truth' (2 Tim. 2:15). The gospel ministry is all about responsibility and hard work, bearing burdens and proclaiming truth that many do not want to hear. It is not about prestige, status, a great career or a life of ease. The blessing of God is certainly going to be experienced in the ministry, but it is the fruit of costly, sacrificial faithfulness. Those men who seek the ministry for its influence, usefulness and privileges ought to weigh carefully its responsibilities. 'Not many of you should presume to be teachers, my brothers,' warns our Lord's brother, 'because you know that we who teach will be judged more strictly' (James 3:1).

The principle of accountability applies, of course, not only to the ministers and elders of the church in their calling, but to *all* believers with respect to their lives, their witness and callings. Above all, the 'priesthood' of believers is, as Peter put it, a 'holy' one (1 Peter 2:5). It is both our privilege and our responsibility to live for our Lord.

A shared ministry (18:2-4)

The appointment of the Levites to be the helpers of the Aaronic priests exemplifies another fundamental aspect of the ministry, namely, that it is a shared work. There are diverse and distinct roles to be filled and they are all complementary and indispensable to one another. This theme comes to its fullest expression in the New Testament church, which is variously described as a house built of 'living stones' fitted together in their places (1 Peter 2) and as a 'body' comprised of various parts, each with its particular gifts and capacities (1 Cor. 12). Each believer has a place in God's scheme of things, with the ultimate purpose of the whole people of God coming to maturity and attaining, as Paul puts it, 'to the whole measure of the fulness of Christ' (1 Cor. 7:20; Eph. 4:11-13).

A serving ministry (18:5)

The purpose of priestly and Levitical faithfulness was not, however, merely to fulfil a set of professional responsibilities. It was, the Lord told Aaron, **'so that wrath will not fall on the Israelites again'.** Just as Aaron had literally stood between the dead and the living, so the exercise of faithful ministry is the holding forth of the word of life about Jesus Christ to a dying world. You will notice that God's ministers were not called to lord it over the people, but to *serve* them in the Lord's name. In New Testament terms, the eldership is not to be seen as primarily a command structure (although it does have authority for the government and discipline of the church), but as the work of pastoral service, in which the Word of God is ministered faithfully in the shepherding of the sheep. 'For we do not preach ourselves,' says Paul, 'but Jesus Christ as Lord, and ourselves as your servants for Jesus' sake' (2 Cor. 4:5). This too, is the attitude of all believers and not just apostles and preachers.

A God-given ministry (18:6)

God himself had **'selected'** the Levites to be **'dedicated to the Lord to do the work at the Tent of Meeting'.** This is the universal law of all ministry for God. 'No one takes this honour upon himself; he must be called by God, just as Aaron was' (Heb. 5:4). 'Should you then seek great things for yourself? Seek them not' (Jer. 45:5). 'The truth is,' writes James Philip, 'it is possible to covet a place in the work and the service of God, and to do so as a means of self-expression, or for the gratification of personal ambition, or as the indication of a lust for power, or even merely for the prestige it seems to bestow.'² It is also possible to be mistaken as to God's call as a result of a lack of spiritual discernment and self-knowledge. If more attention is paid to inward feelings and enthusiastic impulses than to objective evidence of real gifts and spiritual maturity, there is no doubt that an excess of the former will always overwhelm a lack of the latter. We can too easily call ourselves to the ministry on a wave of emotional self-persuasion. To aspire to the eldership is 'to desire a noble task'. But the tests of the Word must then be honestly and rigorously applied by the individual *and* the church, for the blessings of both the body of Christ and the men themselves (1 Tim. 3:1-7).

A separated ministry (18:7)

The servants of God must also be thoroughly committed to their task. They are to be separated to God. 'I will give you shepherds after my own heart, who will lead you with knowledge and understanding' (Jer. 3:15). The Aaronic priests, and they only, ministered **'inside the curtain'**. The principle of exclusive devotion is at the heart of the gospel itself. Christ commands our total obedience. And he promises the fulness of his enabling grace to his disciples: 'Never will I leave you; never will I forsake you' (Heb. 13:5; Deut. 31:6). 'And surely I am with you always, to the very end of the age' (Matt. 28:20).

The five foregoing aspects of the ministry together amount to a massive affirmation of the love of God for his people — and, indeed, for the world that he has determined to save to himself. To an Israel smarting under his recent judgements, the Lord's exposition of the doctrine of the ministry of the priests and Levites said in unmistakable terms that God had a purpose of grace for them. The absence of a sound ministry of the Word is always, in Scripture, seen as a curse (Prov. 29:18; Amos 8:11-13; Rom. 10:14). The ministry of the Word of God is the proof of God's gracious purpose to seek and to save the lost. Those who are converted to Christ through the ministry of the Word and Holy Spirit are themselves made into a royal priesthood and a holy nation scattered throughout the world to 'live such good lives' that people may see their 'good deeds and glorify God on the day he visits us' (1 Peter 2:9, 12). God's gift of ministry is a gift of grace.

The support of the ministry — God's gift of himself (18:8-32)

The focus now shifts from the duties of the priests and Levites to the matter of their support — their compensation for serving the tabernacle and having no inheritance in the land of promise. It is important to see this as more than an economic arrangement. It is, in fact, the means by which God involved the whole congregation of Israel in the ministry given to the priests and Levites. The gift of that ministry is acknowledged, received and enjoyed and shared through faithful participation in sustaining God's ministers by means of their offerings and tithes to the Lord. The heart of these gifts was devotion to the Lord. As is still true in the New Testament church, worship 'in spirit and in truth' is vitally connected with practical support of the work of God. The offerings and tithes, which are the fruit of obedient faith, simultaneously sustain the extension of the faith through a dedicated ministry.

An everlasting covenant of salt (18:8-19)

The **'offerings'** given to the Lord as the sacrifices at the tabernacle were given to the priests as their **'portion and regular share'** (18:8). These included the portion of the **'grain or sin or guilt offerings'** not burnt on the altar (18:9-10); the **'wave offerings'**(18:11); the **'first-fruits of their harvest'** — new **'olive oil'**, **'new wine and grain'** (18:12-13); and **'everything ... that is devoted to the Lord ... the first offspring of every womb'** (18:14-18). This repeats in substance the details of the various sacrifices and procedures set down in Leviticus 1-7 and 27. First-born children, it should be noted, were to be redeemed by a payment of five silver shekels — a not inconsiderable sum, equivalent to about six months' wages.[3] This provision was to be **'an everlasting covenant of salt before the Lord'** for the Aaronic line (18:19). Salt symbolized permanence, no doubt on account of its utility in retarding food spoilage.[4] 'As long as the priesthood should continue,' comments Matthew Henry, 'this should continue to be the maintenance of it, that this lamp might not go out for want of oil to keep it burning.'[5]

We should note that these offerings for the tabernacle sacrifices are not the equivalent of what we call 'the offering' in today's church. The latter is the descendant of the Old Testament tithes. The former is fulfilled for ever in Jesus Christ as the once-for-all sacrificial offering for sin. What does continue is the principle underlying the apportioning of some of that offering to the priests — namely, that God will sustain the ministry of his church as long as the world will last.

I am your share and your inheritance (18:20-32)

The **'tithes'** were that one-tenth portion of the produce of the land which the twelve landed tribes were to give to the Lord (18:20-24; Lev. 27:30-33). These were to be given to the Levites for the reasons that, first, they had no land and, second, they were to be compensated for their work in connection with the tabernacle. Another tithe, collected every third year, was also received by the Levites but was at least in part for the relief of the poor (Deut. 14:22-29). Tithing was already of great antiquity by Moses' day and is properly regarded as a universal principle governing our service to the Lord (Gen. 14:17-21; 28:20-22) The New Testament lays aside the specific Mosaic rules of tithing, but clearly builds upon the pre-Mosaic tithing principle by recasting the believer's liberality in terms of the love of Christ and a free sanctified conscience. Christian giving, which in absolute terms cannot properly be conceived of as *less* than the ten per cent of Leviticus and Numbers, is joyful (2 Cor. 9:7), systematic and proportionate (1 Cor. 16:2), substantial (Acts 2:45), voluntary (Acts 5:3-4), and is related to the twin blessings of supporting the ministry of the gospel (1 Cor. 9:13-14) and helping those who are in need (Gal. 2:10; 2 Cor. 8:13-15; 1 John 3:17).

The Levites, then, received the tithes as their inheritance, in lieu of a portion of the land, and for services rendered (18:20-24). The meaning of this reached beyond the necessities of life. The tithes were an indication that God himself was their **'share and ... inheritance among the Israelites'** (18:20). The normal aspirations of the mass of God's people were denied them in favour of the rigorous responsibilities of the ministry of God's house. They must therefore find the Lord all the more precious — and they would do so, as they looked to him in faith.

The Levites, in turn, were to give tithes to the priests out of the tithes they received from the twelve tribes (18:25-32). The Aaronic priests were, of course, also descendants of Levi and could rightly expect to share in the tithes. Why, then, did the Lord insist that the priests' share be mediated through the Levites in terms of a distinct tithe? Surely, it was to highlight the distinctive separation of the priests to God as the ministers 'at the altar and inside the curtain' (18:7) and so to exalt the Lord who proclaimed his salvation from the altar and the curtain.

What does this say to us in the New Testament era? Certainly, as already noted, it teaches that the support of the work of the gospel is to be regarded as *a precious privilege* — the proper response of Christians to the grace of the God who saved them, in Christ, to be his people. This is also, as we have seen, based on the tithing principle of *10% plus* and is designed to provide adequately for a *full-time ministry* — 'Scandalous maintenance makes scandalous ministers,' says Matthew Henry. This points very clearly to the necessity for whole-hearted devotion in the body of Christ. It is a 'holy' and 'royal priesthood' (1 Peter 2:9), in which *every member* is mobilized for the glory of God and the extension of his kingdom. The tithes — what people actually give to the Lord and his church — are, in the last analysis, a measure of personal commitment to Christ. They are the *part* with which we testify that God gave the *whole* in the first place — and all by his free grace. Hence, not to tithe faithfully is, God says, to 'rob' him. Why? Because, as the first answer of the *Heidelberg Catechism* so beautifully puts it, my 'only comfort in life and in death,' if I am really a Christian, is 'that I am not my own, but belong — body and soul, in life and in death — to my faithful Saviour Jesus Christ'. Furthermore, 'Because I belong to him, Christ, by his Holy Spirit, assures me of eternal life and makes me wholeheartedly willing and ready from now on to live for him.' Faith is more than words. Belonging to the Lord means living for him. We love him, because he first loved us. We give to him, because he first gave to us. So the tithes are always a test of practical faith: '"Bring the whole tithe into the storehouse, that there may be food in my house. Test me in this," says the Lord Almighty, "and see if I will not throw open the floodgates of heaven and pour out so much blessing that you will not have room enough for it"' (Mal. 3:10).

Faithful ministry is always a gift of God's grace and it calls for faithful response. 'Remember your leaders, who spoke the word of God to you. Consider the outcome of their way of life and imitate their faith. Jesus Christ is the same yesterday and today and for ever' (Heb. 13:7-8).

15.
The water of cleansing

Please read Numbers 19
'It is for purification from sin' (19:9).

So many of the rules and rituals of the Old Testament seem strange and oppressive to our way of thinking. It all seems so complicated, arbitrary and rigorous, that we have difficulty, even as we read of it in Scripture, getting the details straight in our minds. The thought of what it meant to keep all these regulations to the letter beggars our powers of imagination. The great temptation is, of course, to gloss over it all, to brush off any significance it might have, and dismiss it all as an era of shadows and obscurities, the explanation of which is irrelevant to our time. It is to say, in practice, if not in theory, that whatever these might have meant then, they have little to teach us now. In countless Christian homes and churches, unthumbed, unread and unassimilated Old Testaments bear mute, but irrefutable, testimony to the triumph of this outlook. It must be said, however, that there is no justification for New Testament Christians looking at the Old Testament with a superior smirk. Given that it is the Word of God, it is vital that we do not neglect the riches of divine revelation and so miss the truth the Lord has been teaching his people from the past, to the present and into the future.

The 'secret' to understanding the Old Testament's ceremonial rules is to recognize that 'Such ceremonies ... express the deepest truths about life ...'[1] They present pictures of deeper realities about God and humanity. These pictures consist of symbolic elements, the understanding of which is essential to the correct interpretation of the ceremonies as a whole. The rituals represent truths that the Lord wants his people to see, believe and do. They were not merely to 'go through the motions' of some strange ceremonial actions: they were to respond in faith to the doctrinal content of these actions. This is very clearly illustrated by the ceremonies of purification in Numbers 19. These ceremonies involved the peculiar procedure of mixing water with the ashes of a cow and then sprinkling the resultant 'water of cleansing' on the ceremonially unclean, in order to cleanse them. But behind these rituals lay the most profound of truths: namely that sinners must be saved and sanctified in order to enter the presence of a holy God. In other words, this peculiar ritual points us to the very heart of the gospel of Jesus Christ.

God's provision: the ritual of the red heifer (19:1-10)

This ritual was quite unique, in that it was not a formal sacrifice. Whereas all of the designated sacrifices were performed by the priests in the Tent of Meeting, this animal was killed **'outside the camp'** and only **'in [the priest's] presence'** (19:3). The characteristics of sacrifice are evident in all five main elements of the ritual.

1. The heifer to be *chosen* was to be without blemish and never to have been yoked (19:1-2). Here are echoes of the Passover lamb (Exod. 12:5; Lev. 22:22-24; 1 Peter 1:19).
2. The animal was, as we have seen, to be *killed* outside the camp in the presence of the priest (19:3; Heb. 12:12-13).
3. A token portion of the cow's *blood* was to be sprinkled seven times towards the door of the Tent of Meeting (19:4; Heb. 9:22). The cow itself was the colour of blood.
4. The heifer was *burned* whole — a complete offering (19:5-8). The addition of cedar wood, hyssop (i.e. sprigs of marjoram) and scarlet wool to the fire has sacrificial overtones, although it is uncertain what is meant specifically by these elements.[2]
5. The *ashes* were gathered and stored for the preparation and use of **'the water of cleansing'** (19:9-10).

What does this say to the church today? Clearly, the whole ceremonial system has passed away under the gospel. There is just no such category in biblical teaching and practice under the New Testament. Why? Because these ceremonies symbolized in picture form a work of God's grace which has been revealed in fulness in Jesus Christ. The substance has superseded the shadow. The reality has replaced the representation! That being the case, it is all the more important that we understand what, if anything, is relevant to the Christian era. What connections of substance come into the light, and therefore remain for our instruction in godliness, when the shadows have receded? The elements of the ritual surely suggest some answers. Let me offer four in particular.

First of all, the most obvious theme is that of *purification from sin and its effects*. The recurrent necessity for an Israelite to resort to the water of cleansing for his ceremonial uncleanness underscored the fundamental problem of the human condition. Sinners could not stand on any merits of their own before a holy God, because they simply had none — the demerits of sin placed them under the sentence of death from a just and holy God, whose 'eyes are too pure to look on evil' (Hab. 1:13). Cleansing was absolutely essential and it had to be the work of God. This is the meaning of the ritual: God provides cleansing for his people.

This is, of course, precisely the symbolism that underlies the New Testament sacrament of baptism. The water of baptism speaks of the work of the Holy Spirit in *regeneration* — the 'washing of regeneration' (Titus 3:5, AV) — and of the flow of 'streams of living water ... from within' — the words with which Jesus describes the *sanctification* of the believer (John 7:38). Water baptism speaks of cleansing in terms of the entire process of salvation (the *ordo salutis*), from regeneration and effectual calling, through repentance and faith, to sanctification and the day-to-day experience of the Christian life. Water baptism, as the sign and seal of the covenant of grace in the New Testament, corresponds to circumcision in the Old Testament. It is theologically and experimentally a much richer and more comprehensive symbol of what God has done and will yet do for believers, but it nevertheless shares — indeed, absorbs — the idea of purification central to the 'water of cleansing' under the law of Moses.

Secondly, the 'water of cleansing' speaks to us of *the necessity of atonement* for sin, even if only in an almost incidental way. The sacrifices of the tabernacle were, of course, the repositories in Israel of the doctrine of the atonement. The red heifer ritual did not add anything to that doctrine. What it did, though, was to link the idea of atonement to the provision it made for dealing with the minor uncleannesses of everyday life. The sprinkling of a very few drops of blood, seven times (seven is the number symbolizing God's covenant dealings with us), and in front of the Tent of Meeting told the Israelites that the basis of all cleansing was sacrifice: 'Without the shedding of blood there is no forgiveness' (Heb. 9:22). And, of course, that is precisely the teaching of the New Testament. It is the blood of Jesus Christ which alone purifies from all sin (1 John 1:7).

Thirdly, like everything else in the ceremonies of the law, rightly understood, the 'water of cleansing' was actually pointing to *Jesus Christ*. Aaron and Israel would not have seen this clearly at all, but even they recognized that it spoke of a greater salvation to come. They knew symbolism when they saw it and rightly believed that there was a substance hidden behind these symbols. And look at that symbolism: an unblemished animal, blood that is shed, death of a substitute outside the camp (Heb. 13:12). These are echoes of more explicit Old Testament foreshadowings of Christ. If, by comparison, they glow rather than shine with the promise of the gospel, they are nevertheless a genuine foretaste of the Lord Jesus Christ.

Finally, the 'water of cleansing' speaks of *the grace of God*. The supply of ashes was ample for the future. It was stored up and readily accessible. This was God's provision. Again Jesus comes into this symbolism, for he is that 'fountain ... opened to the house of David and the inhabitants of Jerusalem, to cleanse them from sin and impurity' (Zech. 13:1).

The need for cleansing (19:11-22)

The 'water of cleansing' was designed as a readily available means of meeting the necessity for dealing with ceremonial uncleanness without the expensive procedure of making sacrifices at the tabernacle. Ceremonial uncleanness was a factor in everyday Israelite life (see Lev. 12-15 for cases). Whatever the cause — and often this was quite accidental — it was always inconvenient, disruptive, time-consuming and involved temporary exclusion from the camp (Lev. 5:2-4; 12:4; 13:45-46).

The specific cases in view concern contact with dead bodies

(19:11-16; Lev. 21:1-3). Why? This is hardly a moral question. In fact, it is good and necessary to dispose reverently of the dead. Why, then, was death considered to be so defiling — so much so that tombs in biblical times were whitewashed, to warn pious Jews so that they could avoid proximity with the dead? (Matt. 23:27; Acts 23:3).³ The answer lies in the meaning of death. Death is not a normal part of life. It is certainly all-pervasive, but it is an abnormality, 'the wages of sin' and the 'last enemy' (Rom. 6:23; 1 Cor. 15:26). This form of ceremonial uncleanness reminded the Israelites of the reality of sin and the necessity of cleansing from sin for communion with the Lord. Furthermore, this ceremonial uncleanness was a reminder that the law could not conquer death. All through life, death was very near. It took God's grace to overthrow the effects of death. The ritual of using the 'water of cleansing', repeated over and over again through life, pointed to the need of a greater, deeper provision of God's grace to transform death into life.

The means of purification was for a man who was ceremonially clean to sprinkle the 'water of cleansing' with a sprig of hyssop onto the people, furnishings and tent tainted by uncleanness, on the third and seventh days of the period of uncleanness. Rightly understood, this is a distant picture of the gospel of Christ. The writer to the Hebrews makes the direct connection from shadow to substance: 'The blood of goats and bulls and the ashes of a heifer sprinkled on those who are ceremonially unclean sanctify them so that they are outwardly clean. How much more, then, will the blood of Christ, who through the eternal Spirit offered himself unblemished to God, cleanse our consciences from acts that lead to death, so that we may serve the living God' (Heb. 9:13-14). We are called, in other words, to the Messiah, Jesus Christ, as the only means of real cleansing. If we confess our sin and our lostness, cast ourselves upon the mercy of God in Christ and believe in the Lord Jesus Christ, we shall be saved.

> Do thou with hyssop sprinkle me
>> I shall be cleansed so
> Yea, wash thou me and then I shall
>> Be whiter than the snow.⁴

Part IV

From Kadesh to the River Jordan

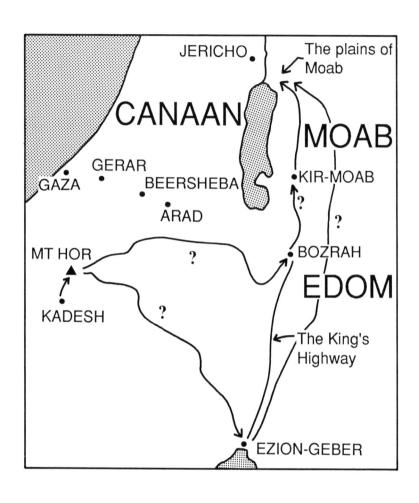

Map 3. — Israel's march from Kadesh to the Jordan

16.
Turning-point

Please read Numbers 20 and 21
'So Israel settled in the land of the Amorites' (21:31).

We almost always expect an easier ride in life than we actually get. Yet, even if things are harder than anticipated, they can often seem a lot worse to us than they really are, just because we were not realistic from the outset. We tend to swing from unreal optimism to irrational pessimism, because in both cases our (mis)interpretations of the facts were largely shaped by our feelings.

Perhaps Israel expected a walk-over in the conquest of Canaan. What is certain is that they were so shaken by reports of Canaanite military power that they forgot everything God had done for them and were ready to give up and go back to slavery in Egypt. The Lord was not to be denied, however, and so in the end they suffered more severely from his righteous chastisements for their unfaithfulness than they would ever have done at the hands of the enemies of the Canaanites! It was to take thirty-eight years of wandering in the desert before God's time arrived for a second try at the conquest of Canaan. Hundreds of thousands died, mostly of old age, as the Kadesh backsliders lived out the Lord's decree that none of them, except Joshua and Caleb, would enter the promised land.

The day did dawn, however, when Israel again arrived at Kadesh (20:1) and was confronted with her calling to conquer Canaan. To do so, she had to leave the rebellion and irrational fear of the past and approach the task with the realism of a living faith in the promises of God. This turning-point — from the impotence of compromised faith to the effectiveness of faith-driven realism — is recorded in Numbers 20 and 21, which show successively how the shadows of past sins cast their discouraging influence upon Israel's progress and how the shimmerings of salvation lit the way to victory for God's people.

Shadows of sins past (20:1-29)

The past so often returns to haunt the present. Even the memories of past weaknesses conspire to sap our present strength. Forgotten problems rise, as if from the dead, to undo the progress of years of faithfulness. Satan sees to this: he is a roaring lion seeking whom he may devour (1 Peter 5:8). The closer we get to God's goal for our lives, the harder the Evil One tries to get us to stumble. As Israel again approached the promised land, she was subjected to a barrage of discouraging events, which, humanly speaking, might well have led her to turn back again. But God had other, better plans.

The four events in view are all shadows of past sins and, as such, they largely represent the passing of an era in Israel's history. God's people were not deflected from their path, but went on to 'grasp the nettle' of God's call to possess the land of promise.

The death of Miriam (20:1)

With her brothers Moses and Aaron, Miriam was part of the triumvirate whom the Lord had raised up to lead his people (Micah 6:4). She was a prophetess, whose privilege it had been to sing the victory song at the crossing of the Red Sea. She had, however, 'once been a murmurer (12:1) and must not enter Canaan'.[1] In a sense, her death pointed both ways: it reached back to her sin and reminded the people that even the best cannot avoid responsibility for their actions, and it looked forward to the imminent fulfilment of the promise that the next generation would succeed where their parents had failed (14:31). If we are inclined to think God harsh in thus depriving her of entrance into Canaan, we should remember that Miriam was a believer, dying at a great age and passing into glory to be for ever with the Lord. Nevertheless, death is always the wages of sin and hers did mean that she forfeited a real blessing she would otherwise have enjoyed. In this life, even God's redeemed cannot escape something of the temporal consequences of their sins. Heaven alone is the wiping away of all our tears.

The failure of Moses and Aaron (20:2-13)

A second shadow from the past arose with a water shortage affecting the whole community. Once more, Israel voiced self-pitying recriminations against their leaders and their God (20:3-5). As before, Moses and Aaron interceded with the Lord and he commanded Moses to **'Take the staff'** — evidently symbolic of his office — and, having gathered the assembly, **'speak to that rock'** and it would **'pour out its water'** 'for the community and their livestock (20:6-8). This was virtually a repeat of the incident at Rephidim forty years before, with the difference that Moses had then been told to *strike* the rock (Exod. 17:1-7). Moses and Aaron duly gathered the people. Moses rebuked them, struck the rock twice and **'Water gushed out, and the community and their livestock drank'** (20:9-10). There was no judgement from God: only a merciful answer to their need, which had been very real indeed.

On this occasion, it was Moses and Aaron who were to receive God's rebuke (20:12-13). This is not to say the people were innocent and did not deserve to be corrected for their complaining spirit. It was just that, this time, Moses and Aaron stood in the most urgent need of correction. If the leaders are not called to account for their sins, how can the people ever be expected to follow them?

God's *sentence* on Moses and Aaron joined them to the Kadesh rebels by debarring them from leading Israel into Canaan (20:12). They too would die in the wilderness.

God's *reason* was made plain: **'You did not trust in me enough to honour me as holy in the sight of the Israelites'** (20:12). Why did God say this? For three reasons, I believe.

First of all, *Moses did not speak to the rock*; he struck it twice. This may seem a little thing, especially to people who sin a lot more boldly every day. It was, however, a clear contravention of God's plainly stated will. As such, it indicated a distinct disregard for the Lord. When we are bold to modify God's known will, we effectively humiliate the Lord and hold him to public shame. It is irreverence and rebellion. It is saying either, 'I know better than God,' or 'God doesn't care how I do things for him.'

Secondly, *Moses showed little of his famous humility* in his address to the people: '**Listen you rebels, must we bring you water...?**' (20:10) There is an arrogance here. He labels the people 'rebels' in obvious contempt. He speaks as if he and Aaron, rather than the Lord, were providing the water they asked for. The whole tone is devoid of grace. God was ready to give them a miracle, but his servants had the poison of asps under their tongues.

Finally, *it was a bad example to the people* from leaders who had been given not only great responsibilities, but great gifts. God brought them down a peg, because greater things were rightly to be expected from them! The Lord is just in all his ways. He sees our real character and motives and sins. And he expects us to follow him with holy and humble resolve.

The waters, like those of forty years before on the other side of Sinai (Exod. 17), were called '**Meribah, where the Israelites quarrelled with the Lord and he showed himself holy**' (20:13). The last clause is the key: the character of God as the Holy One who inhabits the praise of his people. In the last analysis, it is not fear of punishment or rebuke and correction that cause people to obey God, but rather a large view in the soul of the holiness and perfection of God. It is seeing him and knowing him in the perfect excellence of his self-revelation that draws believing hearts into wanting earnestly to be holy as he is holy.

The rebuff by Edom (20:14-21)

The most convenient way to Canaan was through Edom (south-east of the Dead Sea) to the plains of Moab and then across Jordan to the west bank. The 'short' route, 'as the crow flies,' was north through the Negev, but the terrain was decidedly inhospitable. Moses therefore negotiated with the King of Edom for passage through his country, taking care to offer assurances that would protect the Edomites' interests (20:14-17,19). The Edomites refused and mobilized their army to bar the Israelite passage. Israel had no mandate from God to fight Edom, so they turned away and began their march around Edom to the east (20:20-21).

The significance of this, apart from the test of faith it offered to Israel, is that it represented another piece in the emerging mosaic of the enmity between the descendants of Esau (Edom) and those of Jacob (Israel) — sins of the past returning to blight the present and the future. This would later issue in warfare and, ultimately, the extinction of Edom as a nation (Amos 1:11-12; Obad. 10-14). In New Testament terms, it reminds us that God is sovereign in salvation. 'Jacob I loved, but Esau I hated' (Rom. 9:13-16). There are two destinies operative in God's dealings with the human race: election and reprobation, heaven and hell, redemption and condemnation, saving faith and lost unbelief.

The passing of Aaron (20:22-29)

Israel advanced north-east to Mount Hor. There the Lord revealed to Moses that Aaron would be **'gathered to his people'**.

First, *we see the shadow of past sins falling upon the present.* Aaron was to die, said the Lord, **'because both of you rebelled against my command at the waters of Meribah'** (20:24). Aaron's death presented Israel with a vivid demonstration of the certain fruition of God's will. It also showed them that God is the real leader of his people. Human leaders are his servants and even the best are less than perfect. All soon pass from the scene. It emphasized afresh the need for the Lord's people not to put their trust in princes or in the arm of the flesh, but to take the Lord to be their Prince and Saviour.

Secondly, *a new era was dawning for Israel.* Even taking account of the 'untimely' nature of Aaron's death, it was majestic in its solemnity and its significance. Aaron was 123 years of age. He was a believer, taken to glory for all eternity, and his passing was marked by the transfer of his priestly office to his son, Eleazar: **'Moses removed Aaron's garments and put them on his son Eleazar'** (20:28). With Eleazar's investiture, the future beckoned and the light of living hope burned more brightly. We have every reason to believe that Aaron's heart burned with a sense of that hope as he went to be with the Lord.

Thirdly, *we are challenged to consider our own death:* **'Aaron died'** (20:28). Even if we live to be over 100, life will be short! We are all 'destined to die once, and after that to face judgement' (Heb. 9:27). Aaron was told the day of his death. Charles Simeon asks, 'What if God were now to issue the command to any one of us, "Go to your bed, and die"? How would it be received among us? Should we welcome such an order? Should we rejoice that the period has arrived for our dismission from the body, and for our entrance into the presence of our God?'² That time is coming soon for everyone who reads these words. Aaron was ready. How about you?

Finally, in the light of the New Testament, we can say that *we are actually pointed to Jesus Christ as our great High Priest.* The Aaronic priesthood is clearly a foreshadowing of the work of Christ in his atoning death upon the cross (Heb. 4:14 - 10:18). If, then, the shadows of past sin recorded in Numbers 20 seem rather dismal and discouraging, it should be noted that they were in fact passing shadows. God was at work to unfold his plan of redemption for Israel, but also, in Jesus Christ, for the whole world. This did not, then or now, mean an end to problems for God's people. Israel had, however, reached a turning-point. God's time had come for them to enter the promised land, and in Numbers 21 we see the first steps that were to bring the people to the edge of Jordan — the shimmerings of the future progress that God had in store for his people.

Shimmerings of salvation (21:1-35)

Future progress in life often means having to slay the dragons of past failure. It is always more difficult, at least in the mind, to defeat an opponent who has previously beaten us. A good coach, for example, will take particular care to prepare an athlete to cope with the challenges, physical and psychological, which proved too great in earlier contests. The promise that God's 'grace is sufficient for [us], for [his] power is made perfect in weakness' (2 Cor. 12:9) finds its most potent application as the Lord gives us victory over the very thing in which we earlier experienced defeat. Sin can be defeated and it is God's enabling grace that clothes our weakness with his strength. As Israel prepared, at last, to enter Canaan, her experience was something of a mirror image of earlier failures. A new victory at Hormah reversed the defeat of the first battle of Hormah (21:1-3). A new healing, through looking to a bronze serpent, contrasted with the death attending the rebellion of Korah (21:4-9). The long, hard march to Jordan turns round the forty-year exile in the desert (21:10-20). The conquest of Sihon and Og overcomes once and for all the fears of Kadesh Barnea (21:21-35). All of these provide a picture of spiritual growth, from repentance, to faith, to obedience and ultimately to glory. Spiritual renewal means taking possession of once lost battlefields. New holiness kills old sins and kindles new fires that light the way to heaven itself.

Repentance — dying to old sins at Hormah (21:1-3)

The kingdom of Arad lay to the north of the Negev, towards which the Israelites were advancing. The king heard of Israel's approach and put in a pre-emptive strike and took some prisoners. Israel's reaction was evidence of a new spirit — they immediately turned to the Lord, sought his aid and covenanted to fight and to destroy the Canaanites. The result was the total destruction of Arad.[3] Recognizing this to be a reversal of the earlier battle of 'Hormah' (14:45), this place was also named Hormah. So began God's predicted proscription of the Canaanites — the cup of Amorite iniquity had filled up (Gen. 15:16-19). It remains a solemn foreshadowing of the eternal punishment of the wicked to be effected on the coming day of the Lord. To Israel then and for Christians now, Hormah speaks of dying to old sins and living to new righteousness. Sin will not have dominion over the Lord's people!

Faith — looking to a saviour in the bronze snake (21:4-9)

Israel did not venture north through the Negev to Canaan, but decided to go around Edom and approach Canaan from the east, across the Jordan from Jericho. This first took them south **'along the route to the Red Sea'** (i.e., the Gulf of Aqaba), before turning east and north to Moab. It was on this journey that murmuring once more arose against the Lord and Moses. Once again, they provoked the Lord to anger and he **'sent venomous snakes among them; they bit the people and many Israelites died'** (21:6).

The people were convicted that they had sinned and asked Moses to pray that the Lord would take away the snakes. Moses did pray on their behalf, but the Lord did not grant the request. Instead, he told Moses to make a snake of bronze and put it on a pole. Then, **'When anyone was bitten by a snake and looked at the bronze snake, he lived'** (21:7-9).

The meaning of this incident is not difficult to discern. Clearly, God's employment of an irruption of poisonous snakes was designed to teach Israel, once again, that the consequence of rebellion against God is death and that they were not able in their own strength to save themselves from these consequences. Without the mercy of God, they would all perish.[4]

God's solution to the problem, at first sight, looks rather strange. As with all the sacrifices and many of the events of the Old Testament period, the key to understanding is in the symbolism employed. For example, the connection between the animal sacrifice and human beings, for whom it is a substitute, is particularly symbolized in the shedding of blood — because 'the life of a creature is in the blood' (Lev. 17:11). Man's life is forfeit because of sin. The substitute is the life of the sacrificed animal. The equation is: its blood (life) for man's blood (life). So it is no surprise to find the same principle of symbolic parallelism in connection with the solution to the problem of the snake bites. 'Those inflamed and dying through the bite of living snakes were restored to life through a dead reddish-coloured snake.'[5] The substance, of which this is only the symbol, was healing for those who *in faith* looked to the bronze snake. God promised to heal those who believed enough in his promise to do what he said! There was no magical efficacy in the metal snake. It was not touched. It was not paraded about, or venerated, or later treated as a relic, after the fashion of the superstitious practices of Roman Catholicism, even today. Simple, straightforward faith is the key. This is made clear by our Lord in his conversation with Nicodemus, when he says, with reference to saving faith, 'Just as Moses lifted up the snake in the desert, so the Son of Man must be lifted up, that everyone who believes in him may have eternal life' (John 3:4-16; cf. 12:32-34; 1 Cor. 10:9). Jesus was made 'in the likeness of sinful man to be a sin offering,' dying 'the righteous for the unrighteous' to bring us to God (Rom. 8:3; 1 Peter 3:18). The bronze snake preached gospel grace to Israel and speaks to us of Jesus, the only Saviour of sinners like ourselves.

Obedience — on the move for God to Jordan's edge (21:10-20)

The journey to the Jordan took Israel on a wide arc around Moab, carefully avoiding confrontation with the Moabites. This account — further details of the journey are given in Numbers 33 — is interesting for its quotations[6] from 'the book of the wars of the Lord,' which, like the Book of Jashar mentioned in Joshua 10:13 and 2 Samuel 1:18, was a collection of songs celebrating Israelite exploits over the years. Both books have disappeared and these are the only references to them still extant.

The journey is best seen, in James Philip's words, as 'a parable of deeper spiritual realities', illustrating the necessity of persevering in obedience to the Lord's will.[7]As with the well at Beer, where the **'princes dug'** and the Lord **'[gave] them water,'** so the Christian life is one of divine provision in conjunction with human responsibility. 'Prayer and diligence, dependence and activity,' remarked William Jay, 'harmonize in Scripture, and are only inconsistent in the crudeness of ignorant and foolish men. Paul makes divine influence, not an excuse for the neglect of means, but a motive and encouragement to the use of them — "Work out your own salvation with fear and trembling; for it is God who worketh in you both to will and to do of his good pleasure."'[8]

Glory — entering the inheritance (21:21-35)

Only two obstacles remained on Israel's march to the Jordan. Between the Arnon (Moab's northern border) and the Jabbok (Ammon's southern border), lay the territory of the Amorite kings Sihon and Og. In spite of efforts to pass through peacefully, both kings made war on Israel, but were utterly destroyed and their depopulated lands settled by Israel. The significance of this first conquest and occupation of land was threefold.

First of all, Israel's victory served notice on the surrounding nations that *a new order was dawning on their world.* Moses records the text of an Amorite taunt-song boasting of an earlier triumph of Sihon of the Amorites over Moab, turning it against both the Amorites and Moab to rub in the triumph of God's people (21:27-30).[9]

Secondly, *the annihilation of the Amorites was part of the purpose of God revealed to Abraham* 400 years earlier (Gen. 15:16). It was therefore the first instalment of the fulfilment of the Lord's promise to Israel of their inheritance of the Canaan that loomed large ahead of them beyond the Jordan. For this reason, Sihon and Og were to be mentioned frequently in the Scriptures as God gave them over the years ahead (Deut. 1:4; 2:24-37; 3:1-11; 4:47; 29:7; Josh. 9:10; 12:4; Judg. 11:19-21; Ps. 135:11, 136:19-20).

Last, but not least, *Israel's victory was the fruit of her renewed commitment to her calling as the people of God.* After they had been wandering in the desert for a generation, the Lord had put them back on his track. The gates of hell could no more prevail against the Old Testament people of God than they ever will against the New Testament church. Israel's struggles remind us that there is a spiritual warfare going on behind the observable contendings of the church in the world. 'For our struggle is not against flesh and blood, but against the rulers, against the authorities, against the powers of this dark world and against the spiritual forces of evil in the heavenly realms' (Eph. 6:12). This struggle is to the death — to eternal death — for the Evil One and his unrepentant allies. Victory is beyond the abilities of the best of God's people, for, as Martin Luther observed:

> With force of arms we nothing can,
> Full soon we were down-ridden.

But all is not lost, for the Lord has sent his Redeemer to save the unsavable, to help the helpless, to redeem the lost:

> But for us fights the proper man,
> Whom God himself hath bidden.
> Ask ye who is this same?
> Christ Jesus is his name,
> The Lord Sabaoth's Son;
> He and no other one,
> Shall conquer in the battle.

Part V

On the threshold of the promised land

17.
A curse sought and a blessing given

Please read Numbers 22-24
'Now come and put a curse on these people...' (22:6).

On 23 February 1991, American President George Bush gave notice to Saddam Hussein's Iraq to withdraw from Kuwait or face a land offensive. A few hours later, an Iraqi spokesman denounced this as a 'shameful ultimatum' and described its author as 'God's enemy and Devil's friend Bush'. Iraqi communiqués had regularly used such language and frequently invoked the divine curse on their enemies. It was to the credit of the allied governments that their own official pronouncements were consistently couched in the language of moderation and that where prayer was called for, as it was in the United States, it was either for the avoidance of war, before it broke out, or for swift victory with minimal casualties, after it did.

This was not the first occasion in history when one side sought to invoke the divine curse on an adversary. 3,500 years earlier, Balak, the King of Moab, sought to secure the services of a prophet named Balaam (from Pethor on the Euphrates, in modern Iraq) to put a curse on the Israelite nation, in the hope that this would weaken them to the point where he could defeat them in battle. How this sought-for curse was turned by God into an unexpected blessing is recounted in Numbers 22-24.

A curse sought (22:1-40)

Balaam is probably most widely remembered for his talking donkey. This has been so trivialized in the popular mind that all sight has been lost of what actually happened. The donkey was not the centre of the story and her words, though not unimportant, were ancillary to the main point, which concerned how God dealt with Balaam so as to overthrow Balak's scheme to destroy Israel. Gordon Wenham has captured the essence of the story in a few sentences, unsurpassed for analytical succinctness; 'The charming naiveté of these stories disguises a brilliance of literary composition and a profundity of theological reflection ... [the donkey], proverbial for its dullness and obstinacy, is shown to have more spiritual insight than the super-prophet from Mesopotamia ... Yet this numb-skulled, money-grubbing heathen seer is inspired by the Spirit of God with a vision of Israel's future destiny truly messianic in dimensions.'[1]

The first part of the narrative tells how Balaam came to Moab to curse Israel and is in dramatic form with a prologue, three acts and an epilogue.

Prologue: Balaam summoned from Mesopotamia (22:1-6)

The Moabites were terrified by Israel's annihilation of the Amorites, although there was in fact no threat to them. Moses had been expressly forbidden by the Lord from attacking them, because, as the descendants of Lot, they held their territory by the Lord's donation (Deut. 2:9; cf. Gen. 19:37). Israel therefore avoided intruding on Moabite territory after Moab had denied them passage up 'the King's Highway' (Judg. 11:17). Where the Moabites really had nothing to dread, 'There they were, overwhelmed with fear' (Ps. 53:5). Balak, the King of Moab, accordingly enlisted his Midianite allies and together they sent an embassy to Balaam to come and curse Israel.

Act I: God says 'No!' (22:7-14)

The Moab-Midian axis duly sent a delegation to Balaam. Mention of **'the fee for divination'** effectively evokes the air of the magical and mercenary which surrounds the whole transaction.[2] Balaam asked the Moabite princes to remain for a night, promising, **'I will bring you back the answer the Lord gives me'** (22:8). Balaam's use of the word YHWH (Yahweh/Jehovah) for 'Lord' would seem to indicate that he specifically sought the God of Israel for guidance in the matter. This does not indicate any faith in the living God, beyond a general acknowledgement of his existence, or the possibility of his existence. The world of pagans is populated with gods of all sorts and a diviner like Balaam, far from disbelieving in the gods of other nations, would accept their reality as a matter of course. His job, as he saw it, was to find out the will of the god, or gods, directly relevant to the case. If Israel had a god named 'Yahweh,' then to Yahweh he must go! Balaam therefore sought the will of the God of Israel. And, lo and behold, God answered! And he told Balaam not to go to Moab! He **'must not put a curse on these people [Israel], because they are blessed'** (22:12). Clearly, Balaam was impressed by this for he declined the invitation, indicating that **'The Lord has refused to let me go'** (22:13). So the Moabites had to return to Balak without their super-prophet!

Even though the embassy failed on this occasion, the basic tension of the incident with Balaam can be clearly seen. In Wenham's words, 'Balaam is thus trapped between the demands of Balak and the commands of God. It is this conflict that sustains the whole drama that follows.'³ And it must surely touch a chord in everyone who has a conscience, for this is the most basic tension in human experience: between what *we* want to do and what *God* wants us to do. It is a parable of the universal human condition.

Act II: God permits him to go (22:15-20)

Balak, like temptation itself, refused to take no for an answer. So back came a bigger and better delegation with an even more lucrative offer for Balaam. The prophet's first response was to emphasize his earlier decision: he could not come, so to speak 'for all the tea in China' nor **'do anything great or small to go beyond the command of the Lord my God'** (22:18).

If matters had ended there, we might be extolling Balaam's memory as a great hero of faith. At the very least, we would have been persuaded he truly believed in the Lord. But it is precisely at this point that his true colours begin to shine through. **'Stay here tonight,'** he tells the men, **'and I will find out what else the Lord will tell me'** (22:19). It is the word 'else' that gives him away. It can only mean that he wanted the Lord to change his mind. In his heart — and this is confirmed by all that the Bible later tells us about Balaam — he found that Balak's offer was one that he could not refuse. His earlier protestations were just coyness masking a drooling avarice. He really wanted to go to Moab.

The Lord, surprisingly and without the slightest fuss, now permitted the prophet to go. He only added the proviso: **'Do only what I tell you'** (22:20). As with all apparent changes of mind on God's part, this one masks his deeper purposes, one of which was surely to give Balaam opportunity to expose something of his real attitudes and motives. It thus set in motion the series of events in which both God's purpose to bless Israel and his power to defeat their enemies were dramatically demonstrated. Nevertheless, it must have seemed to Balaam himself — and surely also to the Moabites, after Balaam had told them what God had said — that he was 'a man of great spiritual stature, who can meet with God when he wants and whose words can have tremendous effects on the fate of nations'. Things were now going well for Balaam and Moab and strongly suggested that God was even in favour of what they were doing! This is the inevitable consequence of assuming that an 'open door' to do what you want to do is proof that God wants you to do it! Balaam wanted his 'open door' and God gave it to him — not because he approved of it, but because he was determined to teach Balaam, Balak and all future students of the Bible what happens when opportunism triumphs over right principle. Balak and Balaam were committed to essentially wicked goals — the destruction of Israel and personal enrichment respectively. Yet they went on all the same and felt entirely justified in doing so.

Act III: God rebukes him but still lets him go (22:21-35)

Balaam duly set off with the Moabites. God, we are told, was **'very angry when he went, and the angel of the Lord stood in the road to oppose him'** (22:21). This puzzles many readers. If God was angry, why had he not said so, instead of letting Balaam go? The answer is that while it served God's deeper purposes to let Balaam go, it remained a fact that Balaam was doing something essentially wicked. God does not like everything he permits people to do. He expects us to act on principle. He never removes our responsibility for doing so, and when he lets us make our own decisions and act upon them, this is in no way an approval of our sin. Soon enough, we reap as we have sown. So it was with Balaam. But what happened first showed just how spiritually blind he was.

Balaam did not see the angel, but his donkey did. Three times the donkey baulked on account of the angel and three times an angry Balaam beat her with his staff (22:23-27). On the third occasion, **'The Lord opened the donkey's mouth, and she said to Balaam, "What have I done to you to make you beat me these three times?"'** (22:28). Of all the miracles recorded in Scripture, this one has stirred the most amazement and incredulity. The idea of a talking animal seems ludicrous and out of keeping with the generally majestic tone of biblical miracles.[5] This entirely overlooks the Lord's aim in having the donkey speak to Balaam. God meant it to appear incredible and even ludicrous! Why? To expose Balaam's foolishness! Why, asked the animal, did you beat me? Because, replied the prophet, **'You have made a fool of me!'** 'Have I been in the habit of [making a fool of] you' countered the donkey. 'No,' Balaam had to admit. And **'Then ... the Lord opened Balaam's eyes, and he saw the angel of the Lord standing in the road with his sword drawn'** (22:29-31).

The donkey is a living parable of Balaam's predicament. She was caught between Balaam's stick and the angel's sword — just as Balaam would, in Gordon Wenham's words, 'find himself trapped three times between Balak's demands and God's prohibitions'.[6] God's use of an animal noted for dumb obstinacy to open the eyes of the super-prophet to his own incredible foolishness makes the point in a way that, say, a straightforward appearance of the angel of the Lord would not have done. We all remember Balaam's donkey, don't we? Why is it a case of, 'Once heard of, never forgotten'? Because its images are as incredible as a Bugs Bunny cartoon! And there lies the wisdom of God. His purpose was deadly serious, not only for Balaam and Balak, but for every one of us. He wants us to see the folly of foolishness: and what more winsome way than to expose our blindness by a talking donkey?

He also points to his authoritative word. He, who could speak through a donkey, would speak through Balaam. Balaam had sinned, but he had been spared so far — had it not been for his donkey, the angel would have killed him. The angel told him he could go on to Moab, but made it plain that he was to **'speak only what I tell you'** (22:32-35). God would not be denied!

'He does as he pleases
  with the powers of heaven

and the peoples of the earth.
No one can hold back his hand
or say to him: "What have you done?"'

(Daniel 4:35).

Epilogue: Balaam arrives in Moab (22:36-40)

Balaam at length arrived in Moab and was greeted by his royal employer, who was less than thrilled about the time it had taken for the prophet to agree to come and curse Israel, but nevertheless assured him of an ample reward. In reply, Balaam indicated honestly that he could not say **'just anything'**, but only **'what God puts in my mouth'** (22:38). We are not told what was going through his mind. He must have known that *not* to curse Israel would incur Balak's wrath. Perhaps Balaam hoped against hope that he could pull off a few curses anyway, or maybe that God would change his mind. Perhaps he just felt trapped and, like a man in a dentist's chair, was just determined to tough it out and take his chances. That is how many people live their lives in relation to the Lord — they grit their teeth, do their own thing and, the closer they get to eternity, the more determined they become *not* to come to Christ that they might have life. Balaam knew enough of the truth to know he was on God's wrong side but he still died in his sins.

A blessing given (22:41-24:25)

Balaam was to give no fewer than four oracles — three at the insistence of Balak and the fourth by the spontaneous leading of the Spirit of God. We may call them Balaam's oracles, but they were in fact *God's* oracles spoken by his unwilling mouthpiece, Balaam. Balaam was God's 'donkey,' compelled to bring the Word of God to Moab. Indeed, the scope of the message is far wider. It is God's timeless manifesto for his people with respect to their position in his eyes, relative to the unbelieving peoples and nations of the world.

Oracle I: God will not curse his people (22:41 - 23:12)

Balak took Balaam to **'Bamoth Baal'** (literally, 'high places of Baal'), from which point he could see **'part of the people'**, i.e., of

Israel's camp. Balaam and Balak then undertook a series of seven sacrifices, each of seven bulls and seven rams, and Balaam withdrew to **'a barren height'** in the hope of meeting with God. The Lord did indeed reveal himself and gave Balaam an oracle to proclaim over Israel, all of which shows why he cannot do the job for which Balak hired him. This included four basic truths:

1. *God has not cursed Israel (23:8).* Therefore Balaam cannot curse them.

2. *God has separated Israel* as a **'people who live apart'** (23:9). Among all the nations, Israel has a unique relationship with God.

3. *God has blessed Israel* with manifest power: **'Who can count the dust of Jacob ... ?'** (cf. Gen. 13:16); and great numbers: **'... or number the fourth part of Israel?'** (23:10).

4. *God has made Israel his covenant people.* Balaam's plea says more about Israel than about himself: **'Let me die the death of the righteous, and may my end be like theirs'** (23:10; cf. Gen. 12:1-3). Their character and destiny are bound to the Lord in terms of his covenant of grace.

Small wonder, after all this, that Balak expostulates, **'I brought you to curse my enemies, but you have done nothing but bless them'** (23:11-12).

Oracle II: God is faithful to his promises (23:13-26)

Balak did not give up easily. 'Try, and if you don't succeed,' goes the proverb, 'try, try and try again.' Perhaps a different vantage-point and new sacrifices would do the trick. So off they went to Zophim for a second attempt. As before, Balaam went aside to receive a word from God. And once more, the Lord gave him a four-part oracle to take to Balak.

1. *God keeps his promises (23:19-20).* **'God is not a man, that he should lie, nor a son of man, that he should change his mind'** (23:19). Behind his variable *dealings* with man, as when he let Balaam go to Moab and so seemed to change his mind, lies an unchanging purpose, his eternal decree. This is partly secret and partly revealed — the latter in his Word and in his works.

2. *God has preserved his people (23:21-22).* His promises to Israel in word had been maintained by his mighty acts in history on their behalf — the same combination by which Christ sustains his people in the present, New Testament era.

3. *God continues to reveal himself to his people.* The thrust of 23:23 is future: **'It will now be said ... of Israel, "See what God has done!"'**

4. *God gives the strength his people will need to overcome their enemies.* She will be like a lion who **'devours his prey'** (23:24).

Balak once again was frustrated, and we can well understand why he would rather Balaam shut up altogether than open his mouth to utter oracles such as these (23:25-26).

Oracle III: God blesses the lives of his people (23:27 - 24:13)

Apparently undaunted, Balak insisted on one more attempt to curse Israel. Perhaps he thought it might be 'third time lucky'! This time, the chosen site was Mount Peor, surely that of the worship of 'the Baal of Peor', to which many Israelites were later lured by the charms of the Moabite women (23:27-24:2; cf. 25:3). The usual sacrifices were observed, but this time Balaam apparently did not draw apart to receive the oracle. He **'saw that it pleased the Lord to bless Israel'**, and **'did not resort to sorcery as at other times, but turned his face towards the desert'**. As he saw the Israelite camp, **'The Spirit of God came upon him and he uttered his oracle'** (24:1-2). This third oracle has a twin focus:

1. Balaam speaks of *the clarity of the vision given to him (24:3-4).* This underscored the certainty of the oracle. At the same time, it was not the fruit of any personal commitment to the Lord. His ecstatic experience of the Spirit of God was not the same as the baptism of the Holy Spirit as experienced by Jesus (Isa. 61:1) and believers at their conversion to Christ (Acts 2:1-4).[7]

2. The vision itself was *a poetic description of Israel's future* in Canaan. The picture is of a prosperous and fruitful land, ruled by a powerful king — **'greater than Agag,'** i.e., the kings of the Amalekites (24:5-9; cf. 1 Sam. 15:32).

This was the last straw for a furious Balak. He banished Balaam without his pay, but promptly received another prophecy instead! (24:10-14).

Oracle IV: God gives his people victory over their enemies (24:14-25)

Balaam's final oracle, or group of oracles, turns the attention fully upon Balak and all the enemies of God's people. It is introduced by the formula on the clarity of the vision used in the third oracle (24:15-16; cf. 3-4). The prophecies focus on the coming king and the conquests he will effect:

1. *A king will come from Israel (24:17).* The language is unmistakably messianic. He is **'a star ... out of Jacob'** and a **'sceptre ... out of Israel'**. Jesus is the 'bright Morning star' (Rev. 22:16), the sceptre is Christ's mediatorial rule (Gen. 49:10; Ps. 45:6; 110; Rev. 2:27). In the light of such passages as Psalms 2, 22 and 110, Acts 2:14-36 and Hebrews 1-2, the words of Balaam can only find their meaning and fulfilment in Jesus Christ as the Mediator-King who rules until all his enemies are made his footstool. Some commentators see it as looking ahead to David, but David is himself more of a prophecy than a fulfilment. He too looked forward to the coming of Christ, the final King (Acts 2:30-31).

2. *The Lord's enemies will be destroyed (24:17-24).* Moab and Edom will be crushed; the Amalekites will be destroyed; the Kenites will be taken captive by the Asshurites,⁸ a tribe of southern Canaan; and the Asshurites, together with the descendants of Eber, would in turn be conquered by invaders **'from the shores of Kittim'**, probably the Philistines.

Balaam was finished, he **'got up and returned home'**, while Balak **'went his own way'** (24:25). The comedy was over!

The abiding lessons of Balaam

The whole Balaam episode took place without the knowledge of the Israelites. Only later did they discover what God had done behind the scenes. This has powerful implications for the Lord's people, then and now.

First of all, *God is winning victories as you read these words.* There is a war going on all the time against God and his people (Eph. 6). We see plenty of this in our own lives. Much of it is hidden from our view — something for which we should give thanks to the Lord, because a full knowledge of the evils that threaten us would be depressing, if not crushing, to our souls. We may later learn of them, as Israel later did concerning Balaam. But we may never know, simply because the Lord has turned the threat aside and let it be forgotten. Christians therefore have warrant to believe that they have more reasons than they can ever know for giving thanks to the Lord for his care and protection. We also have cause to trust the Lord in holy confidence, because he is absolutely sovereign and his gracious hand acts for the ultimate good of all who love him (Rom. 8:28).

Secondly, not only will the wickedness of the wicked not thwart God's will, but *the wicked will actually be made to serve God's will.* 'The king's heart is in the hand of the Lord; he directs it like a watercourse wherever he pleases' (Prov. 21:1). Balaam was undoubtedly wicked. It was his advice that led to Israel's sin at Peor (Num. 31:16; cf. 25:1-18; Rev. 2:14), while the New Testament characterizes him as an avaricious hireling, who 'loved the wages of wickedness' (2 Peter 2:15; Jude 11). Nevertheless, he was made, against his every intention, to serve the Lord's purpose for Israel. The lost in hell will have served God's glory, not only in their banishment from his presence for ever, but in the Lord's negation of the damage they might have done, and actually did, to the Lord's people and the cause of Jesus Christ while they lived.

Finally, Balaam was used by God in two quite different ways *to point to Jesus Christ.* He did so prophetically, if unwittingly, in the messianic utterances of the fourth oracle — Jesus is the 'star' that 'will come out of Jacob' and the 'sceptre' that 'will rise out of Israel' (24:17). In another, darker way, Balaam reminds us of the necessity of salvation by the free grace of God through faith in Jesus Christ as our only Saviour. Balaam reminds us of those who will come to the Lord when their lives are over and say, 'Lord, Lord, did we not prophesy in your name, and in your name drive out demons and perform many miracles?' In other words, people will present their good works, their good intentions, the gifts that they exercised in doing people some good and a whole list of qualities that would seem to them to guarantee their acceptance with God and their tenure in heaven. Most people actually believe they are good enough for God to be incapable of turning them away.[9]Yet, Jesus will say, **'I never knew you. Away from me, you evildoers!'** (Matt. 7:22-23). Why? Knowing Jesus Christ, having come to him in repentance and faith as the only Redeemer, receiving his free grace in the gospel and forever putting away the notion that our best works are really 'good' and meritorious — this is what is vital. Not gifts, not ability to prophesy, and not what I do for God (by my way of it), but coming to Christ with nothing but my helplessness and need of a Saviour — this is the need of sad, hurt, lost humanity.

> Not the labours of my hands
> Can fulfil thy law's demands;
> Could my zeal no respite know,
> Could my tears forever flow,
> All for sin could not atone
> Thou must save and thou alone.
>
> Nothing in my hand I bring,
> Simply to thy cross I cling;
> Naked, come to thee for dress;
> Helpless, look to thee for grace;
> Foul, I to the fountain fly;
> Wash me Saviour, or I die.[10]

18.
Balaam's revenge

Please read Numbers 25
'They were the ones who followed Balaam's advice' (31:16).

Entirely unbeknown to Israel, God overthrew the scheme of Balak,
King of Moab, to curse Israel and bring them down to defeat. It was
not for want of effort on the king's part. Balak had hired the
Mesopotamian prophet Balaam to curse Israel. Three times he
called the prophet to deliver that curse, only to hear his hireling utter
words of divine blessing upon his intended victims no less than four
times! (Num. 22-24). The score, you might say, was: God — 4,
Balak — 0!

This, however, was not the end of the matter. Evil is like a weed.
Cut it down, and up it comes again! Balaam was obliged by the Lord
to speak his word, but this was not because he enjoyed doing so or
endorsed the message from his heart. Balaam was no friend of God.
He was powerless to curse Israel, but we know that he was still able
to give to Balak some parting advice, which, Moses later records,
was instrumental in 'turning the Israelites away from the Lord'
(Num. 31:16). This, then, was Balaam's revenge! And it did not stop
there, because it not only wreaked havoc with Israel in the plains of
Moab, but 'eventually brought about the destruction of the nation'
nearly nine centuries later.[1] Even so, this is not the whole story.
Many in Israel fell away (25:1-5), but the Lord saved his people
through the faithfulness of one man (25:6-15) and sealed his hatred
of idolatry by declaring his judgement upon the people who seduced
the Israelites (25:16-18).

The apostasy of Israel (25:1-5)

What was 'Balaam's advice'? (31:16) The most succinct definition is given by the apostle John in his letter to the church at Pergamum fourteen centuries later. There were those in Pergamum, said John, 'who hold to the teaching of Balaam, who taught Balak to entice the Israelites to sin by eating food sacrificed to idols, and by committing sexual immorality' (Rev. 2:14). And how was this to be achieved? By employing what Charles Simeon calls 'the fascinations of abandoned women'![2] 'We are more endangered by the charms of a smiling world,' notes Matthew Henry, 'than by the terrors of a frowning world.'[3]

Playing the harlot (25:1-3)

The result was that **'The people began to play the harlot with the daughters of Moab'** (25:1, NASB). The NIV rendering, 'The men began to indulge in sexual immorality,' is too restrictive an interpretation of an expression which refers not only to the physical act of fornication, but includes the broader and more profound dimension of a spiritual and national harlotry (e.g., Isa. 1:21; Ezek. 16:26-28). The two — the physical and spiritual — are integrally related. In this case, the one leads to the other — illicit sex soon gives way to explicit idolatry. John Calvin, speaking of the women of Moab, notes that, 'By this fan ... Balaam stirred up the fire, which impelled these poor wretches, inflamed by blind lechery, to another crime, by which they might arouse against themselves the enmity of God.'[4]

The women invited the men **'to the sacrifices to their gods. The people ate and bowed down before these gods. So Israel joined in worshipping the Baal of Peor'** (25:2-3). First sex, then false religion. The old doctrines do not allow the new sins, so new 'insights' are needed to restore the lost feeling of being respectable! 'Those that have broken the fences of modesty,' remarks Matthew Henry, 'will never be held by the bonds of piety.'[5] There is a 'domino effect' in personal morality and a spiritual life. One sin does lead to another. It gets easier as time goes on. And the same is true of unbelief. That is why people brought up in orthodox Christian homes, but never converted to Christ in their hearts, fall away with a bang! They often look like instant atheists! Why? Because they were all façade, all outward conformity! It only took one kick on the door to bring the whole house tumbling down! Opportunities to sin are all that is needed for the unconverted, lip-serving, churchy type of 'Christian' to unmask his own hypocrisy! Of course, true conversion from the world can be as dramatic the other way, the difference being that it is the irreversible work of God's saving grace.

The reason that sins follow one another with such ease, rapidity and escalating intensity is that sin is essentially a *complex* — a disposition, a life-style, a condition of heart, a web of interrelated motivation. This, incidentally, is why we find natural networking among the various anti-morality pressure groups in society. They drink at the same fountain and share the same presuppositions about the basic issues — the issues upon which the Lord has delivered his perfect, righteous will in his Word, and to which they are intrinsically opposed.

Answering to God (25:3-5)

'The Lord's anger burned against them' (25:3). God is justifiably angry about evil 'every day', but just as surely loves his Son and his people with an everlasting 'unfailing love' every day (Ps. 7:11; 52:8). But as the unchangeable God deals with us very changeable people, he reveals himself in relation to the need of the moment. When Israel sinned, he revealed his otherwise unvarying anger against sin and withheld any sense of his otherwise unwavering covenant love. What varies is what God *reveals* of himself, not what he *is* in himself. And he communicates his perfect hatred of sin with a variable intensity calculated to awaken those who are listening to him to the gravity of defying the living God.

First, the Lord decreed the execution of **'all the leaders'** (25:4). The implication was that they all bore responsibility for what had happened. This was true whether they were the ringleaders who led their men off to Moab or whether they remained personally clear of this sin, but had failed to exercise their proper authority and discipline over those who did actually transgress. One way or another, whether by commission or omission, the leadership failed and must face the consequences of their dereliction of biblical responsibility.[6]

These leaders were to be put to death and their corpses exposed **'in broad daylight,'** — probably by being impaled on a stake, after their limbs had been broken (25:4; cf. 2 Sam 21:9).[7] The people would thus have visible proof that the wages of sin is death (Rom. 6:23). Furthermore, it would not be lost on the people that this was a representative, exemplary punishment, to be visited upon the responsible leadership of the tribes. It was, in other words, a penalty unmistakably in the nature of an *atonement* for the sin of the people, so that **'the Lord's fierce anger [might] turn away from Israel'** (25:4).

Secondly, Moses instructed the judges that each of them must put to death **'those of your men'** — i.e. those men within their jurisdictions —**'who have joined in worshipping the Baal of Peor'** (25:5). This should be seen, not as a modification to the Lord's sentence on the elders, but as an additional extension of justice to the guilty among the ordinary people.[8] The rigour with which the matter was to be dealt with rather rankles in modern minds that are squeamish especially when it comes to justice and the law. God, however, is perfectly realistic about sin. He knows what it is, what it means and what it will do. Idolatry unchecked would mean the end of Israel as the people of God. Failure to expunge any kind of sin or abuse from anybody whatsoever — church, state, family, your own heart and mind — is tantamount to accepting it as a future norm for all. If God's people can indulge in immoral behaviour at will and worship false gods with impunity, then these become the effective 'standards' for future generations. And so the church of God becomes a synagogue of Satan! God was determined to have a people for himself and so he exercised the discipline a father should to keep his children walking in the truth and not turning aside to lies.

The righteous zeal of Phinehas (25:6-13)

The measures commanded by the Lord were apparently never put into effect, because they were immediately overtaken by events. The mass of the Israelites were powerfully affected by the Lord's word to Moses. They **'were weeping at the entrance to the Tent of Meeting'**. Picture the scene: the wrath of God was about to break upon Israel. The repentant were crying out to God in their sorrow both for the sin and for its tragic effects. And yet, at that very moment a young upper-class Simeonite named Zimri brought his Midianite princess girlfriend, Cozbi, to his family tent **'right**

before the eyes of Moses and the whole assembly' (25:6, 14-15).

At this point, a **'plague'** broke out amongst the people. This is assumed by 25:8, which only mentions the ending of the calamity, but is explicit in the account given in Psalm 106:28-31:

> 'They yoked themselves to the Baal of Peor
>   and ate sacrifices offered to lifeless gods;
> they provoked the Lord to anger by their wicked deeds;
>   and a plague broke out among them.
> But Phinehas stood up and intervened,
>   and the plague was checked.
> This was credited to him as righteousness
>   for endless generations to come.'

Phinehas' intervention arose from his discerning that Zimri's brazen behaviour was the point at which the Lord was provoked to instant judgement upon the people. He moved to exercise the discipline hitherto neglected.

Phinehas stops the plague (25:7-9)

Phinehas was a grandson of Aaron and therefore a member of the priestly family. He saw the young couple go into the tent and correctly concluded that they intended to indulge their immorality right there and then, God, righteousness and judgement notwithstanding. We are reminded of what Jesus says of the end of the age in Matthew 24 — people will go on living their sin-sick lives right up to the brink of a lost eternity. For sinners, judgement, like 'tomorrow' in the common proverb, 'never comes'! Zimri defiantly threw down his gauntlet before the Lord and took the Moabite princess to his guilty bed! Taking **'a spear in his hand'**, Phinehas followed them into the tent and 'pierced them through in the midst of their guilty pleasures'.[9] The plague stopped, but **'those who died in the plague numbered 24,000'** (25:9; cf. 1 Cor. 10:8).

God's 'covenant of peace' with Phinehas (25:10-13)

Although Phinehas took a most draconian action, it is clear that he did not take the law into his own hands. He was a priest among the one people in the world ruled directly and explicitly by God. Even

though judges had been appointed, the priests retained the responsibility to act for God whenever the situation warranted. Civil
government was not yet institutionally separated from the church as
in the New Testament era. Israel *was* the church of its time. A priest
was not disqualified from executing justice by his own hand, any
more than was Samuel the prophet even in the day when Israel had
a king (1 Sam. 15:32-33). Furthermore, Phinehas was deeply
committed to the righteousness of God and was animated by a
profound concern for the welfare of the people as a whole. We have
every reason to believe that it was the impulse of the Spirit of God
that moved him to action. This does not mean that we should expect
to be moved by the Holy Spirit to the same kind of action, for as
Charles Simeon correctly observes, 'Such an act in *us* would be
unjustifiable: because we have received no such commission from
God or man.' But, adds the same writer, *'The spirit from which it
proceeded* would be commendable in whomsoever it were found:
we *ought* to be filled with a zeal for God's honour; we *ought* to be
penetrated with compassion towards those who are in danger of
perishing through the impiety of others; and we *ought* to be ready to
assist the civil magistrate in the suppression of iniquity.'[10]

The Lord who propelled Phinehas to take action certainly
blessed him for doing what he did. He declared that Phinehas had
'made atonement for the Israelites' (25:13). He had saved the
people by executing justice on these two most notorious offenders
and turning **'[God's] anger away from the Israelites'** (25:10). The
Lord also commended Phinehas for his enthusiasm for the honour
of God, comparing it to his own zeal for righteousness, and made
with him a unilateral **'covenant of peace'** promising a **'lasting
priesthood'** to him and his descendants (25:12-13; cf. 1 Chron. 6:4-
15).

Phinehas therefore remains today as an example of enthusiasm
for personal holiness and the honour of God in the church and the
world. His example, understood and applied in terms of the gospel
of Jesus Christ, challenges Christians to stand up, speak out and live
forth their Christian life in all its responsibilities and privileges, with
gentle gusto and militant meekness. Jesus told Peter to put up his
sword, when the latter attempted to protect him from the soldiers in
Gethsemane. Phinehas' spear is not God's chosen weapon for the
priesthood of believers, which is the New Testament church. The
weapons of our warfare are spiritual, but we must have the soul of

a Phinehas and the zeal of the later, mature Peter, if we are to commend our Saviour to a dying world.

The judgement upon Midian (25:14-18)

The formal record of the names of Zimri of Simeon and Cozbi the Midianite sets the scene for the final judgement, which is the command to treat the Midianites as enemies from that day forth. This would soon issue in the campaign against Midian, in which Balaam would die by the sword (31:8,16). The sin of Baal of Peor was Balaam's revenge against the God and people whom he was obliged, against his will, to bless four times. Balaam's death and the defeat of Midian were proof that the long arm of God's justice will reach his enemies sooner or later.

We are warned against the deceitfulness of characters like Balaam and the dangers of the world's seductions. The Lord warns the church against 'the teaching of Balaam', but also promises to 'him who overcomes' some of 'the hidden manna' and 'a white stone with a new name on it, known only to him who receives it' (Rev. 2:14,17). These highly symbolic gifts speak of the Lord's sustaining grace and his everlasting approval — of practical perseverance in the faith and the inward assurance of belonging to the Lord — and they call us every day to love Jesus and follow him.

19.
A new day coming

Please read Numbers 26 and 27
'Take Joshua son of Nun ... and lay your hand on him' (27:18).

It is fashionable nowadays to talk about 'defining moments' in current events. These are events which seem to herald a decisive turn in history, perhaps even a new order of things. The fall of Communism in Eastern Europe and the reunification of Germany were seen as such a moment for Europe — marking the real end of the Second World War. The lightning victory of the United States and her allies in the Gulf War was announced as the 'defining moment' which laid to rest America's national loss of confidence dating from the Vietnam War. This is, of course, 'instant history' (just add 'expert opinion') and it remains to be seen whether or not these analyses will stand the test of time.

From the perspective of over 3,000 years and the record of the Scriptures, it is certainly safe to say that Israel faced one of her great 'defining moments' on the Plains of Moab, across the Jordan from Jericho and the land of promise. There, in connection with a census, arrangements were made for the new land they would inherit in Canaan, even before it was conquered (26:1 - 27:11), and a new leader, Joshua the son of Nun, was appointed to succeed Moses and command the armies of Israel in the conquest of Canaan (27:12-23). In these twin events we see the shape of things to come — the contours of the new Israelite order, an order which was nothing less than God's order for his people. Things would never be the same again. The future was at hand! Finally we shall see the new lessons God taught Israel.

A new land (26:1 - 27:12)

The narrative consists of five distinct sections, which together describe the second census of Israel and a number of matters relative to the apportioning of inheritances in the land.

The census of the landed tribes (26:1-51)

First, we notice that the census was *appointed by God* (26:1-4). Like modern censuses, this one had an economic purpose. It was to organize the people and to give to them — and to future generations, via their history — some understanding of what they were as a nation and what was happening in their national life. More importantly and unlike modern censuses, it was a theocratic exercise, fixing the structure of the nation according to God's direction and setting it in the consciousness of the people. As such it was also eschatological, because it looked ahead to the destiny of the people as the people of God.

In contrast, David's census 500 years later was the subject of God's anger because it had not been commanded by God and it was motivated by David's desire to feel good about his royal power on account of having such a large army. We love numbers — large numbers, that is. They represent a feeling of pride and security and as such are a kind of theology all on their own. 'Big is better than small' translates into 'Big is good, big is blessing', and even 'God approves of big.' It is all false confidence built on a false premise, but still we love numbers. Some count their stamp-collections every week and alternately glow with satisfaction and burn for more acquisitions. Some churches bask in their statistics and dream of bigger and better ecclesiastical barns for their growing membership. But it is really all worldliness. Trust has shifted from God to man, from Christ to numbers, from grace to achievements. Hence the wisdom of God when, with Israel, he only commanded two censuses in forty years and kept the focus upon the practical theological issues facing the nation at those points when such numbering was absolutely necessary for spiritual service. This one was **'after the plague'** and everyone knew that it would represent their numbers after the loss of some 24,000 people. Humility and chastisement, not pride and accomplishment, were the context of this census.

Secondly, this census not only recorded the men **'twenty years**

old or more who are able to serve in the army of Israel,' as at Sinai, but did so **'by families'**. These 'families' were not the same as modern so-called 'nuclear families' (Dad, Mum and two children), but were 'clans' consisting of large groupings of families. They were to be listed for the purposes of apportioning the land, upon their entrance into Canaan.

Finally, we note that, compared with the Mt Sinai census, the total number was about the same — approximately 600,000 — although with different figures for each of the tribes. The percentage increases and declines were as follows: Manasseh, +63.7%; Benjamin, +28.8%; Asher, +28.7%; Issachar, +18.2%; Zebulon, +5.4%; Judah, +2.6%; Dan, +2.1%; Reuben, -6%; Gad, -11.3%; Naphtali, -15%; Ephraim, -19.8%; and Simeon, -69%. It is idle to speculate about the meaning of the figures, but one cannot but wonder if the catastrophic decline of Simeon was the result of the sin of Baal-Peor, in which Zimri, a Simeonite leader, was a prominent actor (25:14). The tribe of Simeon was later not much more than a subdivision of Judah (Josh. 19.9).[1] In absolute terms, Judah remained the largest tribe, with 76,500 fighting men, while all except Simeon and Ephraim could muster in excess of 40,000 warriors each. If there is any lesson for today's churches, it is that while numbers are not to be made the barometer of spiritual health, they may, to a degree and in different ways, reflect God's dealings with us. This is, as already noted, never a simple matter of: growth/ big numbers = blessing; decline/small numbers = something is wrong. False religions are often fast-growing, while solid biblical churches grow very slowly. Nevertheless, it must be said that, in the end, the extinction of church groups is not an evidence of faithful witness, unless as a result of persecution and mass murder. Certainly, in modern Britain, the decline of much of what calls itself the church is largely the evil fruit of a century and a half of preachers and theologians explaining away the Bible, and so giving rise to generations of uncommitted, unconverted pseudo-Christians whose subsequent drift away from the church was thoroughly predictable. On the other hand, such growth as there is has generally been associated with the recovery of the enthusiastic proclamation of the real word from God — both the inscripturated Word, the Bible, and the incarnate Word, the Lord Jesus Christ. That said, we must remember that the 'numbers game' is a snare when it comes to assessing the work of God amongst us. God's *truth* is the measure of faithfulness and blessing — and of the meaning of the numbers themselves, whether great or small. The Lord has his large congregations and his remnants (Ps. 35:18; 40:10; Rom. 11:5). And through them all, he is building his church according to his purposes of grace (Matt. 16:18).

Rules for land allotment in Canaan (26:52-56)

The division of the land was to be equitable — it was **'based on the number of names'** and the tribal allotments were consequently strictly proportional. How any questions as to the relative fertility of land were handled we are not told. Lots were to be cast to resolve the precise distribution of the portions. Tribal groupings were to remain intact, so that each tribe's inheritance would thereafter be fixed as that which God gave them at the time of the conquest of the land of promise. That basic pattern of territorial dispersion was a message to the later generations of Israelites that their life and destiny as a people was both given and guaranteed by God. The very concept of 'the land' was weighty with eternal spiritual significance. In the New Testament era — the one in which we live — 'the land' is the kingdom of God, the inheritance of the saints in light (Col. 1:12, AV). This inheritance is both 'now' and 'not yet'. It is 'now' in the reality of the experience of faith, salvation and eternal life and in the ongoing extension of the gospel throughout the world in the unfolding of human history — the kingdom of heaven at work upon the earth. But it is also 'not yet', in that the consummation of God's kingdom awaits that great day when Christ returns and the final, completed kingdom — heaven itself — is revealed in its eternal glory (1 Peter 1:4).

The census of the landless Levites (26:57-62)

The Levites were **'not counted along with the other Israelites because they received no inheritance among them'** (26:62). The total number of males, one month and older, was 23,000, a slight increase from the earlier tally (3:43). This distinct census, as on the former occasion, emphasizes the separateness of the Levites to their service of the sanctuary. The mention of Nadab and Abihu and their death for worshipping God with **'unauthorized fire'** is a reminder that God is to be worshipped in the way he appoints in his Word and not according to even the sincere and best-meant inventiveness of man. The express will of God is the right rubric for our worship.

The record of the Kadesh generation (26:63-65)

The census is summed up with the solemn declaration that none of those counted in the Plains of Moab had been numbered among the fighting men of Sinai some forty years before — excepting the two faithful spies, **'Caleb son of Jephunneh and Joshua son of Nun'**. These two men were therefore the senior warriors of Israel, the last of their generation and, not least, leaders after God's own heart. Joshua and Caleb were living proof of the Lord's determination to fulfil his promise of a home for Israel in Canaan. The 'democratic' poll among the 'fighting' tribes at Kadesh Barnea had been 2 for, and 600,000 against, God's plan of victory. The Lord, however, is not a democrat. His will is the true 'majority'. His authority is absolute and his sovereignty is not negotiable. His will is going to be served, even if people choose to throw themselves upon God's sword in their determination to have their own way. Think about it, for he is still on his throne!

Rules for the inheritance of daughters and others (27:1-11)

At first sight, the appeal of the five daughters of Zelophehad over the inheritance of their father seems far removed from the census — until, that is, we remember that the main point of the census was to establish the future pattern of land distribution in Israel. Zelophehad had died without sons and his portion of the inheritance of the tribe of Manasseh was being denied to his daughters and, therefore, to his entire posterity. Through the centuries of slavery in Egypt and the wanderings in Sinai, until the giving of the Mosaic law, Israel had had neither land nor rules of inheritance. Nevertheless, the underlying assumption of the time, which they would have shared, appears to have been that inheritances descended through the males (sons, brothers, uncles, etc.), while the females were provided substantial dowries and married off to other families.[2] And, indeed, under the law, primacy was given to the first-born son and the preservation of the family name and inheritance (Deut. 21:15-17; 25:5-10). This was designed, of course, to provide a patrilineal system of inheritance which would maintain the equitable distribution of the land by families as established at the time of the second census.[3]

Now this law did not cover the situation in which there was no son. The inheritance of Zelophehad's daughters is a case in point. Had he left sons, then a portion of the land would have been established in his name. But he only left daughters, so whatever he might have had (it was only theoretical at this stage, since the Canaanites still possessed the land) would be divided between the other male heritors of Manasseh. Zelophehad's name and patrimony would disappear. And this, his daughters could not see as just. Why should their patrimony be lost for ever just because their father only had daughters? For the honour of their father's family, they therefore appealed to Moses: **'Why should our father's name disappear from his clan because he had no son?'** (27:4).

Moses **'brought their case before the Lord'** (27:5). He saw the point, realized that the law did not answer it and thus took it to the Lord according to the prescribed means. Today, we should go to the completed and fully sufficient revelation of God in the Scriptures of the Old and New Testaments. The Lord's answer was to declare the five women **'right'** and command him to **'give their father's inheritance over to them'** (27:7). Henceforth, a daughter was to inherit before her father's brothers and uncles, or any other more distant male relatives (27:8-11). Women have rights too.

New leader (27:12-23)

Only one man was left of the generation that was denied entrance into the inheritance of the promised land and that was Moses himself. What an amazing irony! The great leader of the wilderness wanderings was now, as it were, the very last internal Israelite 'obstacle' to entry to the promised land! The whole history of the forty years in the desert comes to a point — a turning-point — in the person of Moses. We, as it were, stand on Mount Nebo with the patriarch, with the whole desert experience behind us and the prospect of Canaan before us. Moses led Israel thus far, but no further. Now another must take his place and lead them to victory and conquest.

Intimation of death (27:12-14)

God had told Moses that he would not be allowed to enter Canaan, on account of his 'rash words' at Meribah (Ps. 106:33; Num. 20:12). He now intimated to the patriarch that he should ascend **'this mountain in the Abarim range'** (Mt Nebo, Deut. 34:1), from which he would **'see the land'**. He would then **'be gathered to [his] people,'** as had been his brother Aaron. Even though Moses was deprived of entering Canaan, his death has the character of a victorious promotion to a heavenly reward. It was the 'death of the righteous', for which Balaam had cried (in vain, 23:10; 31:8,16). Stripped of the elements which are unique to Moses, it is a model of the death of all God's people.

Like Moses, we shall close our eyes in death having seen, in life, the *promise* of his ongoing work of redemption in the world we are leaving. Moses saw Canaan from a distance, and knew that God would win victories for his people in days to come. We see the promises of God's Word going forward in a new generation of those who love the Lord and in spreading of the gospel to the nations.

Like Moses, Christians have the happy *prospect* of being 'gathered' to the eternal fellowship of the saints in glory. Canaan also pointed to the final glory of God's consummated kingdom. There remains a rest for the people of God, a glory yet to be revealed, a heaven in which all tears are wiped away and the righteousness of God alone is established for ever.

Like Moses, believers have the *comfort* of knowing they are following the redeemed who have gone before them. Moses was preceded by Aaron. He saw the peaceful and submissive way he went to be with the Lord. This is 'an encouragement to us to think of death without terror,' counsels Matthew Henry, 'and even to please ourselves with thoughts of it. It is but to die as such and such died, if we live as they lived; and their end was peace, they finished their course with joy; why then should we fear any evil in this melancholy valley?'[4]

Intercession for the people (27:16-17)

Moses' thoughts immediately turned to the need of the people for sound leadership. He appealed to God as **'the God of the spirits of all mankind'** (27:16; 16:22), thus emphasizing the necessary dependence of the creature upon the Creator. The Lord must provide a leader, he pleads, or the people will be **'like sheep without a shepherd'**.

Inauguration of a successor (27:18-23)

The Lord's answer was to appoint that Joshua be ordained as Israel's leader, in the presence of all Israel and by the laying on of Moses' hands. He was endowed with 'the spirit of wisdom because Moses had laid his hands on him. So the Israelites listened to him and did what the Lord had commanded Moses' (Deut. 34:9). Unlike Moses, who had direct access to God, Joshua was to seek the Lord's guidance through Eleazar the priest. The prophetic ministry of the church is the light for the nations as well as individuals, a truth which civil governments ignore at their peril (Ps. 2:10-12).

New lessons

The meaning of these events and declarations is not difficult to discern.

First of all, we are taught that, sooner or later, *God carries out his revealed will*. The census records and seals the certainty of divine judgement upon human sin. Everyone who rebelled at Kadesh Barnea nearly forty years earlier had died in the desert. They had for the most part lived out their allotted span, so it was not a 'judgement' in quite the same way as the various plagues which had struck down certain people during the various episodes of apostasy. The punishment of the bulk of the Kadesh generation was not a simple sentence of death, implying that they were all lost unbelievers, but was the removal of the privilege of entering into their inheritance in the land. Nevertheless, it was God's judgement upon unbelief (1 Cor. 10:1-6; Heb. 3:17-19). They reaped upon earth what they sowed in their earthly lives and so stand for ever as a parable of the devastating results of sinful behaviour. They chose the rejection of God and they reaped rejection by God.

This is as compelling in its application to people today as it was to ancient Israel. God is calling every one of us to account! Yet this is obviously not heeded by too many. Why? No doubt many reasons could be advanced, not least the most basic fact that men and women are naturally predisposed to resist the Lord and reject his Word (1 Cor. 2:14). There are, however, two common myths which more immediately stand in the way of many people taking seriously this solemn reality.

The first is the myth that 'Time is a great healer.' It seems to work, at least some of the time, because people get tired of quarrelling or just forget. 'So,' we reason, 'why can't it be the same way with God? Isn't there a "statute of limitations" on our sins? Give any problem enough time, we reason, and it will go away.' Time is, however, not a healer, but a period of opportunity for turning around our lives in repentance towards God and faith in the Lord Jesus Christ. Scripture teaches that 'Now' is the time to close with the Lord and, in faith, enter into salvation and new life (2 Cor. 6:2; Heb. 3:7). The time is now! To take your time, on the other hand, is to court disaster (Luke 12:19-20; Matt. 25:1-13). Far from being a healer, time wasted is a way of death!

The second myth is the notion that the absence of immediate judgement means there will be no judgement at all — indeed, that there is no God 'out there' to do any judging. 'In the last days scoffers will come... They will say, "Where is this 'coming' he promised?"' (2 Peter 3:3). The argument is that since the world goes on in its normal way, without, as they say, any evidence of divine intervention, then we are justified in rejecting the warnings and promises of God's Word. If the world ends, it will be through nuclear war or heat death from the demise of the sun — but, a day of judgement? Never! Scripture makes clear, however, that the decisive moment for everyone is the moment of death (Heb. 9:27). In most cases, this is soon enough for the Lord to settle his accounts with people. Again, it must be said that the deferment of wrath is *prima facie* evidence of God's patient longsuffering and his purpose of grace. The correct conclusion is to seek him while he may still be found and to call upon him when he is near (Isa. 55:6).

Secondly, we are taught that *there is no security in numbers*. There is a saying to the effect that '50,000 people can't be wrong'. Well, 600,000 people *were* wrong and died to prove it. Not a man was left, except Caleb and Joshua (26:65). Jesus republished the same message very plainly: 'Enter by the narrow gate; for the gate is wide, and the way is broad that leads to destruction, and many are those who enter by it. For the gate is small and the way is narrow that leads to life, and few are those who find it' (Matt. 7:13-14).

Thirdly, we are taught that *there is no security in lip-service to God*. 'I want to remind you,' writes Jude, 'that the Lord delivered his people out of Egypt, but later destroyed those who did not believe' (Jude 5). Notice it was not 'those who did not believe they were all right with God', but those who did not believe, personally, from the heart, in Jesus Christ (see Jude 1-4, 20-21). Perfunctory church-going and cold moralism are not enough. Talk about God, while denying the teaching of the Bible and living in disregard of Jesus' claims on our daily lives, will not do either. Living faith, faith in Christ as Saviour, faith that gets to work — not mere lip-service — is what God wants of you and me. Christ is our only security and he is everything to those who love him.

Fourthly, we have assurance that *no believer will ever perish*. This is the deeper meaning of the preservation of Caleb and Joshua and, not least, the raising up of a new generation of 600,000 to take the place of those who fell in the desert. 'I will sift the house of Israel among all nations, like as corn is sifted in a sieve, yet shall not the least grain fall upon the earth,' said Amos in a later day, speaking of the salvation of the faithful remnant of Israel (Amos 9:9, AV). Jesus our Shepherd says of his believing sheep, 'I give them eternal life, and they shall never perish; no one can snatch them out of my hand' (John 10:28).

Fifthly, *the Lord guarantees your inheritance,* when you are one of his. This is the significance of the case of Zelophehad's daughters. There are many doctrines here: the sovereign authority of God, the dignity of women and the duty of magistrates to protect the poor and the oppressed (Ps. 82:3), but overarching them all is the assurance of eternal life itself for all who love the Lord. 'We know', says Paul, 'that if the earthly tent we live in [i.e., our bodies] is destroyed, we have a building from God, an eternal house in heaven' (2 Cor. 5:1). 'The promised land,' as James Philip rightly observes, 'is a type and illustration of salvation and eternal life.'⁵

Sixthly, we are taught that *God alone is our indispensable leader*. The change of leadership in anticipation of Moses' death is, at one level, the proof that no leader, however 'great', is indispensable. That Moses' death should occur before entry to Canaan and as a result of his personal sin, underscores the point even more emphatically. The best leaders have clay feet. The true leader is the Lord. On him we must depend.

Finally, we are pointed to *Jesus Christ as the Saviour of all who will believe in him.* Moses' prayer that the people might not be left 'like sheep without a shepherd' (27:17) uses language that was to bridge the two Testaments and lead us to the gospel. It reminds us of what it means to be a lost sheep (Matt. 9:36) and also what it is to know Jesus as our Great Shepherd (John 10:14).

'May the God of peace, who through the blood of the eternal covenant brought back from the dead our Lord Jesus, that great Shepherd of the sheep, equip you with everything good for doing his will, and may he work in us what is pleasing to him, through Jesus Christ, to whom be glory for ever and ever. Amen' (Heb. 13:20-21).

20.
Spiritual worship

Please read Numbers 28 - 30

'Present your bodies a living and holy sacrifice, acceptable to God, which is your spiritual service of worship' (Rom. 12:1, NASB).

The word 'worship' comes from the Old English *weorthscipe* and basically means the recognition of 'worth' or merit. 'Worthship' is worthiness of offered praise. As 'worship' has become more a technical term for religious services, we have lost sight of the experiential thrust of the concept of worship, which is that a worshipper is not just someone present at a church service, but is someone who in the act of worship is expressing a simple, heart-felt acknowledgement of the particular qualities of the person to whom he brings his adoration. When a young fellow 'worships the ground' upon which a certain girl stands, it says something about his innermost feelings for her and about her intrinsic attractiveness. Similarly, to 'worship the Lord in the splendour of his holiness' (1 Chron. 16:29) says something about the character of both the Lord and his true worshippers. It is not a bare description of an ecclesiastical event (a service): it is a window on the doctrine of God and the faith-experience of the believer. This worship is about God — he is worthy to be praised. This worship is about our relationship to God — as creatures coming to their Creator. This worship only happens in a right, reconciled relationship to a holy God — where sin has been forgiven and new life has replaced lostness, unbelief and spiritual death, for the Lord's true worshippers, as Jesus told the woman of Samaria, 'must worship in spirit and in truth' (John 4:24).

For this reason, God gave Israel many instructions as to why, how, when and where he was to be worshipped. These are very remote from our everyday experience and we are perhaps tempted to pass over them with a shrug and the thought that they belong to a bygone age anyway. But they actually afford us profound insights into the timeless principles of the worship of the living God and, as foreshadowings of the gospel of Jesus Christ, they give depth to our grasp of the place of worship in the Christian life today. Four general themes dominate the three chapters which detail the laws on offerings and vows: they teach us that worship is towards God (28:1-2); is through sacrifice (28:3); encompasses our whole life (28:3 - 29:40) and is a matter of heart-commitment (30:1-16).

Worship is God-centred (28:1-2)

God is the originator and initiator of all true worship. **'The Lord said to Moses...'** God commands us to worship him. Worship means being in complete submission to him. He says four things about this worship.

First, the Lord says that worship is to be offered, **'to me'**: not to whomever you may regard as your 'god,' not to whatever may be called 'God' by somebody somewhere, still less (with easy blasphemy) to 'the man upstairs'! Worship is to be given exclusively, and with the utmost sincerity and personal reverence, to the living God who reveals himself in his Word. 'You shall have no other gods before me,' says the Lord in the First Commandment (Exod. 20:3). 'Without faith it is impossible to please him; for he that cometh to God must believe that he is, and that he is a rewarder of them that diligently seek him' (Heb. 11:6, AV).

Secondly, God is to be worshipped at **'the appointed time'**. Not any old time that suits us will do! God's times were as much part of godliness and instruction as the symbolism and teaching in the actions of worship themselves — hence the elaborate daily, weekly, monthly and annual cycles of specific offerings and festivals as required by 28:3 - 29:40 (see Fig.3). This sacrificial system has been entirely fulfilled in Jesus Christ, the once-for-all sacrifice for sin, and so, in the New Testament, we find only the day of Jesus' resurrection — the 'first day of the week' or 'Lord's day' — mandated as a weekly Christian sabbath set aside for the assembled public worship of the church (John 20:19; Acts 20:6-12; Rev. 1:10; Heb. 10:25).

Thirdly, God prescribes how he is to be worshipped. His people are to bring **'my offerings'** — those which he commands — which are to be **'made by fire, as an aroma pleasing to me'** (cf. 2 Cor. 2:14-17). There is not the slightest hint in Scripture (in the Old or New Testaments) that we may worship the Lord as *we* please. What God has commanded is the regulative pattern for what we are to do. God initiates, inhabits and instructs the worship of his people.

Worship requires sacrifice (28:3)

The presentation of sacrifices was central to Israel's worship. God was always approached with some specified sacrifice. The daily offering at the tabernacle was an **'offering made by fire'** of **'two lambs a year old without defect'**. The only animal sacrifice made by families in their homes — all others were made by the priests at the tabernacle — was the Passover lamb, remembering the original deliverance from Egypt. In these and other sacrifices for sin, three great points were being made over and over again in the life of God's people — points that are even more clearly applicable today, since they all have their perfect focus and fulfilment in Jesus Christ.

The first point is that *sin requires atonement.* Perfect justice requires the punishment of sin. The wages of sin against God is death. Life offered can alone pay for life forfeit. Hence animal sacrifices were to be offered in the place of men and women. The shedding of blood was at the very heart of sacrificial death, for 'The life of every creature is its blood' (Lev. 17:14), and so, 'Without the shedding of blood there is no forgiveness' (Heb. 9:22).

Secondly, *God in his grace provides a Saviour*, who is the perfect, once-for-all sacrifice. The dead animals and their blood actually saved nothing and no one. They were symbolic of the need of a Saviour and of God's promised provision of a Saviour at a future date. The animal sacrifices proved that man could not save himself. Pagans, like the Aztecs, sacrificed human beings precisely because they believed in the efficacy of human sacrifice in appeasing the gods. God never required his people to atone for their sins with their own bodies because he knew it could not be done. To be saved, they needed a sinless Saviour to die in their place. Hence the symbolism of the sacrificial lambs, which pointed to the last Lamb, 'slain from the creation of the world,' Jesus 'our Passover lamb' (Rev. 13:8; 1 Cor. 5:7-8).

Finally, *believers are themselves called to be living sacrifices,* 'holy and pleasing to God' (Rom. 12:1). The sacrificial system called for a yielding of the worshipper to the Lord. The offerings of animals, grain, oil and wine, and the concepts of the first-fruits and the tithes, all spoke of devotion to God. Of course, this self-offering is not atonement, but the fruit of atonement already made. Christ's righteousness is the only meritorious work under heaven. It is the root, of which our devotion is the practical fruit.

Worship encompasses our whole life (28:3 - 29:40)

Nothing in the Bible is more confusing to the modern Christian than the multitude of rules and regulations governing the ceremonies and rituals of Old Testament worship and sacrifice.[1] It is important, however, that we grasp the meaning of these things and see them in the clear light of the Christ to whom they pointed. The fundamental point is that Israel's life was built upon worship. Every day, every week, every month and at particular times every year, the priests offered these sacrifices at the tabernacle on behalf of the nation. Israel's life was lived in the context of God.[2]

Daily worship (28:3-8)

The morning and evening sacrifices each consisted of a lamb, together with a grain offering and a drink offering. The latter offerings spoke of the worshippers giving themselves to the Lord, while the lamb speaks of God's provision of salvation through sacrifice for sin. The meaning, then, is that God's people were to live every day for him. Biblical piety begins and closes each day in devotion to the Lord. 'Awake, my soul!' sings the psalmist, 'Awake, harp and lyre! I will awaken the dawn' (Ps. 57:8). And again, 'I will lie down and sleep in peace, for you alone, O Lord, make me dwell in safety' (Ps. 4:8). Worship is not only for the church or on Sundays. Every day, whether privately in the secret place of individual prayer, or as families, singing praise, reading Scripture and praying together, God calls you to worship him and receive his blessing, just as surely as he blessed Israel through the daily sacrifices of the tabernacle.

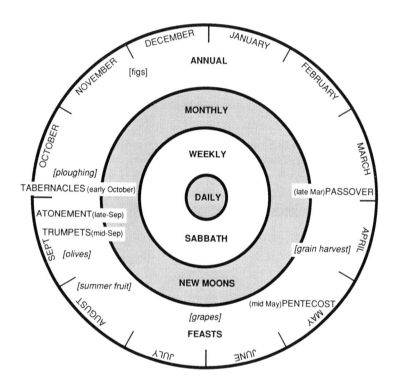

Figure 3. The cycles of Israel's worship

Weekly worship — the sabbath (28:9-10)

The Old Testament sabbath was the seventh day of every week — our Saturday. On that day, a double sacrifice was required. This was in addition to the daily sacrifices. This double service emphasized the vital significance of the Fourth Commandment of the moral law — to 'remember the sabbath day by keeping it holy' (Exod. 20:8-11; Deut. 5:12-15). Today, as we have already seen, the Fourth Commandment continues in the New Testament's only 'holy day' — the weekly celebration of our Lord's resurrection, known as the Lord's day or the Christian sabbath.[3]

Monthly worship — the new moons (28:11-15)

The Lord gave the moon, says the psalmist, to mark the seasons and be a 'faithful witness in the sky' (Ps. 104:19; 89:37). Perhaps in recognition of the Lord's providential upholding of his creation, the **'new moon'** was marked by even greater sacrificial offerings and heralded by the trumpets of joy and celebration (10:10; cf. Isa 1:13; Ezek. 46:6-8).

Annual worship — the five festivals (28:16 - 29:40)

The five great festivals of the Hebrew year echoed the rhythm of the agricultural year, but were wholly dominated by the twin themes of redemption and the mighty acts of God (See Fig. 3).

1. The *Feast of Unleavened Bread*, which began with the Passover, was observed for eight days in late March and/or early April, by our calendar — 14-21 Nisan, in the Hebrew reckoning (28:16-25; Exod. 12; Lev 23:5-8). This celebrated the deliverance from Egypt and pointed to redemption in the coming of the final Lamb, the Messiah, Jesus Christ (1 Cor. 5:7-8).

2. The *Feast of Weeks*, which began with Pentecost, took place fifty days after Passover, in our mid-May, and celebrated the first-fruits of the wheat harvest (28:26-31; Exod. 23:16; 34:22; Lev. 23:15-22).

3. The *Feast of Trumpets* was the 'new moon' celebration of the seventh month (1 Tishri) — our mid-September (29:1-6; Lev. 23:23-25). This is the Jewish 'New Year,' literally the 'head of the year' or *Rosh Hashanah*. By this time, the harvests were in and there was a lull before the next ploughing. There was cause for rejoicing

in God's provision for the coming year, hence the trumpets, as on all 'new moons'.

4. The *Day of Atonement, Yom kippur,* took place nine days later (10 Tishri). Here, the emphasis was on confession of sin and atonement (29:7-11; Lev. 16; Heb. 9:6-14). One might have thought that a special 'day of atonement' was utterly redundant in a ceremonial system that was to sacrifice lambs every day for nearly 1500 years. Precisely the opposite is the case. The Day of Atonement actually underscored the imperfection of the animal sacrifices as atonements for sin. 'For what the law could not do, weak as it was through the flesh, God did: sending his own Son in the likeness of sinful flesh, and as an offering for sin, he condemned sin in the flesh, in order that the requirement of the law might be fulfilled in us, who do not walk according to the flesh, but according to the spirit' (Rom. 8:3-4, NASB). 'Christ is the end [i.e., goal] of the law so that there may be righteousness for everyone who believes' (Rom. 10:4).

5. The *Feast of Tabernacles,* or Ingathering, began five days after *Yom Kippur* and lasted a week (15-21 Tishri, our early October, 29:12-39; Lev 23:33-43). This celebrated the *joy* of salvation as they remembered the forty years in the desert and the provision of the harvest in the promised land. The people lived in booths made of branches. It was 'on the last and greatest day of [this] feast' that 'Jesus stood and said in a loud voice, "If anyone is thirsty, let him come to me and drink. Whoever believes in me, as the Scripture has said, streams of living water will flow from within him"' (John 7:37-38). Jesus probably took his cue from the practice, in his day, of a priest taking a pitcher of water from the Pool of Siloam and pouring it out on the ground, with the words of Isaiah 12:3: 'With joy you will draw water from the wells of salvation.' In this way, Jesus expounded the meaning of the feast in terms of the work of the Holy Spirit (John 7:38-39). While *Yom Kippur* focused on the *accomplishment* of redemption through atoning sacrifice, the Feast of Tabernacles celebrated the *application* of redemption — which is, of course, the work of the Holy Spirit in the lives of believers from their conversion to Christ until they come to heaven.

The whole sacrificial system — daily, weekly, monthly and annual observances — brought Israel before their God as the one who provided their salvation in his sovereign and free grace. How anyone could reasonably believe that the naked observance of these ceremonies was a means of meriting salvation — a kind of works-righteousness — is a testimony to man's spiritual blindness. Godly Old Testament believers certainly had no illusions that their salvation was earned or self-generated. They knew they could not keep the law and that the very promise of the Messiah — the meaning of the sacrifices — spoke of the need for this Saviour who would come in the fulness of the time and do for sinners what they could not do for themselves.

Worship involves a heart-commitment (30:1-16)

A chapter on vows may look out of place beside regulations on sacrifices, but a moment's reflection will soon persuade us that this is in fact another element in the spectrum of worship. The vows and oaths in view are those voluntary, gratuitous promises to do certain things, good in themselves, which God did not require in his Word. The Nazirite vow is a classic case (Num. 6; see also Lev. 5:4-5; 7:16; 27:1-29; Deut. 12:11,17).

Ordinarily, such vows are to be kept to the letter (30:1-2). God holds us to our word, even if we contrive to forget it or explain it away. God expects our word to be our bond. You did not need to make the promise, but once made, simple honesty requires following through on it.

Nevertheless, there are certain circumstances when vows may be revoked (30:3-16). These involve women who were under the authority of their father or a husband. In a case where the woman makes a vow — a **'rash promise'** (30:6) — and the father or husband disapproves, then the vow is revoked. If the father or husband raises no objection, the vow stands. In both instances, the authority of the head of the family is thereby honoured and preserved. A widow, however, must keep her vow(s), because she is no longer under the authority of any man (30:9).

Several abiding principles shine through in these regulations and are applicable to us today as to the Israelites of old.

First is *the necessity for a heart-commitment* to our worship and service of the Lord. The point of any vow to God is that it must arise from a profound inward commitment to him. And, of course, we know very well from experience that it takes just that to keep our promises. We are to serve the Lord with *all* our heart, *all* our soul and *all* our strength (Deut. 6:5).

Secondly, this should act as *a healthy caution against making rash promises and vows* on extra-biblical duties. 'No man,' the Westminster Assembly counsels, 'may vow to do anything forbidden in the Word of God, or what would hinder any duty therein commanded, or which is not in his own power, and for the performance whereof he hath no promise of ability from God. In which respect, popish monastical vows of perpetual single life, professed poverty, and regular obedience, are so far from being degrees of higher perfection, that they are superstitious and sinful snares, in which no Christian may entangle himself.'[4] To which might be added, the evangelical-fundamentalist equivalent — vows of total abstinence from fermented beverages. You may choose, if you wish, to remain unmarried or to be a teetotaller. These are good and honourable options for Christian people. But they are neither required by Scripture nor marks of superior godliness.

Thirdly, *fathers and husbands are responsible for their wives and children.* The responsibility/authority structure of the family has not changed under the New Testament. The family too is an arena in which obedience to the Lord calls for conscientious submission to those whom God has called to exercise headship. It calls also for heads of houses to exercise their responsibility so as to serve, with love, the best interests of those under their charge.

Conclusion — living sacrifices and spiritual worship

Virtually every regulation in the chapters we have just discussed is about blessings that were, at the time of being revealed through Moses, yet in the future! They required faith in Israelite hearts and victory in battle from Israelite arms!

Ultimately, they looked to their fulfilment in the unfolding of the gospel of the new covenant in Jesus, the promised Messiah (Jer. 31), and their realization in the experience of the new life of believers, in Christ received as Saviour and Lord. 'Therefore, I urge you, brothers, in view of God's mercy, to offer your bodies as living sacrifices, holy and pleasing to God — this is your spiritual act of worship. Do not conform any longer to the pattern of this world, but be transformed by the renewing of your mind. Then you will be able to test and approve what God's will is — his good, pleasing and perfect will' (Rom. 12:1-2).

21.
Your sin will find you out!

Please read Numbers 31 and 32
'But if you fail to do this ... you may be sure that your sin will find you out' (32:23).

Of all the sayings that the Authorized Version of the Bible has contributed to the English language, few are more striking than that drawn from Numbers 32:23: 'Be sure your sin will find you out.' Even for the many who did not know that this came from Scripture, it has been a witness to some powerful truths and has probably been a significant restraining influence. It taught generations that *actions have consequences,* that *bad* actions have *punishing* consequences and that there is a *God* who is watching us and will hold us *responsible* for what we do!

This was designed to put the fear of God in us. Now, fear — and by this we mean the straightforward fear of punishment — is not the highest motive to keep us on the straight and narrow. Love for the Lord and a heart-felt conscientious desire to be holy as he is holy is the best way to serve God and keep ourselves from sin. And, indeed, every believer knows that he is to love the Lord his God with all his heart, with all his soul and with all his strength (Deut. 6:4). Yet, the *fear* of the Lord is at least *the beginning* of wisdom (Prov. 1:7). It is even a motive for evangelism, as Paul tells the Corinthians, 'Since, then, we know what it is to fear the Lord, we try to persuade man' (2 Cor. 5:11). The fear of God is not a bad thing, for as long as we are sinners and God is perfectly righteous, human fear of the consequences of sin and bad deeds must remain a powerful restraining, if not even a reforming, motive in our lives.

The two major incidents recorded in Numbers 31 and 32 — the defeat of Midian and the agreement to permit the Israelite tribes of Gad and Reuben to settle in Gilead — are basically an extended exposition of this theme. The first is an example of what it means, in the final analysis, for the sins of the wicked to find them out, while the second demonstrates what happens when, by God's grace, we first find out our own sins and deal with them in terms of the Lord's provision for their cancellation and forgiveness. And so, Midian and Balaam perish under God's just judgement, whereas the Gadites and Reubenites enjoy the blessing of God as the fruit of faithfulness to his covenant of grace.

Sin finds out Midian — too late for change (31:1-12)

The Midianites had been instrumental in leading Israel into idolatrous worship and sexual immorality in 'the affair of Peor'. In consequence of this, God had commanded Israel to 'treat the Midianites as enemies and kill them' (25:16-18). The point is that the sin of Midian — or, at least, this particular section of Midian[1] — had in effect reached the same point as that of the inhabitants of Canaan, in the view of the Lord. Their sin had reached its full measure (compare Gen. 15:16) and the reckoning had come. It is important to note in these days of squeamishness about God's judgements, that there is a moment in the rebelliousness of every individual and of whole communities and nations, beyond which the striving of God's Spirit will not go (Gen. 6:3). God is longsuffering and plenteous in mercy, but he will not be resisted and reviled by sinners for ever. One day the openly unbelieving become the irretrievably lost. God takes them at their word. They do not want the Lord's will, or the Lord's salvation. They say so in thought, word and deed. They resist the gospel, they despise the Saviour, they oppose, obstruct and oppress the Lord's people. And God, who is jealous of his name, his Son, his Word and his people's welfare, decrees an end of them, temporally and eternally. Vengeance is his and, one day, he does repay (Rom 12:19). On this occasion, God chose Israel to be the instruments of his wrath upon certain, named, reprobate peoples. This task was uniquely revealed to Moses and Israel at that time and was bound up with the conquest of the land of promise.

No such revelations are given to the church today, for the weapons of New Testament church warfare are spiritual. But it remains true that God still reveals his wrath from heaven against human wickedness (Rom. 1:18). He keeps to himself his secret will for specific men and nations and his judgements, like his saving grace, operate in the movements of history, personal and international. But move they do! Judgements are at work in the world. People die under these judgements and are going to the real, eternal hell. Nations rise and fall. The finger of God squashes the puny presumption of peoples who think themselves invulnerable in their rejection of the living God. Communist Russia goes the way of Nineveh and Tyre after less than a century of triumphalist atheism. The so-called 'American century' is already over after forty-six years! These blows to human pride and certainty may be analysed in terms of secondary causes — economic, political, military and so forth — but the deeper meaning is in the mind of God and his sovereign disposition of historical events. Part of this is the way in which he sees to it that men and nations are 'found out' by their own sin! And in this respect the destruction of Midian is a warning to men and nations today to 'kiss the Son (i.e., Jesus as Saviour and King), for if they do not, they will perish in his wrath (Ps. 2:12). This, in the last analysis, is the meaning of the history of the human race!

The destruction of Midian was to be the last campaign of Moses' leadership. He was not to be 'gathered to [his] people' without the scent of victory in his nostrils and the sight of Canaan fresh before his eyes (31:1-2). 'God sometimes removes useful men when we think they can ill be spared,' comments Matthew Henry, 'but this ought to satisfy us, that they are never removed until they have done the work which was appointed them.'[2] This is true — and a great encouragement — for every Christian. It is also a consolation for those who are left when a greatly used servant of the Lord is removed. Moses must depart, but Joshua takes his place.

Intriguingly, the Moabites escape the imposition of this ban, in spite of their involvement. Their time would come, but, probably because of their descent from Lot and near relationship to God's people, they were spared for the moment. They had not yet filled up the cup of their iniquity.

An expeditionary force of 12,000 men, 1,000 from each tribe, was despatched. This was commanded by the formidable Phinehas, who had earlier demonstrated his qualities of leadership in executing God's justice on the Simeonite and his Midianite Delilah (25:6-13). This force invaded the enemy's territory, annihilated the Midianite forces, killed their five kings, destroyed their towns and took their women, children, livestock and possessions as plunder. Balaam the prophet, whose influence lay behind the original Midianite-Moabite plot (Rev. 2:14), perished by the sword — his sin had found him out.

This terrible event is not to be written off as the 'barbarism' of a primitive, bygone age. We too easily adopt a superior tone, implicit in which is the thought that if God told *us* to kill people, we would not be able to comply, on account of *our* higher moral standards! The abolition of the death penalty in the United Kingdom is a case in point — here is autonomous man telling off God for being too harsh in his judgements! The same society, however, slaughters millions of unborn babies in the womb and thinks itself compassionate and caring! This patent reversal of true justice — the guilty live while the innocent die — cries out to heaven for the vengeance of God and it is difficult to believe it will be long delayed, in the absence of revival and national repentance and reformation. 'There is a way that seems right to a man, but in the end it leads to death' (Prov. 14:12) — eternal death, that is, under God's just wrath against sin.

Israel finds out sin — repentance and reward (31:13-54)

The Israelite army returned from their campaign with the spoils of war, including the captured Midianite women and children. They were met with great ceremony by the entire assembly of Israel. It must have been all the more surprising when Moses greeted them with anger and a stinging rebuke.

Rebuke (31:13-18)

The cause of Moses' anger was the captured women and boys. Many of these women were the very people who had seduced Israel and succeeded in **'turning the Israelites away from the Lord in what happened at Peor'** (31:15). If anyone deserved to be executed, it was these women! Yet they had been spared! Moses immediately ordered the execution of **'all the boys'** and **'every woman who has** slept with a man', but they could **'save for [themselves] every girl who has never slept with a man'** (31:17-18). This draconian measure thus ensured the extinction of that portion of Midian, for the young girls would be assimilated into Israel (Deut. 21:10-14). Again, it is well to remember that the only conceivable justification for this is that 'This was *God's* holy judgement, not *man's* arbitrary retaliation.'[3] The last judgement will be even more thorough.

Renewal (31:19-24)

After contact with death, God's people were required to engage in a seven-day ritual purification (19:11-22). Even the spoils were to be purified. Furthermore, the soldiers were excluded from the camp until this was complete (5:1-4; 12:14-15). The ceremonies, as we have noted many times in these studies, were not merely perfunctory observances. They symbolized a deeper reality in the lives and experiences of the people involved. The need for atonement for sin and for sanctification in living daily life before the Lord, was, and still is, of the essence of the self-knowledge of any human being. The ceremonies ministered God's grace to the consciences of men and women who knew that they were accountable to a holy God. They point us to the sole sufficiency of Jesus Christ as our Saviour.

Reward (31:25-47)

Midian discovered her wealth to be 'worthless in the day of wrath'. Its falling to Israel as spoils of war bore eloquent testimony to the truth that the 'sinner's wealth is stored up for the righteous' (Prov. 11:4; 13:22). The captured booty was shared among the whole nation. The people were given 50%., while the soldiers retained the other 50% (31:25-27). The practical value of this windfall was as timely as it was substantial. Israel's GNP[4] received a massive boost, just at the point at which she faced the necessity of settling a land which would be ravaged by war. These resources would sustain her through some difficult times.

As with all the income of God's people, a portion was to be set aside for the Lord. This usually took the form of a tithe (10%), payable to the Levites. A tithe of this tithe was then given by the Levites to the priests (18:21,28). With respect to the Midianite spoils, the priests were to receive 0.2% (one-five-hundredth) of the soldiers' share, while the Levites took 2% (one-fiftieth) of the people's portion: considerably less than the usual tithe, but maintaining the 10:1 ratio between the Levites and the priests (31:28-47). The central point is that these were offerings to the Lord. They were expressions of faith in him. He had given the victory. He was therefore due the praise of his people. How appropriate then, when Christians today set aside not only a tithe of their regular income, but also a portion of the surprise windfall and the unexpected inheritance!

Rejoicing (31:48-54)

'I rejoice in your promise,' exulted the psalmist, 'like one who finds great spoil' (Ps. 119:162). God loves to bless his own people and he loves to see them rejoice in that blessing. On checking their roster, the Israelite officers found that not one man had been killed in the battle with Midian. This moved them to make an entirely voluntary offering of **'gold articles'** they had acquired, together weighing about 190kg.[5] The men gave this **'to make atonement … before the Lord'** (31:50). They proclaimed that it was God's grace that had spared them from suffering casualties. They did not ascribe the success to their brilliant leadership or superior weaponry — how often were these reasons trumpeted for the coalition victory over Iraq in the Gulf War? They thanked the Lord and gave him the glory: 'Not to us, O Lord, not to us but to your name be the glory, because of your love and faithfulness' (Ps. 115:1).

The Lord, for his part, accepted the gold as **'a memorial for the Israelites'** (31:54). What a contrast with the man-centred, even egocentric, memorials we raise to ourselves! University campuses are littered with buildings named for the benefactors who gave the money to build them. Church buildings named for the great and the forgotten are found in all our cities. Israel's gold memorial was 'a monument of God's goodness to them.'[6] It pointed to the Lord. It reminded them of his power to give them victory over their enemies. It encouraged them for their approaching clash with the Canaanites. It preached that God is able to keep his people, and called them all to trust in him as they sought to serve him day by day. The true memorials of the modern Christian are similarly simple, spiritual and God-centred. They are the sacrifices of praise, the worship of full hearts, the grateful remembrances of signal blessings in our past and the present testimonies of the Holy Spirit to our spirit that we are children of God.

Gad and Reuben face the issue — God's gracious warning (32:1-42)

The destruction of Midian showed the ultimate result of the sinner being found out by his sin. On the other hand, Israel's receiving of the spoils of Midian and drawing near to the Lord in worship demonstrated the fruit of God's redeeming grace. Israel, in effect, found out her own sin and it was dealt with in terms of God's way of salvation. Numbers 31 lays out very starkly the consequences of sin and the fruit of faithfulness.

Numbers 32 may seem to be about something altogether different, but it is in fact the third piece of the one picture. In the episode in which Gad and Reuben expressed their desire to settle east of the Jordan in Gilead, we are confronted with an illustration of the practical question as to which way we will go with our lives, day by day. Will it be the way of Midian or the way of Israel, the way of curse or the way of blessing? Centuries later, the Lord posed the question with respect to a matter of simple obedience, or disobedience: 'See, I am setting before you the way of life and the way of death' (Jer. 21:8). This is the principle at the heart of God's law: life versus death — which will you choose? The theme of Numbers 32, **'You may be sure that your sin will find you out'** (32:23), is the application of the lessons of Numbers 31. Are you listening? God is speaking to *you*, now, wherever you are!

The passage is divisible into five sections, which not only tell the story but develop the message. First is the request of Gad and Reuben (32:1-5); second, Moses' rebuke (32:6-15); third, the submissive response of Gad and Reuben (32:16-19); fourth, Moses' requirement for faithfulness (32:20-24); and finally the re-affirmation of the agreement by both parties (32:25-42).

Request (32:1-5)

The defeat of the transjordanic kings, Sihon of the Amorites and Og of Bashan, left Israel in sole occupation of land that was **'suitable for livestock'** (32:1; 21:21-35). This lay outside the borders of

Canaan and was not part of the promised land. Israel was not warranted to settle the area at all, but 'Possession is,' as they say, 'nine-tenths of the law.' Someone was bound to be tempted to stay put and avoid the effort of crossing the Jordan and subduing the Canaanites. This is exactly what occurred to the tribes of Reuben, Gad and half of Manasseh. They saw the potential of the land and went to Moses with the dual request that they be given this land as their inheritance and not be required to cross the Jordan with the other tribes.

Rebuke (32:6-15)

It was a clear case of self-interest triumphing over known duty. Moses asked the obvious questions and exposed this covenant-breaking selfishness.

First of all, this was *a betrayal of their own people.* Moses asked: **'Shall your countrymen go to war while you sit here?'** (32:6). They thought only of their prosperity in Gilead and their avoidance of the cost of taking Canaan. They wanted to quit while they were ahead — an understandable impulse to be sure — but a cheap and wholly unjustified abandonment of those to whom they were bound in fellowship as the people of God. They would be spectators of the struggle for Canaan, without so much as raising a finger to help — shades of the 'spectator Christians' in the church today, who will come to meetings, but let the 'old faithfuls' do all the work! This is sin, not faith, in action and calls for repentance no less than did the request of Reuben and Gad!

Secondly, this was also *an incitement of others to sin.* It as good as suggested that the Lord need not be obeyed and that his promises could be set aside. Moses asked, **'Why do you discourage the Israelites from going over into the land the Lord has given them?'** (32:7). If it was all right for Reuben and the others to drop out, then why not all? An example was being set — and it was a bad one. It proclaimed the primacy of self-interest, immediate gratification, avoidance of responsibility and unilateral reneging on solemn commitments.

Finally, it was, in effect, *a proposal to rebel against the Lord* (32:8-13). It was a replay of their fathers' attitude at Kadesh Barnea some four decades earlier. Like them, Reuben and Gad wanted to take the line of least resistance and avoid the impending clash with the Canaanites. Well, said Moses, **'Here you are, a brood of sinners'** (have you ever heard such language from a modern preacher?), **'standing in the place of your fathers and making the Lord even more angry with Israel. If you turn away from following him** [in this way] **he will again leave all this people in the desert, and you will be the cause of their destruction'** (32:14-15).

We come away from this with a sense that Reuben and the others were not so much intent on rebelling against God and letting their own side down, as they were thoughtlessly carried away in their captivation by Gilead's lush pastures. They had not thought things through. This is, of course, how sin often begins. An overwhelming passion is allowed to blot out disquieting thoughts about the implications. Hence Matthew Henry's timeless advice: 'If men did but consider, as they ought, what would be the end of sin, they would be afraid of the beginnings of it.'⁷ Shallow enthusiasms sooner or later produce deep problems. Too many things that 'seemed like a good idea at the time' end up on the scrap-heap of shipwrecked lives. Reuben, Gad and Manasseh stood at the same old crossroads that, one way or another and to one degree or another, confront people most days in life. Will it be God's way or our way? Or rather, are we willing for our way to be God's way? Do we care to test our wishes against God's Word? Are we ready to think it all through, to seek the mind of God in prayer, to weigh the advice of wise counsellors and to follow, where the Lord is calling us to go?

Response (32:16-19)

Some people resent a rebuke, but the spiritually discerning know that 'Wounds from a friend can be trusted' (Prov. 27:6). It seems clear enough that Reuben, Gad and Manasseh took Moses' words in good grace, for after some discussion **'They came up to him'** and declared themselves ready to **'go ahead of the Israelites until we have brought them to their place'**. They would forego their inheritance west of the Jordan in favour of the other tribes and be content to settle in Gilead. Their families would settle there in the meantime, while the bulk of their men campaigned in Canaan. This response, says Matthew Henry, is 'an instance of the good effect of plain dealing; Moses, by showing them their sin, and the danger of it, brought them to their duty without murmuring or disputing'.⁸ Too often, we are hesitant to bear testimony to the Lord and his Word, for fear of rejection.

Requirement (32:20-24)

Moses accepted this proposal, presumably after seeking God's will in the prescribed manner. He made it unmistakably plain that they were required to keep their word and continue to fight in Canaan until the land was subdued. Only then would Gilead be their inheritance **'before the Lord'**. In laying their own commitment squarely before their consciences, Moses uttered the words that are indelibly inscribed in our language: **'Be sure that your sin will find you out'** (32:23). This has sometimes been restricted in its application to secret sins, as if to say, 'Be sure your secret sins will be found out' — on the strange assumption that furtive sinning is especially heinous, while open sinning is hardly worth worrying about. Some folk like to think that 'honest' sinning makes it 'sort of' all right. The point Moses emphasizes explodes such unethical contortions. Any and all sin will find out the sinner. The chickens will come home to roost! God will satisfy his perfect justice right down to the least infringement of his perfect holiness. Moses therefore wanted the people of God to know that there was an unbreakable obligation upon them to keep their word and do what God required of them, in the sure knowledge that punishment would surely catch up with them if they did not.

This word still stands today. The sins of sinners are finding them out in this life, sometimes sooner, sometimes later, but always and inevitably. And those who die unrepentant and without a saving knowledge of Jesus Christ are irreversibly found out by their own sin. Every single person in hell, right now as you read this, has been found out by his or her unbelief and actions. Do you want to escape that just judgement? Then listen to the message of the gospel of Jesus Christ. There is no other way.

Reaffirmation (32:25-42)

The remainder of the chapter records the re-affirmation of the covenant between the Lord and the tribes of Reuben, Gad and Manasseh. For a second and a third time, they declare their resolve to **'cross over to fight before the Lord'** (32:27,32; cf. 32:17). In due course, this is exactly what they did (Josh. 4:12-13). Their reward was the permanent settlement of Gilead and, with it, the effective enlargement of Israel's inheritance to include the lands east of the Jordan — a circumstance reflected in the historic region of Palestine, which was only divided into what is now Israel and Jordan in the aftermath of the break-up of the Ottoman Empire following the First World War.[9]

The heart of the matter is *keeping covenant with the Lord*. The avoidance of sin is one thing, but it only has reality when it is expressed in the performance of what is right according to God's Word. We must remember that the consequences of our personal godliness will be as fruitful in blessing as the entail of our sins will be sad and ruinous. This is why it is so vital that we find out our sins before they find us out. 'It is not sin lamented, but sin unrepented of, which will find us out,' proclaimed Charles Simeon. 'There is a city of refuge provided for those who flee to it [Heb. 6:18]. The man Christ Jesus is a hiding place from the impending storm [Isa. 32:2]. If we flee to him, we may be sure that our sin will *not* find us out.' The Day of Judgement, he reminds us, 'is appointed no less for the justification of believers than for the condemnation of unbelievers. Let this blessed assurance then dwell richly on our minds. Let it encourage us to take refuge under our Saviour's wings. Let an holy confidence inspire those who have committed their souls to him. And let all rejoice and glory in him as able to save them to the uttermost' (2 Thess. 1:9-10; Matt. 23:37; 2 Tim. 1:12; Heb. 7:25).[10]

22.
Preparing for victory

Please read Numbers 33 - 36
*'Take possession of the land and settle in it, for I have given you
the land to possess'* (33:53).

One of the enduring images of the closing hours of the Vietnam War
is that of an American helicopter landing on the roof of the U.S.
Embassy in Saigon to evacuate people frantic to escape from the
advancing Communist forces. Some Christians think of the end of
the world this way. In these 'last days', they would say, we see a
pattern of intensifying struggle and creeping defeat for the church.
Sure, there are localized successes and revivals. But, by and large,
the spiritual skies are darkening, the gospel is receding and
tribulations of one kind or another are multiplying for God's people.
But, hold on, Jesus is coming and, like the helicopter in Saigon, he
will lift us off in the nick of time, just as God pours out his last
judgements upon this wicked world. There is certainly a plausibility
to this scenario. The Scriptures predict a last judgement like nothing
anyone has ever seen before. They also predict an intensification,
towards the end, of the struggle between the kingdoms of light and
darkness. And what passes for 'Christianity', especially in Europe,
is in precipitous retreat. The embattled, 'escape from Saigon'
outlook strikes many as the way things are!

Things looked that way to Israel at Kadesh Barnea, only eleven
days after they marched away from Sinai. Israel had God's promises
still ringing fresh in their ears. But the heat, the desert, the diet and
the size of the opposition plunged them into pessimism and

defeatism and they turned back. They believed, in effect, that God could not keep his Word, that the Canaanites were too powerful and that they were simply doomed to defeat!

Even so, there is sometimes another way to look at the data of Scripture and experience, than the one which right now seems so monolithically certain. Yes, there is judgement coming. Yes, much of European Christianity is an apostate dead duck. But why should we assume that *we* are the last generation in history — the one to whom Jesus is coming? The 'last days' have lasted quite a time. No one knows when they will end. Anyway, they encompass all of New Testament history. The 'signs of the times' are seen in every generation. The spiritual state of the church ebbs and flows as the winds of the Holy Spirit blow across unfolding human history. And nowhere in Scripture is there any warrant for an 'escape to Saigon' or 'US cavalry to the rescue' attitude to the coming of Christ and the consummation of the kingdom of God. Winston Churchill said of the rescue of Britain's army from Dunkirk in 1940 that wars were not won by evacuations. The same can be said of God's war with the powers of darkness. Jesus is not coming again just to evacuate the elect, but rather to renovate his creation radically, as 'a new heaven and a new earth', in which his righteousness, exclusively, will flourish. He will take possession of his creation, raise his people to resurrection glory and banish the lost to perdition.

The biblical perspective on the life and witness of God's people in the meantime is thoroughly positive. It is: 'Occupy till I come' (Luke 19:13, AV) — in military language, 'Take the high ground.' Spiritually, morally, in family and business life, in witnessing and doing good, in expecting blessing and extending love, we are to be alive in working for Christ's kingdom. This is where the closing chapters of Numbers offer a highly relevant perspective. Israel was being prepared for victory. The sinful pessimism of Kadesh had been buried in the sand with a whole generation who wanted Canaan without casualties. The land of promise lay before a new Israel. Yes, there would be a struggle. Many would die. The effort would be painful. But victory and conquest were the goal and the expectation. The physical factors had not in fact changed since the report of the spies forty years before: Israel was no larger and the enemy no weaker. What was different was Israel's attitude. She expected blessing. She believed God. She scented victory. This is the message the true church of Jesus Christ needs in the neo-pagan West as the twenty-first century dawns upon the world. Victory will come! But heaven will not be won without a fight!

The four chapters of this closing section survey the past experience (33:1-49), present calling (33:50-56) and future destiny (34:1-36:13) of God's people as they stand at the threshold of the promised land.

Past experience — hitherto has the Lord helped us (33:1-49)

The narrative consists of Moses' record of Israel's journey from Egypt to the Plains of Moab. There has been a great deal of inconclusive and unprofitable debate among the commentators as to where most of these places are located. Gordon Wenham's discussion is thorough and unsurpassed, but really only serves to prove just how little we know for certain about the details of their itinerary.[1] A glance at the list of camp-sites (see Fig. 4) will show that it is generally consistent with such Scripture cross-references as exist in both Exodus and Numbers and ought to be regarded as an accurate record of the contours of Israel's journey, even if many details are lost, as they say, 'in the mists of time'.

The question is, what does it all mean? What did it mean to Israel as they looked back on the wilderness wanderings? And what is this to mean for us, who are so removed by time and culture from Israel's experience?

Perhaps most obvious, this afforded a unique sense of *history* to Israel. This was no merely sentimental notion of having a past — like the 'Mary, Queen of Scots, slept here' version of history presented to visiting tourists. It was not history as 'facts' — places, battles, artefacts and heroes — but history as the movement of God's eternal purpose and revealed will. For Israel this involved mighty acts of God which could not be ascribed to natural or secondary causes. Even in the absence of definable miracles, the hand of God may be discerned in the providential unfolding of history. The Bible presents history as God's *telos* — that which proceeds to a goal. The New Testament period, which lies between the first and second comings of Jesus Christ, is 'the end [*telos*] of all things' (1 Peter 4:7). Providence and purpose are evident in the flow of history for those with eyes to see (1 Cor. 2:14).

Closely allied to this is a sense of *destiny*. Israel's desert itinerary

Fig. 4 — Israel's camps from Egypt to the Plains of Moab (Numbers 33)

1.	Rameses	**Exodus**	12:1-36	Passover
2.	Succoth		12:37-39	Flight from Egypt
3.	Etham		13:20	
4.	Pi Hahiroth		14:1-31	Crossing the Red Sea
5.	Marah		15:23	Bitter water/grumbling
6.	Elim		15:27	Twelve springs/seventy palms
7.	Red Sea			*no mention elsewhere*
8.	Desert of Sin		16:1	
9.	Dophkah			*no mention elsewhere*
10.	Alush			*no mention elsewhere*
11.	Rephidim		17:1-16	Water from rock/Amalek defeated
12.	Desert of Sinai		19:2	The giving of the law
13.	Kibroth Hattaavah	**Numbers**	11:34	Objections to the manna
14.	Hazeroth		11:35 - 12:16	Aaron & Miriam's complaints against Moses
15.	Rithmah		13:26	Kadesh Barnea/rebellion[2]
16.	Rimmon Perez			
17.	Libnah			
18.	Rissah			
19.	Kehelathah			
20.	Mount Shepher			*no mention elsewhere of*
21.	Haradah			*these stops in the thirty-eight years*
22.	Makheloth			*of wilderness wandering.*
23.	Tahath			
24.	Terah			
25.	Mithcah			
26.	Hashmonah			
27.	Moseroth			*Deut. 10:6-7 records a second*
28.	Bene Jaakan			*journey through these places*
29.	Hor Haggidgad			*at the time of Aaron's death,*
30.	Jotbathah			*c.38 yrs after Kadesh (33).*
31.	Abronah			*no mention elsewhere*
32.	Ezion Geber			*Deut. 2:8; 1 Kings 9:26; 22:49*
33.	Kadesh		20:1	Second visit after thirty-eight years
34.	Mount Hor		20:22 - 21:3	Death of Aaron/defeat of Arad
35.	Zalmonah		21:4	The bronze snake
36.	Punon			*no mention elsewhere*
37.	Oboth		21:10	
38.	Iye Abarim/Iyim		21:11	
39.	Dibon Gad			*no mention elsewhere*
40.	Almon Diblathaim			*no mention elsewhere*
41.	Abarim		21:20?	Mount Nebo/Pisgah
42.	Plains of Moab		22:1	Arrival on the banks of Jordan

pointed to the fulfilment of God's promise of a land in which to settle permanently. Wenham notes that if the forty-two stations are arranged in six groups of seven, then certain parallels emerge, most notably the miracles of the exodus and the manna at stages 1 and 8, the victories over Egypt and Amalek at 4 and 11, the provision of water at 6 and 13 and the appearance of Miriam at 7 and 14 (compare Fig. 4). Is it 'just coincidence', he asks, 'that at the twelfth station the law was given? Twelve is the number of election (12 tribes, 12 apostles, 144,000 (12^2 x 1000) saints in heaven, Rev. 14:1), and in the covenant of Sinai, Israel's election as God's holy people was sealed (Exod. 19:5-6).'[3] If this is so, than it is altogether possible that the six groups of seven stations constitute an open-ended symbolism, in which the six stages of desert wandering lead to the seventh and final stage — the entrance into the land of promise, the inheritance and, after conquest, the rest for God's people, a Sabbath in real estate. Whether in explicit promises and prophecies, or in simple symbolism of the historical events themselves, the Bible sets out the calling and destiny of God's people. The history points to the future. We look back in order to look forward. We march from promise to fulfilment.

For this reason, this itinerary also conveys a sense of *God's presence* with his people, to guide them in his appointed path. It was the work of God. 'Though from a human point of view, nothing memorable may have happened at Dophkah or Alush, these are recorded as places where the Lord of hosts, the Lord's army, marched through on their way to the promised land.'[4] For all their failings, Israel was never left to itself. The pillar of cloud by day and the pillar of fire by night led them throughout their epic odyssey. Christians today have no such pillars, but in fact they have the Holy Spirit leading them into the truth, according to the promise of Jesus. And this sense of guidance is no less real for being something unseen (John 14:16, 26; 16:13; Heb. 11:1).

Finally, at the heart of the whole Sinai experience there was a manifest sense of *God's unmerited favour*. Even the fact that no mention is made of the failure at Kadesh Barnea emphasizes the point. This dwelling on the positive side of things, far from putting out of mind all thoughts about their sins and failings, vividly reminded Israel that they had, as John Calvin put it, been 'rescued from impending death ... and a way of life opened to them'.[5] Robert Murray M'Cheyne (1813-43), expressed this with fragrant poignancy, in these verses from his poem, 'I am a debtor':

When this passing world is done,
When has sunk yon glaring sun,
When we stand with Christ in glory,
Looking o'er life's finished story,
    Then, Lord, shall I fully know —
    Not till then — how much I owe.

When I stand before the throne,
Dressed in beauty not my own,
When I see thee as thou art,
Love thee with unsinning heart,
    Then, Lord, shall I fully know —
    Not till then — how much I owe.

When the praise of heaven I hear,
Loud as thunders to the ear,
Loud as many waters' noise,
Sweet as harps' melodious voice,
    Then, Lord, shall I fully know —
    Not till then — how much I owe.

Even on earth, as through a glass,
Darkly, let thy glory pass;
Make forgiveness feel so sweet;
Make thy Spirit's help so meet;
    Even on earth, Lord, make me know
    Something of how much I owe.[6]

Present calling: take possession of the land (33:50-56)

From the past, attention then moved to the present. Through Moses, the Lord now gave Israel a command (33:50-53), a commitment (33:54) and a caveat or caution (33:55-56).

A command (33:50-53)

The Lord renewed the commission to Israel to **'cross the Jordan into Canaan, drive out all the inhabitants... Destroy all their**

carved images and their cast idols, and demolish their high places.' They were to **'take possession of the land and settle in it,'** because the Lord had **'given [them] the land to possess'** (33:50-53). Israel was called by God to be the instrument of his judgement upon peoples whose sin he had deemed to have 'reached its full measure' (cf. Gen. 15:16; Exod. 23:23; 34:11-14; Lev. 20:22-24). It is important to interpret and apply this law with sound biblical proportion.

First of all, *it was a law for Israel from God.* There is no evading the fact and therefore no reason to be squeamish about what it required. We are not superior to God. Our justice is not fairer than his. We have no reason to be embarrassed by his destruction of reprobate peoples. No judgement is easy to contemplate and God himself takes no pleasure in the death of the wicked. Protestations, for example, about the innocence of children have a powerful emotional appeal but fail to establish that God is unjust, for the plain teaching of God's Word is that, regardless of age, there is amongst us 'no one righteous, not even one,' by nature (Rom 3:10). The doctrine of the 'the ban' is unutterably solemn. It is awful, in the exact sense of the word. It was imposed upon nations whose wickedness was evidently deemed by the Lord to be beyond redemption.

Secondly, *the ban was unique,* in that it was revealed of, and applied to, particular peoples, and no others. There is no general principle here for the international relations of nations. No nation — not Israel, not any nation today, nor the church — is warranted to wage 'holy war' or mount a 'crusade' on any nation that it may deem a suitable target.

Finally, we ought to recognize that *God is at present judging nations* and a day will come when 'the saints' will 'judge the world' (1 Cor. 6:2). This is the abiding principle at the heart of the ban on Canaan. Some commentators individualize and spiritualize this into a message about putting our own sins to death, all of which is true in itself but is not the focus of the passage.[7] Redemption is, after all, found in the gospel, not in a 'ban' that cannot be escaped. The destruction of Canaan points to the inevitability of the last judgement and, while that must warn those who have ears to hear to 'flee the wrath to come', its true application stops with the starkly simple point that God is just and his justice will not be denied.

A commitment (33:54)

God promised success to Israel's faithful exercise of her commission. The command to **'distribute the land by lot'** was in the nature of a promise. Canaan would be divided according to the tribes and their clans. We are pointed to the wider truth that 'The earth is the Lord's, and everything in it' (Ps. 24:1) and that, ultimately, it is the Lord's people that inherit the earth (Matt. 5:5). More specifically, the Israelite tribes would enter into that which God promised to Abraham, and would do so in confirmation of Jacob's prophetic blessing of his descendants (Gen. 17:8; 49:1-27). Thus, notes John Calvin, 'Zebulon obtained his portion on the seashore' and Asher 'a district productive of the best corn,' all according to the ancient prophecies.[8]

A caveat (33:55-56)

There is, however, nothing automatic about God's promises. They are attached to faith and to obedience. Hence the warning that if they did *not* drive out the Canaanites, those they allowed to remain would **'become barbs in [their] eyes and thorns in [their] sides'** and give them **'trouble in the land'**. In such circumstances, says the Lord, **'I will do to you what I plan to do to them'** — i.e., dispossess them! Subsequent history confirms the sad fact that Israel never did completely drive out the Canaanites and, after many troubles — not least their repeated adoption of the idolatrous practice of Baal-worship — the Lord destroyed their national independence and exiled them to Assyria and Babylon. Here again, a general principle is dramatically demonstrated: if we are not killing sin, it will be killing us. This is where mortification of sin comes in (not in 33:50-53). Our sin will find us out, if we do not deal with it faithfully.

Future triumph — settling the land (34:1 - 36:13)

The last three chapters may be surveyed very briefly. They record a number of laws which would come into operation in the future, after the conquest of Canaan. As such, they would set their seal upon Israel's future victory.

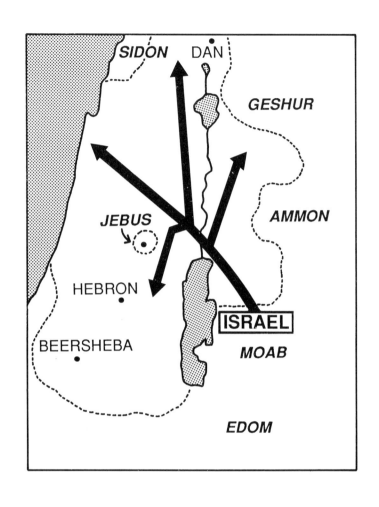

Map 4. — The boundaries of the promised land
(Numbers 34)

Land distribution (34:1-35:5)

The borders of the land were defined, orders for its assignment to the tribal groupings were given, the tribal leaders who were to oversee the final distribution of the various portions were appointed and arrangements were made for cities to be allocated to the otherwise landless Levites.

The description of Israel's new land generally conforms to an area encompassing modern Israel, the West Bank and Gaza strip, south Lebanon, southern Syria and northern Jordan (34:1-12; see Map 4). This was never completely settled. Much of it was only subjugated in the reigns of David and Solomon and some of it not at all. James Philip observes that this reveals the 'simple fact that the children of Israel never entered into their full inheritance because of their inability or refusal to be thorough enough in dealing with their enemies, and because they were content with small things ... they could have been a much greater nation ... if only they had risen to the challenges of the divine promise.'[9] How sadly true this is of many a Christian's life — to miss the blessing that might have been! Paul sets out the guiding principle for our discipleship to Christ: 'For God did not give us a spirit of timidity, but a spirit of power, of love and of self-discipline' (2 Tim. 1:7). The Lord is not stingy in his blessings. The language of abundance fills the Scripture: 'All things are yours' (1 Cor. 3:21,23); 'Now to him who is able to do immeasurably more than all we ask or imagine ...' (Eph. 3:20); 'My son ... you are always with me, and everything I have is yours' (Luke 15:31); and not least, 'Ask and it will be given to you; seek and you will find; knock and the door will be opened to you' (Matt. 7:7).

This land was to be distributed to the tribes, remembering that Reuben, Gad and half of Manasseh had already taken their inheritance in Gilead. This was to be achieved by two co-ordinate means: the casting of lots (34:13-15) and the decisions of a boundary commission appointed from the tribal leadership (34:16-29). Divine revelation (lots) and responsible human intelligence (leadership) were to combine in resolving the practicalities of serving the Lord in the new land. So, today, God has given us his Word (the Bible) and his Counsellor (the Holy Spirit), and has called men to lead his church (elders and deacons) in step with the Spirit and the Word.

The Levites were landless. They were to be scattered throughout the territories of the other tribes and settled in forty-eight Levitical cities (35:7). They were provided with pasturage, extending 1,000 cubits (about 450m.) from the walls of each city.[10] God had called the Levites to 'teach [his] precepts to Jacob and [his] law to Israel' (Deut. 33:10). Their dispersion ensured that their ministry reached the whole nation. The Lord's pastors are to shepherd their sheep in the field, where they live. True churches are bodies of people who live and work in personal and living fellowship with one another, pastored by men after God's own heart (Jer. 3:15). The contemporary phenomenon of an 'electronic church', in which 'television pastors' minister to people in their homes over the airwaves, flies in the face of every biblical norm for the life of God's people and the pastoring of the flock of God through personal ministry.

Criminal justice (35:6-34)

Six of the Levitical cities were designated as **'cities of refuge'** (35:6; Josh. 20). These were provided as sanctuaries, to which anyone who had **'killed another accidentally'** could flee (35:15). The context for this gracious provision was the 'right of revenge' on the part of the relatives of someone who had been murdered — called here **'the avenger of blood'** (35:19; Gen. 9:5-6). The purpose was that the land should not be polluted, for **'Bloodshed pollutes the land, and atonement cannot be made for the land on which blood has been shed, except by the blood of the one who shed it'** (35:33). The perennial problem was no doubt the tendency for the 'avengers of blood' to exact an over-hasty, ill-considered, disproportionate vengeance and so perpetuate injustice in the name of doing justice. The cities of refuge allowed a breathing-space in which justice according to law could be invoked and the accused **'[stand] trial before the assembly'** (35:12).

The rules for judgement in such cases — and certain others — were specified by the Lord.

1. Anyone guilty of premeditated murder was to be given no refuge (35:16-21). The death penalty was mandatory. This rested on the Sixth Commandment, is therefore still in force and ought to be the penalty of law under modern civil governments.

2. If the killing was accidental — what we call 'manslaughter' today — the guilty party was to remain in the city of refuge as his

place of exile until the death of the high priest, at which time he would receive an amnesty and could leave (35:22-25). The death of the high priest, who was the embodiment of mediation between God and man under the Old Testament, stood as an emblem of atonement for sin — hence the freedom for the convicted party. In the meantime, he was subject to the ministry of the Levites and would have worked with and for them.

3. If he left prior to such an amnesty, he would lose his protection and risk the wrath of the 'avenger', who would incur no guilt if he took the convicted person's life in such circumstances (35:26-28). Notice that the emphasis was on the responsible action of the convict. He was in exile, but not in prison. He could leave, but would have to face the consequences — which could well be his execution, for that was what his death at the avenger's hand was in God's eyes.

4. Conviction for murder required more than one witness, and a convicted murderer could not be ransomed: **'He shall surely be put to death'** (35:30-31).

The reason for these measures is made very clear in Scripture. The Word of God teaches the sanctity of human life. The murderer therefore appropriately forfeits that protection of life which he wrested from his victim and is, through his execution, summoned before the highest court of all, the judgement seat of God.

'Whoever sheds the blood of man,
    by man shall his blood be shed;
for in the image of God
    has God made man'

(Gen. 9:6).

The absence of such stringent penalties for murder means that the land, now as then, is polluted with blood, which like the blood of the first murder victim, Abel, cries to God from the ground. It is impossible not to tremble for our country — a country in which convicted murderers walk free in less than a decade, where men recently were convicted on the testimony of one well-rewarded witness and where unborn children, made in the image of God, have perished in their millions in the womb, because they were inconvenient, unwanted or deficient in some way. O Lord, in wrath, remember mercy!

Inheritance rights (36:1-13)

The final set of regulations takes us back to 27:1-11 and the daughters of Zelophehad. Their late father's inheritance would have been lost on account of his having no sons, had they not secured it for his descendants through the establishment of their right as daughters to the inheritance. The problem now arose that if any of them married men from other tribes, then their own tribe, Manasseh, would lost those portions of what was supposed to be an inviolable tribal inheritance. Accordingly, they referred the matter to Moses (36:1-4).

Moses found Manasseh's plea justified and it was decreed that the five heiresses should marry only within their tribe, so as to preserve the tribal territories intact. This might seem very strange to us today, unless, say, one of the great landowners of our country were to marry a foreigner and her estates were annexed by her husband's country! Israel's legislation was consistent with the will of God and held before the people not only the inviolability of the tribal inheritances, but also the certainty of all the Lord's promises for his people.

Journey to victory

The book of Numbers is all about the forty-year journey of the Old Testament church, Israel, from Egypt to the land of promise. The story of this great trek is told with transparent candour, as success and failure, blessing and curse, victories and defeats, pour from the pages of inspiration and reach across the centuries to challenge our own pilgrimage in life. Numbers asks each of us, 'Where have you been? What are you learning from your journey? How is it going? Where are you heading? What are your goals? Who is the Lord?'

For all of Israel's set-backs and failures, Numbers records a *journey to victory* ... to *God's* victory. There is a great deal of the gospel lying latent in the mighty acts of God along the way, as we have seen, and there is in this yet another example of the truth of what the apostle Paul said about the Old Testament law — that it is a schoolteacher to lead us to Jesus Christ. Without the promise of the Messiah and its fulfilment in the advent of Jesus, the Old Testament is no more than a collage of ancient spiritual lore. We might visit this now and again, as tourists of our cultural heritage, but it would have nothing to say about our destiny and little of relevance for our present. But here is the glory of the Old Testament in general, and of a book like Numbers in particular: it continues to shine brilliantly in the light of the New Testament revelation of Jesus Christ. In Christ, we understand the meaning of the Tent of Meeting and the multiplied sacrifices of Israel's worship. In Christ, we grasp the grace which was poured upon sinners in spite of their sins, in manna and quail, in water from dead rocks. In Christ, we see the unquenchable purpose of God to save a people, in plague stopped by priestly intercession or atonement of blood, in a new generation brought from defeat in the desert to triumph in the promised land. Paul points out that these things 'occurred as examples, to keep us from setting our hearts on evil things as they did' (1 Cor. 10:6). But, he adds, there is more here than learning moral lessons about what to do and what not to do in life. We need to learn from them, he says, because we are those 'on whom the fulfilment of the ages is come' (1 Cor. 10:11) — namely the era of Jesus Christ, the last days, the days which will issue in the consummation of God's plan of redemption on the day when Christ returns to judge the living and the dead. Our destiny, the goal of everything in the universe, and the culmination of all of history is, in the last analysis, the theme of Numbers. However distantly or faintly it may seem to point to Christ, it is in him alone that it has meaning for any of us, from the Israelites of long ago to the whole human race at the threshold of the twenty-first century.

> Advancing still from strength to strength
>   They go where other pilgrims trod,
> Till each to Zion comes at length
>   And stands before the face of God.
> Lord God of hosts, my pleading hear;
>   O Jacob's God, to me give ear.
>
> Look thou, O God, upon our Shield;
>   The face of thine Anointed see;
> One day within thy courts will yield
>   More good than thousands without thee.
> I'd rather stand near my God's house
>   Than dwell in tents of wickedness.

For God the Lord is shield and sun;
   The Lord will grace and glory give.
No good will he withhold from one
   Who does uprightly walk and live.
O Lord of hosts, how blest is he
   Who places all his trust in thee![11]

References

Chapter 1   Stand up and be counted!

1. The case to reduce the numbers as recorded in the text of Numbers is thoroughly — but in my view unconvincingly — discussed by Gordon J. Wenham in his fine commentary, *Numbers: an Introduction and a Commentary*, IVP, 1981, pp. 60-66.
2. Matthew Henry, *A Commentary on the Whole Bible*, World Bible Publishers, 6 vols., vol. 1, pp. 563-4.
3. The mediatorial kingship of Jesus Christ is that lordship which he exercises over 'all things' (Eph. 1:22). See A. A. Hodge, *Outlines of Theology*, Banner of Truth, pp. 428-44.
4. James Philip, *Numbers,* Word (Communicator's Commentary), 1987, p.36.
5. J. Calvin, *Commentaries on the Four Last Books of Moses,* Baker, 1979 (22 vols), vol. III, p. 442.

Chapter 2   God's order of battle

1. Henry, *Commentary*, vol. 1, p. 568.
2. Philip, *Numbers,* p. 44.
3. Irving Jensen, *Numbers — Journey to God's Rest-Land (Everyman's Bible Commentary)*, Moody Press, 1964.

Chapter 3   Saved to serve

1. Wenham, *Numbers,* p. 69.
2. As above.
3. Henry, *Commentary*, vol. 1, p. 571.
4. Psalm 119: 33 (1650 Scottish Psalter).
5. C. F. Keil and F. Delitzsch, *Biblical Commentary on the Old Testament.* vol. III, the Pentateuch, Eerdmans, p. 25. (This is in vol. 1 of the Eerdmans reprint, where three volumes are in one).
6. Wenham, *Numbers,* p. 73.

7. Henry, *Commentary*, vol. 1, p. 577.
8. From 'Onward! Christian soldiers' by S. Baring-Gould.

Chapter 4   Outside the camp
1.   Philip, *Numbers,* p.72.
2.   As above. For an interesting discussion of 'Restitution' see R. J. Rushdoony, *The Institutes of Biblical Law*, Craig Press, 1973, pp.272-7.
3.   Jensen, *Numbers — Journey to God's Rest-Land,* p.34.
4.   Wenham, *Numbers*, p.80.
5.   As above, p.85.
6.   Philip, *Numbers*, p.68.

Chapter 5   Consecration and blessing
1.   Wenham, *Numbers*, p.89.
2.   For example, prior to 1980 my own denomination, the Reformed Presbyterian Church of North America, *required* a pledge of total abstinence for membership in the church.
3.   The symmetry is remarkable: the three lines have 3, 5 and 7 words; 12, 14 and 16 syllables and 15, 20 and 25 consonants.
4.   Wenham, *Numbers*, p.90.
5.   Keil and Delitzsch, *Commentary*, p.42.
6.   Wenham, *Numbers*, p.91.

Chapter 6   Gifts for God's altar
1.   *The Constitution of the Reformed Presbyterian Church of North America*, RPCNA, 1990, p. G-1. (This is from one of the questions put to prospective church members.)
2.   Wenham (*Numbers*, pp.91-92) gives a clear account of the chronology and the reasons for the inclusion of Numbers 7-9 at this point in the narrrative, rather than in Exodus 40 or somewhere in Leviticus.
3.   Material in this section is drawn from G. J. Keddie, 'The Biblical Basis for Church Finance,' published in *The Minutes of the Synod of the Reformed Presbyterian Church of North America, 1980* (Pittsburgh: RPCNA, 1980), pp.209-30.
4.   Henry, *Commentary,* vol. 1, p.589. 'The great change' is, of course, our death and passage into eternity.
5.   In the well-known American children's show, *Mr Rogers' Neighborhood*, one of Fred Rogers' theme-statements is 'I like you just the way you are.' Mr Rogers is an ordained minister of the Presbyterian Church (USA), but, significantly, his TV 'neighbourhood' has no church.
6.   G. J. Wenham, *The Book of Leviticus*, Eerdmans (NICOT), 1979, p. 71.
7.   Wenham, *Leviticus*, pp.63-66, gives a fine account of the NT theology of the burnt offering.
8.   As above, pp. 101-103.
9.   As above, p. 81.

10. Wenham, *Numbers*, p.94.
11. *The Heidelberg Catechism,* Bd of Publ. of the Christian Reformed Church, 1975, p.12.

Chapter 7   Living lamps
1. Henry, *Commentary*, vol. 1, p. 594.
2. J. G. Murphy, *A Critical and Exegetical Commentary on the Book of Exodus,* James Publns, 1976 [1868], p.295.
3. W. H. Gispen, *The Bible Student's Commentary — Exodus,* Zondervan, 1982, p. 251.
4. Wenham, *Numbers*, p.95.
5. There is no ground for concluding that Exodus 12:24 proves that the Passover was not celebrated *until* Israel arrived in Canaan (e.g., Henry, *Commentary*, vol. 1, p. 598).
6. *The Book of Psalms for singing,* Selection 27A (Ps. 27:1,4).

Chapter 8   Guided by God
1. William Williams (1717-1791) of Pantycelyn is known outside Wales today only for his famous hymn (which was translated from Welsh by Peter Williams), but he published some ninety works in his native language and remains the most prolific of Calvinistic Methodist authors.
2. Henry, *Commentary*, vol. 1, p.600.
3. For a wonderful exposition of this theme, see Robert L. Dabney, 'Meditation a Means of Grace' in his *Discussions: Evangelical and Theological,* Banner of Truth, 1967, vol. 1, pp.643-53.

Chapter 9   Promise and Compromise
1. Joshua and Caleb.
2. Henry, *Commentary,* vol. 1, p. 603.
3. Wenham, *Numbers*, p.105.
4. Henry, *Commentary*, vol. 1, p.604.
5. Philip, *Numbers*, p.130.
6. William Carey's famous aphorism was 'Expect great things from God, attempt great things for God.'
7. Jeremiah Burroughs, *The Rare Jewel of Christian Contentment,* Banner of Truth, 1964 (1648), p.138.
8. This verb, the Hebrew *anan,* occurs only here and in Lamentations 3:39 and in a particular form (the *hitpa'el*), which is reflexive — thus, it may have the sense, 'They complained to one another' or 'They complained amongst themselves.'
9. Henry, *Commentary*, vol. 1, p.606.
10. Taberah is mentioned in Deuteronomy 9:22, but the location is unknown today.
11. R. K. Harrison: *The Wycliffe Exegetical Commentary: Numbers,* Moody Press, 1990, p. 182.

12. Henry, *Commentary*, p.606.
13. Harrison, *Numbers*, p.183.
14. J. C. Ryle, *The Upper Room*, Banner of Truth, 1970 [1888], p.378.
15. Harrison, *Numbers*, p.195.
16. Philip, *Numbers*, pp.133-4.

Chapter 10   So near and yet so far
1. Harrison, *Numbers*, p.202.
2. As above, p.206.
3. Henry, *Commentary*, vol. 1, p.622.
4. As above, p.623.
5. Wenham, *Numbers*, p.121.
6. Henry, *Commentary*, vol. 1, p.627.
7. Philip, *Numbers*, p.164. Philip, with uncharacteristic infelicity of expression, says the children 'atone, as it were' for the parents' sin. 'Atonement' is substitutionary, expiatory sacrifice for another's sin. The children suffered *because of* their parents' sins, but they certainly did not in any sense *'atone for'* their sins. All atonement is suffering, but not all suffering is atonement.

Chapter 11   Reminders of God's goodness
1. F. B. Huey, *Numbers, Bible Study Commentary*, Zondervan, 1981, p.58.
2. Harrison, *Numbers*, p.221.
3. Henry, *Commentary*, vol. 1, p. 632.
4. Wenham, *Numbers*, p.129.
5. The American *conservative evangelical* average for the 'tithe' was 3.8% in 1990. A biblical tithe is what the word means: a straight 10%. Words, like the coin of the realm, are easily devalued. And so, the word 'tithe' has become a cover for shrinking practical devotion.
6. Henry, *Commentary*, vol. 1, p.634.
7. As above.
8. Harrison, *Numbers*, p.227.
9. John Murray, *Collected Writings of John Murray, vol. 1, The Claims of Truth*, Banner of Truth, 1976, pp. 193-228. Four excellent chapters on the biblical teaching on the Christian sabbath/Lord's Day and its continuing relevance.
10. Philip, *Numbers*, p.183.
11. Charles Simeon, *Expository Outlines on the Whole Bible*, Baker, 1988 [1847], 20 vols, vol. 2, p.76.
12. A 'royal warrant' in the United Kingdom is a privilege granted to a business that has provided services for the Crown. The firm may display the royal Coat of Arms on its premises and its products, with the logo, 'By appointment to Her Majesty the Queen, manufacturer of …'

Chapter 12   Showdown in the desert
1. Simeon, *Expository Outlines*, vol. 2, p.91.

Chapter 13   In wrath, remember mercy ...
1.   Henry, *Commentary*, vol. 1, p. 645.
2.   As above.
3.   Simeon, *Expository Outlines,* vol. 2, p.93.
4.   As above, p.97.
5.   As above, p.95.
6.   As above, p.97.
7.   One of the seminal works on the doctrine of church government takes its title from this event: George Gillespie's *Aaron's Rod Blossoming; or, the divine ordinance of church government vindicated...* (1646). Gillespie was one of the Scottish Commissioners to the Westminster Assembly.
8.   Harrison, *Numbers*, p.243.
9.   Wenham, *Numbers*, p.140.
10.   Philip, *Numbers*, p.202. Philip rightly sees the staff as pointing ahead to future blessings, but perhaps makes too fine a point when he identifies Christ's resurrection as 'the budding and blossoming of the almond rod all over again'.
11.   Simeon, *Expository Outlines*, vol. 2, p.100.

Chapter 14   A gift of grace
1.   Harrison, *Numbers*, p.247.
2.   Philip, *Numbers*, p. 205.
3.   Wenham, *Numbers*, p.144.
4.   Harrison, *Numbers*, p.250.
5.   Henry, *Numbers*, vol. 1, p. 651.
6.   As above.

Chapter 15   The water of cleansing
1.   Wenham, *Numbers*, p.146.
2.   F. B. Huey, *Numbers*, p.68.
3.   Harrison, *Numbers*, p.258.
4.   Psalm 51 in the Scottish metrical version of 1650.

Chapter 16   Turning-point
1.   Henry, *Commentary,* vol. 1, p.658.
2.   Simeon, *Expository Outlines,* vol. 2, p.119.
3.   Wenham, *Numbers*, pp. 153-5, 216-30, discusses at some length the problems associated with the location of Arad, Hormah and Mount Hor, as well as the movements of Israel.
4.   Simeon, *Expository Outlines*, vol. 2, p.127.
5.   Wenham, *Numbers*, pp.157-8.
6.   The song of the well (21:16-18) is probably also from the Book of the Wars of the Lord (Wenham, *Numbers*, p.159).
7.   Philip, *Numbers*, p.236.
8.   William Jay: *Morning and Evening Exercises for the Closet for every day of the year,* Harper & Brothers, 1858, 'Morning,' p.177.
9.   Harrison, *Numbers*, p.285.

Chapter 17   A curse sought and a blessing given

1.   Wenham, *Numbers*, pp. 165-6, gives a masterly outline of the threefold repetition, in terms of which the Balaam narrative is structured.

2.   Peter's rebuke of Simon the Sorcerer, when the latter offered money for the same healing powers as the apostles, states the relevant biblical principle succinctly: 'May your money perish with you, because you thought you could buy the gift of God with money!' Balaam was a 'rent-a-prophet' hireling, while his prospective employer apparently thought he could buy a curse!

3.   Wenham, *Numbers*, p.170.

4.   As above.

5.   The common reaction to this miracle is to feel uneasy and think of difficulties, such as the donkey's lack of mental and physical equipment for speaking. We then get into tangles about whether it really made the sounds of the words with real vocal chords, or if the sound was 'dubbed on' an otherwise normal donkey (like the hero — a talking horse — of the American TV series *Mr Ed*), or if it was only in Balaam's mind. The answer is that a miracle is a miracle and it is futile to speculate as to mechanisms which *all* defy normal feasibility. If God could oblige Balaam to speak his words, why is it more difficult to have a donkey speak? If he raised Jesus from the dead, why is any miracle surprising?

6.   Wenham, *Numbers*, p.171.

7.   Harrison, *Numbers*, p.317.

8.   As above, pp.326-7.

9.   The American news magazine *Newsweek* reported on 25 March 1991 (p.57) that while 78% of Americans thought they had an 'excellent or good chance' of going to heaven, only 4% thought they might end up in hell!

10.   From 'Rock of Ages' by the English preacher Augustus Montague Toplady.

Chapter 18   Balaam's revenge

1.   Huey, *Numbers*, p.90.

2.   Simeon, *Expository Outlines*, vol. 2, p. 161.

3.   Henry, *Commentary*, vol. 1, p. 687.

4.   John Calvin, *Harmony of the last Four Books of Moses*, vol. 4, p.233.

5.   Henry, *Commentary*, vol. 1, p.687.

6.   Henry (*Commentary*, vol. 1, p.687) Calvin, (*Harmony*, vol. 4, p.235), and Keil & Delitzsch (p. 204) restrict God's sentence of death to those leaders who were directly involved as ringleaders in the apostasy. Wenham (p.186.) and Harrison (p.337) insist that 'all' the leaders means *all* of them. None was innocent, for the reasons given above.

7.   Harrison, *Numbers*, p.337. Somewhat similar to this was the fearful medieval penalty of being 'broken on the wheel'. Tied across a wheel, the victim's limbs were smashed with a sledgehammer, and he was left to die on the wheel, which was lifted on a pole.

8.   G. J. Wenham (p.186) and Harrison (p.337) see Moses 'modifying' God's

earlier decree, basically to avoid executing anyone who did not actually engage in idolatrous worship. It would seem more consistent, however, to regard Moses' order as a second part of the judgement. In the event, neither the execution of the leaders or the guilty in the tribes seems to have been carried out, because they were overtaken by the 'plague' (25:8), which was precipitated, at the very moment the sentences were being pronounced, by the son of a Simeonite leader, named Zimri, and his Midianite girlfriend flaunting their sin in sight of the Tent of Meeting!

9.   Simeon, *Expository Outlines,* vol. 2, p.162.
10. As above.

Chapter 19   A new day coming

1.   Matthew Henry (*Commentary,* vol.1, pp.691-2) doesn't mind speculating a bit and has some interesting opinions on the numbers.
2.   Harrison, N*umbers,* p.356.
3.   G. J. Wenham (*Numbers,* p. 192) ties this in with the jubilee legislation (Lev. 25) as fundamental to biblical law.
4.   Henry, *Commentary,* vol. 1, p.696.
5.   Philip, *Numbers,* p.282.

Chapter 20   Spiritual worship

1.   Far and away the best treatment of the intricacies of the Old Testament ceremonies is in Gordon Wenham's Tyndale Commentary, which really is *the* standard commentary on Numbers today. See pages 195-205 for a clear and precise exposition of the subject.
2.   The passages which deal with the festivals and sacrifices are Exodus 23:14-17; 29:38-42; 31:12-17; Leviticus 23; Numbers 25:1-2; 28:1 - 29:40).
3.   It is not surprising that, in a day when the distinctiveness of the sabbath is being expunged from the life of Western nations, voices are being heard increasingly *from evangelical churches* proclaiming the death of the Fourth Commandment and insisting that the sabbath should have disappeared with the Mosaic ceremonies (and even that Jesus didn't keep the sabbath!). Bad consciences are thus relieved of the (wholly justified) guilt of sabbath-breaking, and bolstered with the (wholly unjustified) assurance that God is pleased with this (early) retirement of one of the Ten Commandments. 'Watch this space,' as they say, 'for future developments.' The euthanasia of the sabbath will prove to be the harbinger of a full-blown denial of the perpetuity of all the Ten Commandments. You can count on it. It's coming soon to an evangelical church near you!
4.   *Westminster Confession of Faith,* 22, section 7.

Chapter 21   Your sin will find you out!

1.   There were other Midianites who would be a thorn in Israel's flesh for centuries to come (e.g. Judg. 6:6), so it is clear that the annihilation of the whole of Midian was neither planned nor executed on this occasion.
2.   Henry, *Commentary,* vol. 1, p.706.
3.   Irving L. Jensen, *Numbers: Journey to God's Rest-Land,* Moody Press, 1964, p.115.

4.   Gross National Product — a common modern index of the wealth of a nation.

5.   About £1,000,000 at the 1991 melt-down price for gold!

6.   Henry, *Commentary*, vol. 1, p.711.

7.   As above, p.713.

8.   As above.

9.   David Fromkin, *A Peace to end all peace: the Fall of the Ottoman Empire and the Creation of the Modern Middle East*. Avon Books, 1989, pp.148, 504-5.

10.   Simeon, *Expository Outlines*, vol. 2, p.189.

Chapter 22   Preparing for victory

1.   Wenham, *Numbers*, pp. 216-30.

2.   Keil & Delitzsch, *Commentary*, p.143.

3.   Wenham, *Numbers*, p.218.

4.   As above, p.219.

5.   Calvin, p.297.

6.   Andrew A. Bonar, *Robert Murray M'Cheyne: Memoir and Remains*, Banner of Truth, 1966 [1844], pp.636-7.

7.   For example, Wenham, p.231, Philip, p.338, and C. S. Lewis, *Reflections on the Psalms*, London: Collins, 1958, pp.113-14.

8.   Calvin, p.302.

9.   Philip, *Numbers*, p.341.

10.   G. J. Wenham, *Numbers* (pp.234-5) discusses the technical complexities at some length.

11.   *The Book of Psalms for Singing*, 84B.